23941808

THE CIO's LEFT-LED UNIONS

A volume in the

CLASS AND CULTURE series

Milton Cantor and Bruce Laurie, series editors

THE CIO's
LEFT-LED UNIONS

edited by
STEVE ROSSWURM

 RUTGERS UNIVERSITY PRESS
New Brunswick, New Jersey

Library of Congress Cataloging-in-Publication Data

Rosswurm, Steven,
    The CIO's left-led unions / Steve Rosswurm.
        p.   cm.—(Class and culture series)
    Includes bibliographical references and index.
    ISBN 0-8135-1769-9 (cloth)—ISBN 0-8135-1770-2 (pbk.)
    1. Congress of Industrial Organizations (U.S.)—History.   2. Trade
unions and communism—United States—History—20th century.
I. Title.   II. Series.
HD8055.C75R67   1992
331.88'33'0973—dc20   91-19467
                                                                        CIP

British Cataloging-in-Publication information available

For

Antonio Cavorso (1901–1971), FE
Thomas J. Fitzpatrick (1903–?), UE
John W. Nelson (1917–1959), UE

Lo, I am about to create new heavens and a new earth; the things of the past shall not be remembered or come to mind.

Instead, there shall always be rejoicing and happiness in what I create; for I create Jerusalem to be a joy and its people to be a delight; I will rejoice in Jerusalem and exult in my people. No longer shall the sound of weeping be heard there, or the sound of crying; no longer shall there be in it an infant who lives but a few days, or an old man who does not round out his full lifetime; he dies a mere youth who reaches but a hundred years, and he who fails of a hundred shall be thought accursed.

They shall live in the houses they build, and eat the fruit of the vineyards they plant; they shall not build houses for others to live in, or plant for others to eat.

As the years of a tree, so the years of my people; and my chosen ones shall long enjoy the produce of their hands. (Isaiah 65:17–22)

CONTENTS

PREFACE

"That is that," pronounced Philip Murray, CIO president, after the 1950 CIO convention officially expelled nine left-led unions, having ousted two others in 1949.

Murray meant this brief sentence, I think, in two ways. One is obvious: a drawn-out, bitter, and enervating controversy—the problem of the "Communist-dominated" unions in the CIO—had ended. But he also meant that which is signified by our contemporary slang phrase "They're history"—so obscenely wrongheaded, but so indicative of life in contemporary American society.

Murray, however, was wrong.

His literal meaning overstated the matter: the CIO's initial expulsion decision, taken at its 1949 convention, merely had established a precondition for the left-led unions' demise. The federation's leadership then had to commit sizable resources to *destroy* the expelled unions, which did not obligingly disappear. Several of them, including the International Fur & Leather Workers Union (IFLWU), the International Longshoremen's & Warehousemen's Union (ILWU), the United Electrical, Radio & Machine Workers of America (UE), and the International Union of Mine, Mill & Smelter Workers (IUMMSW), remained powerful enough to be targets of CIO "raiding" into the mid-1950s and beyond. The IFLWU merged with the Amalgamated Meat Cutters & Butcher Workmen in 1955, IUMMSW with the United Steel Workers of America in 1967, and the ILWU reaffiliated with AFL–CIO in 1988. The UE, which left the CIO before being ejected, still remains independent and, in Frank Emspak's words, "a moral beacon of the labor movement."[1]

And what about Murray's figurative meaning? That which has happened in the past, history, is not dead, is not gone. It continues to shape our lives—indeed, it establishes the boundaries of our existences—no matter how unaware we are of its influence. The record and experiences of the expelled unions speak to us, as working people and as citizens, across the decades.

They may reach us in many ways. Some of the men and women of these unions, still alive, can talk directly to us. We can listen to the recorded words of others who were interviewed before their deaths. The expelled unions address our lives in still another way: not only are we still experiencing the long-range results of the expulsions, but many of the goals that the expelled unions set for their members and their country have yet to be accomplished.

Perhaps, however, the expelled unions speak to us most pertinently in an abstract sense. They remind us that the collective struggle against the boundaries of our existence—for they understood that there *were* boundaries out there—is the essence of a meaningful life. They prod us to recall that in the effort, sometimes successful, often not, to change the world—for they understood that the world *could* be transformed—barriers to equality can be lowered and attitudes can be altered. Each struggle, moreover, helps create the conditions for the next one.

This book of essays, none previously published and all based upon exhaustive research, is a collective effort to listen to the expelled unions. What then, ever so briefly, do they tell us? Rather, what do I, as editor, think they tell us? No contributor has seen this preface and none, therefore, is in complicity in its viewpoints.

My introduction provides an overview of the history of the expelled unions as well as a preliminary assessment of their significance. I discuss the unions' social composition and leadership and their relationship to the CIO. Both the immediate and long-run implications of the expulsions are examined in the last section of the introduction.

The body of the book begins with Bruce Nelson's essay on the ILWU's effort to organize the predominantly African-American longshoremen in New Orleans in the late 1930s. ILWU organizers went into the South with tremendous courage, flush with the elan of successful struggles against obdurate employers and state and city officials up and down the west coast. Attitude and experience was not enough: the ILWU was soundly defeated in a 1938 NLRB election. Nelson's analysis of this defeat is appropriately complex. On the one hand, he stresses the massive violence, from virtually every conceivable source, that greeted the ILWU's efforts. On the other, he emphasizes the specificity of the black experience on the New Orleans docks during Jim Crow and the ILWU's lack of familiarity with that history. Nelson's ultimate conclusion—that the ILWU's opponents simply had too much state-sanctioned power—draws our attention to the "state's vital role in influencing the outcome of events." But he also points out that the defeat "demonstrates the complexity of working-class consciousness and the complicated ways in which race has affected the social relations of production and the development of unionism."

Nancy Quam-Wickham, the first scholar to use the numerous oral histories done under joint ILWU–National Endowment for the Humanities sponsorship in the 1980s, takes up similar issues in her discussion of the ILWU's defense of the hiring hall during World War II. Despite the class-collaboration rhetoric of some ILWU leaders, particularly Harry Bridges, job-control struggles continued on the docks. For various reasons, some patriotic, some self-interested, there was relatively little opposition to the no-strike pledge. Yet the " '34 men," in Howard Kimeldorf's evocative phrase, continued to defend jealously their hard-won rights.[2] One of those rights, however, was to work with men of their own choosing; during the war, that came to mean other whites. In some cases, it is difficult, if not impossible, to separate job control, ethnic identity, and racism; that the bosses historically had used race to divide working people made the situation even more complicated. The general trend, however, is clear: The '34 men used job control to enforce their restricted vision of who constituted the American working class. The ILWU leadership, although committed to interracial unionism, seldom used their power to effectively oppose such actions—partly because of their intense commitment to job control and partly because of their egalitarian, but economistic, reading of race relations.

Karl Korstad's essay, the reminiscences of a Southern, postwar organizer for the Food, Tobacco, Agricultural & Allied Workers (FTA), takes us into the next decade. Right from its origins, the FTA understood that a confrontation with racism and the institutions that subordinated and segregated people of color was essential to successful organizing. Sometimes explicitly, but more often through the adroit use of memorable anecdotes, Korstad shows the ways in which this fundamental insight became democratic practice in the South from 1945 to 1951. Korstad gives us a good sense of what it was to be a left-wing organizer in the postwar South; he describes the kinds of leaders, men and women, earlier FTA organizing had brought up and the growing anticommunism that increasingly circumscribed FTA's efforts to build militant interracial unionism. He concludes rather somberly with the destruction of Local 22 in Winston–Salem, North Carolina, and the fruitless efforts in 1950 and 1951 to rebuild the local. Showing strength even in defeat, however, FTA never flinched in speaking the truth to those it was organizing: without rank-and-file "self-activity," to use George Rawick's phrase, all the work in the world by a full-time paid staff would not (and could not) produce unions worthy of the name.[3]

The essays of Nelson, Quam-Wickham, and Korstad contribute much to our understanding of how the CIO's expelled unions handled the issue of racial inequality. If the ILWU's approach to this issue was problematic in some places before 1946, thereafter it clearly joined the left-led unions' consensus: the battle for equality, waged on "diverse terrains of struggle," was integral to building solid unions. It is not surprising, then, that the most thorough study of Operation Dixie, the CIO's postwar effort to organize the South while excluding Communists and most independent leftists, points out that it was two expelled unions, the FTA and the IFLWU, and one union heavily influenced by Communists, the Packinghouse Workers, that developed successful southern organizing strategies.[4]

Secrecy was the Achilles heel of the Communist Party (CP): Relatively few Communists, apart from full-time Party functionaries, willingly admitted to their membership. Nowhere was this more true than in the CIO. The subsequent essays, which deal with communism and anticommunism and their implications, are led off by Rosemary Feurer's study of William Sentner, who violated this norm throughout his career.

Feurer's study of a major portion of the career of Sentner, an "open" CP member and UE leader in St. Louis, raises fundamental questions about the CP's strategy of keeping membership secret. Normally written off as a Stalinist whose World War II "alliance" with W. Stuart Symington mocked his commitment to communism, Sentner understood that the CP's policy was politically wrongheaded. The responsibilities resulting from Sentner's proud avowal of his CP membership probably had much to do with his effort, unmatched by any Communist trade-union leader I know of, to come to grips with the "is"—the realities of the capitalism he confronted—and the "ought"—the ultimate goal of democratic socialism. To effect this mediation, Sentner, drawing upon his experiences in St. Louis in the early 1930s and an acute understanding of previous labor struggles, especially those of the Knights of Labor, developed an organizing strategy that revolved around "civic unionism" and "industrial democracy." Class struggle was central to Sentner's trade-union work, but he never assumed that in and of itself class struggle could produce socialist consciousness, nor that as a rhetorical device it provided answers to the most difficult challenges posed by a resilient capitalism.

My own essay shows that Paul Weber, a Detroit leader of the Association of Catholic Trade Unionists (ACTU), was as exceptional in the Catholic Church as Sentner was in the CP: he, too, developed a mediation between the "is" and the Catholic "ought." Weber's conceptualization of the theory and practice of "economic democracy" emerged from the Catholic Church's institutional turn to its working-class constituency in the 1930s and the solidly proletarian character of the Detroit ACTU. Part of the motivation for that turn—indeed, inseparable from it—was the Church's deeply rooted anticommuism. This anticommunism, so understandable—even inevitable, given the conflict between secularism and religiosity—cannot be reduced simply to procapitalism. From 1945, however, the Church's commitment to economic democracy was overwhelmed by laborists' move to anticommunism as the paramount trade-union issue. By the mid-1950s, the Church's secular commitment to its working people had diminished to rhetoric and Weber's economic democracy had become "history." In the intervening years, the Catholic Church, both clerics and laity, played a central role in isolating, defeating, and ultimately destroying the CIO left, both Communist and non-Communist.

Ellen Schrecker shows the integral role the federal government played in this destruction. If anticommunism cannot be reduced to the activities of the government, it is, as Schrecker argues, hard to imagine it succeeding without federal leadership, aid, and legitimization. Sometimes pursuing their own agenda, sometimes reacting to popular anticommunism, sometimes working hand in glove with industralists, and always espousing the highest patriotism, federal officials waged a battle on every front against left trade unionists. Schrecker's discussion of the critical role that the National Labor Relations Board (NLRB) played in this battle is especially important. While its enforcement of the anticommunist provision of the Taft–Hartley Act never accomplished what its officials and other opponents of the left wanted it to, the NLRB kept up its attack throughout the 1950s, thus ensuring that money sorely needed for organizing the unorganized or warding off raids went instead to defense work. Schrecker also implicitly periodizes the role of the federal government in her numerous indications that Dwight D. Eisenhower's election to the presidency brought into office bureaucrats whose commitment to the Bill of Rights, whether principled or pragmatic, was considerably less fervent than that of their predecessors.

Gerald Zahavi's set of interviews with anticommunist activists who defeated an important IFLWU local in upstate New York turns our attention to opponents of left unionism at the local level. Those researching the expelled unions have given short shrift to searching out and talking with anticommunists; Zahavi shows how rewarding such efforts can be. His interviews with those who directed the employers' offensive reveal an astounding level of class consciousness: observe their appropropriation of the working-class language of solidarity; observe their recognition of the necessity to financially support the weakest employers to ensure that the IFLWU could not divide and conquer. Note, too, their perception that they had captured local historical memory—had inflicted a defeat so overwhelming as to be never forgotten.

The interviews with the labor anticommunists are just as revealing. In the case of the more experienced opponent of the left, it shows, on the one hand, how dependent this sort of activist was upon the balance of class forces at the local and national level, as well as in the CIO; on the other, it demonstrates the importance of the leader who had long been jousting with the left. The interview with the final participant provides insight into those who probably were the pragmatically inclined base for labor anticommunism: the younger worker who took for granted the gains of the past and whose greatest concern was whether his/her union could "deliver the goods." Is it surprising that he has second thoughts about the IFLWU's destruction?

Mark McColloch's study of collective bargaining at Westinghouse is an appropriate closure to the collection. Although battered by the brutal attacks of the federal government (as Schrecker shows) and the prime target of the Catholic Church (as I show), the UE built a bargaining record with Westinghouse in the 1950s that compares more than favorably with that of the International Union of Electrical Workers (IUE). On issue after issue, as McColloch shows, the IUE, although representing the vast majority of the company's workers, made significant concessions to Westinghouse, especially on shop-floor issues and equality for women workers. The UE, anchored in the chain by its

Lester, Pennsylvania, local, generally held tough on these aspects of its contracts, though forced to concede on some points. McColloch's essay will force historians and students of industrial relations to re-think time-worn arguments: that there was little difference in the collective bargaining strategy of the UE and IUE in the 1950s and that the heroic period of labor history ended with the expulsion of the left-led unions and Walter Reuther's 1950 contract with General Motors. It, moreover, sets in sharp relief the CIO's decision to devote millions of dollars to replacing the UE with the IUE, especially under the leadership of the erratic, opportunistic, and incompetent James B. Carey.

What remains on the research agenda? Virtually everything, since we know so little about these unions. Most of them—the exceptions, I think, being the FTA, the Farm Equipment Workers (FE), the United Office & Professional Workers of America (UOPWA), and the United Public Workers (UPW)—are represented by substantial national office records (as well as by numerous related collections of locals and indi-viduals), but scant research has been done on the expelled unions. There are exceptions, particularly in the case of the UE and ILWU, but even here there is much to be done. Path-breaking studies of the FTA and the FE soon will appear, along with several works that promise to deepen our understanding of the UE, but even these will barely scratch the surface of what can be known and what needs to be known about the history of these left-led CIO unions.

We especially need studies of the UPW and the UOPWA, two unions that organized large numbers of women and white-collar workers. The most glaring hole in this collection—one which I regret, but for which I make no apologies—is that it contains no essay on these two expelled unions. This is partly due to the serendipitous way in which a collec-tion like this evolves; partly because, as far as I know, no collection of UPW or UOPWA national offices records remains extant. But it is proba-bly more than this. Most labor historians of the CIO period concentrate on the industrial proletariat (which they implicity define as male)—and even here primarily the largest and most organized shops—to the exclusion of the majority of working people in this country. Such a focus is myopic in the extreme. If my suppositions in the introduction are on the mark, perhaps the greatest tragedy of the expulsions was the role they played in the CIO's missed opportunity, produced by a con-juncture of the ideological and the material, to organize those who performed mental labor—especially women.

An analysis of the gendered history of the expelled unions also deserves much attention. Many labor historians, at least of the CIO period, have not quite caught up with the fact that the study of gender and the study of women are not the same thing, that gender relations are embodied in virtually everything we do. These essays, to varying degrees, reflect this underdevelopment; they contain insights, but not nearly enough. Conceptions of gender lay at the heart of the organizing strategies that the CIO and the CP pursued; likewise, it is becoming increasingly apparent that it is difficult to understand anticommunism without comprehending the shifting relations of gender in postwar America.

I was trained as a seventeenth- and eighteenth-century historian. The publication of this collection, then, marks my debut as a twentieth-century historian. I am thankful to many colleagues who generously shared their knowledge, especially the Chicago Area Labor History Group, which has been meeting at the Newberry Library for well over a decade. My department chairs and the dean of the faculty at Lake Forest College, moreover, encouraged and generously supported my switch in chronological workplaces.

Conversations with the following have been useful in framing the issues of this collection: Elizabeth Eudey, Joshua Freeman, Toni Gilpin, Mollie West, and Seth Wigderson. My discussions with Stephen Meyer, David Roediger, and Ellen Schrecker were especially helpful, as were those with James Livingston and Michael Meranze, who with good humor accept my undertheorization. Thanks to Bert Zelman for his copyediting, his enthusiasm, and his help with the title. Marlie Wasserman's straightforwardness, seriousness, and professionalism make it a pleasure to work with her. Susan Figliulo's wit, wisdom, and editorial skills continue to amaze me.

I am especially thankful to Tom Juravich for permission to reprint his wonderful song, "An Old Soldier."

Finally, the dedication—I never knew them, but their hard work, courage, perseverance, and discipline often speaks to me: Tony Cavorso and Tom Fitzpatrick undoubtedly would be surprised to see their names associated with a Bible passage, though both might appreciate the irony; Johnny Nelson, who combined his Catholic faith and his trade-union commitment in ways rare before the days of the theology of liberation, would understand. This collection is an effort to ensure that their years of struggle and those of their compatriots, in the words of the band Midnight Oil, "shall not be forgotten years."

Steve Rosswurm

ACRONYMS

Unions

ACA	American Communications Association
AFL	American Federation of Labor
CIO	Congress of Industrial Organizations (initially called Committee for Industrial Organization)
CIO–PAC	Congress of Industrial Organizations–Political Action Committee
DPO	Distributive, Processing & Office Workers of America
FE	United Farm Equipment & Metal Workers
FTA	Food, Tobacco, Agricultural & Allied Workers
IAM	International Association of Machinists
IBEW	International Brotherhood of Electrical Workers
IFAWA	International Fishermen & Allied Workers of America
ILA	International Longshoremen's Association
IFLWU	International Fur & Leather Workers Union
ILWU	International Longshoremen's & Warehousemen's Union
IUE	International Union of Electrical, Radio & Machine Workers
IUMMSW	International Union of Mine, Mill & Smelter Workers
IUMSWA	Industrial Union of Marine & Shipbuilding Workers of America
NMU	National Maritime Union of America
NTWIU	Needle Trades Workers Industrial Union
NUMCS	National Union of Marine Cooks & Stewards
SWOC	Steel Workers Organizing Committee
TWU	Transport Workers Union
TWIU	Transport Workers International Union
UAW	United Automobile Workers of America

UE	United Electrical, Radio & Machine Workers of America
UFWA	United Furniture Workers of America
UMW	United Mine Workers of America
UOPWA	United Office & Professional Workers of America
UPW	United Public Workers of America
UTSE	United Transport Service Employees

Other Organizations, Agencies, etc.

ACTU	Association of Catholic Trade Unionists
AEC	Atomic Energy Commission
ATS	Army Transport Service
CP	Communist Party [of the United States of America]
CPUSA	Communist Party of the United States of America
FBI	Federal Bureau of Investigation
FEPC	Fair Employment Practices Commission
GE	General Electric Company
HUAC	House Committee on Un-American Activities
ICP	Industry Council Plan
INS	Immigration & Naturalization Service
IRS	Internal Revenue Service
IUC	Industrial Union Council
IWW	Industrial Workers of the World
MVA	Missouri Valley Authority
NAACP	National Association for the Advancement of Colored People
NCWC	National Catholic Welfare Conference
NLRB	National Labor Relations Board
NNLC	National Negro Labor Council
OSV	*Our Sunday Visitor*
PCMIB	Pacific Coast Maritime Industry Board
SACB	Subversive Activies Control Board
SAD	Social Action Department
TUUL	Trade Union Unity League
TVA	Tennessee Valley Authority
UEMDA	UE Members for Democratic Action
USES	U.S. Employment Service
WLB	War Labor Board
WPA	Works Progress Administration
YCL	Young Communist League

THE CIO'S LEFT-LED UNIONS

INTRODUCTION:

An Overview and Preliminary Assessment of the CIO's Expelled Unions

STEVE ROSSWURM

In 1955, at its last convention before merging with the American Federation of Labor (AFL), the Congress of Industrial Organizations (CIO) staged a pageant titled *Image of Freedom.* This hosanna was meant to "portray the history and spirit of the CIO," but its script presented a severely edited version of that history: it completely omitted any mention of the 11 left-led unions expelled in 1949 and 1950. Even their expulsion, still fresh in memory, was not worth noting.[1]

Historians of the United States' recent past, not just labor historians, cannot accept the effort this anecdote represents to obliterate the memory and record of the left-led unions. As part of its revitalization, moreover, the labor movement must come to grips with the significance of these unions and their expulsions.

What follows, then, is a preliminary assessment of the expelled unions. Three general topics will be addressed: an evaluation of their accomplishments; an appraisal of the role of the Communist Party (CP) in them; finally, a discussion of the implications of the expulsions for the development of the American labor movement and American society generally from 1950 to the present.

In 1949, the CIO national convention expelled two unions, both of which already had left it, for being "Communist-dominated": the United Electrical, Radio & Machine Workers (UE) and the United Farm Equipment & Metal Workers (FE). It also leveled the same charge against ten other unions: American Communications Association (ACA); Food, Tobacco, Agricultural & Allied Workers (FTA); International Fishermen & Allied Workers of America (IFAWA); International Fur & Leather Workers Union (IFLWU); International Longshoremen's & Warehousemen's Union (ILWU); International Union of Mine, Mill & Smelter Workers (IUMMSW); National Union of Marine Cooks & Stewards (NUMCS); United Furniture Workers of America (UFWA); United Office & Professional Workers of America (UOPWA); United Public Workers of America (UPW). "[D]emocratic forces" in the UFWA ousted its "Communists," but the CIO tried the other nine and expelled them at its 1950 convention.

How many union members were dumped? CIO officials used divergent figures—from 675,000 to 1 million—and the semiofficial numbers run from about 750,000 to more than 900,000. Whatever the case, the CIO expelled between 17 and 20 percent of its total membership in 1949.

What kind of working people did the CIO expel? First, there were those in what was known as "basic industry." The UE, keystone of the CIO left, was the largest and most important of the expelled unions. Representing men and women who worked in plants manufacturing electrical products as well as those in small machine shops, it had at its height 499,800 members. When expelled, it numbered 427,000. Two other expelled unions primarily organized workers in heavy industry: The FE covered agricultural implement-manufacturing plants, primarily International Harvester, but also small machine shops. At its height, it had 50,000 members and 43,000 when expelled. IUMMSW, concentrated in noncoal mining and the brass and copper industries, numbered 114,000 at its peak and 74,000 when expelled.[2]

Most of the expelled unions, however, comprised working people outside basic industry. First, there is the group that organized what came to be called "blue-collar" workers. The ILWU, which had originated among west coast longshoreman, soon began organizing warehouse workers; by the end of World War II, moreover, its greatest concentration of membership outside the west coast docks was in the Hawaiian Islands, where it had about 20,000 members, primarily in the sugar and pineapple industries. At its height it numbered 62,100, and it had 43,900 members when expelled. Likewise, the IFLWU, which began in New York City's fur shops, expanded to organize tanneries east of the Mississippi; it had 60,300 members at its height and 44,800 when expelled. The NUMCS, which represented those who worked in west coast shipping, was a relatively small union, whose membership peaked at 14,300; it had about half that when expelled. The IFAWA, another small union whose peak size was 10,000 and the same when expelled, covered not just fishermen but also some cannery workers on the west coast. The FTA's membership at its high point was 50,000; in 1949, it had 22,500 members. It organized a wide variety of agricultural and food-processing workers throughout the country.

The remainder of the expelled unions organized white-collar workers. The ACA concentrated on the telegraph industry; at its height, it numbered 12,000 and had 10,000 members when expelled. The UOPWA organized insurance agents and clerical workers as well as white-collar workers in various communication industries. Its peak membership was 50,800; it had 31,500 members when expelled. The UPW organized a wide variety of state, county, and federal employees; it peaked at 61,100 members and had declined to 14,000 at its expulsion.

How one judges the accomplishments of the expelled unions has a great deal to do with what perspective one brings to the viewing. For most contemporary trade-union leaders, who were overwhelmingly white and male, most of the expelled unions were insignificant, for their memberships were tangential to basic manufacturing and its primarily white male work force. This focus was not limited to liberal and conservative union officials; CP leaders, in their strategic thinking, often shared it. Lee Pressman, for example, who probably had been a CP member at some time and who worked with it during his long tenure as CIO general counsel, thought that, outside of the UE and ILWU, the expelled unions "didn't amount to a row of pins."[3]

Viewed from a different perspective—one that sees the American working class as not just male but rather comprising both women and men; not just white but also including African-Americans, Asian-Americans, and Hispanics; not just the steel mills and auto plants but also the offices and classrooms—accomplished a great deal. The American working class in 1950 was an extraordinarily diverse group, laboring in an even greater variety of settings.

The expelled unions, from what can be determined from imprecise figures and impressionistic evidence, reflected the diversity of the American working class to a greater degree than those unions that remained in the CIO. The membership of the ILWU, for example, probably was close to 50 percent nonwhite—primarily Filipino and Japanese sugar and pineapple workers in Hawaii, but also African-Americans in its warehouse division. The NUMCS was at least 50 percent African-American, while there were sizable numbers of Mexican-Americans and African-Americans in IUMMSW, especially in the Southeast and Southwest. There were many Asian-Americans in the IFAWA. The UPW probably was 35 to 40 percent African-American because of its large numbers of poorly paid government workers. Even in the FE, which consisted primarily of white men, there were substantial numbers of African-Americans in its key Chicago locals. Of these unions, the UPW probably had the greatest number of women. There also were sizable percentages of women in the UE as well as the ACA.[4]

An examination of the FTA and the UOPWA sheds further light not only on the issue of composition but also on the development of female and nonwhite leadership in the expelled unions. Philip Murray, CIO president, had nothing but contempt for the small left-led affiliates, and at the 1948 CIO convention he vehemently denounced them for poor organizing records. In an effort to isolate them, the CIO executive board sponsored a resolution, which the convention passed, empowering it to investigate those unions that had "failed to make substantial progress in organizing the unorganized." Both the FTA and the UOPWA came under particular attack during these discussions.[5]

There was much evidence to support Murray's criticisms of the FTA. Its continuing financial problems often made it dependent upon the CIO national office for funds, and it had a small and declining membership. The CP, moreover, probably played as important a role in the FTA's affairs as it did in those of any other expelled union. Donald Henderson, the union's president, was an open Communist and, if we are to believe the Federal Bureau of Investigation (FBI), as we should in this case, many of its staff and executive board members also were CP members. There was, moreover, a financial scandal involving the union's treasurer, and Henderson's personal habits were often troublesome.[6]

Recent scholarship on the FTA, however, seriously undermines this negative appraisal. No other CIO union could begin to match the FTA's accomplishments in organizing some of the most downtrodden and dispossessed in the U.S. working class: at cotton seed plants in Memphis, Tennessee; at Campbell Soup plants in New Jersey and Chicago; at a citrus processing plant in Dade City, Florida; at tobacco-processing plants in North Carolina, Ohio, and Pennsylvania; in the Arizona and California agricultural fields; at salmon-processing plants in Alaska. Women constituted about 50 percent of FTA's membership and people of color probably 75–80 percent, but this, in and of itself, was no guarantee that leadership from women, African-Americans,

Asian-Americans, and Mexican-Americans would emerge. But it did develop at the national and local level, as in no other CIO union.[7]

The CIO trial board stressed the FTA's declining membership after 1946, though much of that membership loss resulted from systematic and semiofficial raiding. By September 1949, six CIO unions had raided more than 20 FTA locals, forcing FTA to spend about $225,000 defending itself against the raids that had cost it more than $100,000 in lost annual income owing to the decline in membership. To put the entire blame for this loss of membership on the FTA was, as Bert Cochran has put it, "like a police officer taking a victim's wallet and then writing out a charge against him for having no visible means of support."[8]

We see similarly important accomplishments in the UOPWA, another union that came under attack at the 1948 convention. There is little research on this union, but it successfully organized white-collar workers in a way never seen before. By the late 1940s, it had organized thousands of insurance agents and clerical workers, and had begun to make gains in New York City banks and on Wall Street. Perhaps the best indication of the serious inroads the UOPWA was making into the nation's offices was the attention management groups began giving white-collar unionization in the mid-1940s, when a spate of articles called attention to the dangers of declining white-collar morale and the growth of unions as well as delivering basic lessons in trade unionism to neophytes.[9]

Women must have comprised a large percentage of the UOPWA, though not as many as one might suppose because most of its insurance agents were male. The UOPWA's male leadership was more sensitive to the issue of women's equality than those of most contemporary unions, but unsurprisingly it was not committed to feminism and the very structure of the organization sometimes reflected gendered divisions of prestige and power within the white-collar work force. In a calculated retreat from industrial unionism, for example, the leadership had granted the insurance agents their own semiautonomous locals and division. Yet women had moved into important leadership positions and there was an incipient feminism within its ranks, particularly within its secondary leadership. The UOPWA's organizing style, which differed from the leading AFL white-collar affiliate, may well have focused on the issue of process, in an implicit recognition of feminist labor-organizing strategies developed in the 1970s.[10]

Many of the expelled unions, then, organized working people who were largely peripheral both to basic industry and to the concerns of most trade-union leaders because of the labor they performed. The relationship also worked the other way around: because of the way in which the labor markets were structured, these people also were peripheral because of the kind of workers they were—often people of color and/or women. This organizing accomplishment alone suggests that most historians have seriously misjudged the expelled unions.

We, so far, have discussed the expelled unions without mention of the CP. What, then, was the role of the Party in the expelled unions?

Party members were very active in the formation of the expelled unions in the 1930s, just as they were involved in the formation of many other CIO unions. Recent work on the Transport Workers Union (TWU), which was left-led until 1948, and the ILWU suggests, in great and complex detail, how deeply the CP was involved in the earliest and formative years of the CIO unions. The Communist leader William Z. Foster's assertion of the key role of Party members in the Steel Workers Organizing Committee in the late 1930s—there were "some" 60 Communists on the committee's full-time staff of 200—suggests the importance of CP cadre to the formation of even a mainstream CIO union like the United Steel Workers of America.[11] We will not discuss, however, the formation of the expelled unions, but rather the CP's role in them from the point when they became CIO affiliates until the mid-1950s.

It is difficult to provide precise figures for the number of CP members in the expelled unions, but we know it was small. In 1948, the FBI, which undoubtedly had obtained CP information, asserted that the Party had 59,000 members. Almost half of these were in unions, and 16,520 were in the CIO—less than 1 percent of the total CIO membership that year. If we assume that only the expelled unions had CP members in 1948, that would mean that less than 2 percent (actually 1.8) of their total membership were Party members, or about 1,502 members per union.[12] (There were, of course, Party members in other CIO unions, so, on the one hand, there were fewer than 1,502 members per expelled union; on the other, CP membership had fallen by 1948, so there many more Party members in the CIO in, say, 1945, than in 1948.)

Figures for most individual unions suggest the same small CP membership. Louis Merrill, UOPWA president, asserted that out of a membership of 85,000, the UOPWA had a CP membership of 2,000—about 2.35 percent. Earl Browder, longtime CP leader, noted that the IFLWU had 600–700 Communists—just over 1 percent—of whom about 200 were "very active." (Local 555, the Teachers Union in New York City that was affiliated with the UPW, is an exception here. Nathan Glazer suggests that 25 percent of its membership may have been Communists at any one time.)[13]

That there is no necessary relationship, however, between numbers and influence is certainly true in the case of the CP and the expelled unions. First, the evidence suggests that CP membership was heavily concentrated in the full-time staff and national officers of these unions. Merrill, for example, attested that 50 of UOPWA's organizers were Party members, while the IUE, which the CIO chartered to destroy the UE and which had access to FBI material, argued in May 1950 that 200 Communists or former Communists were on the UE's payroll. The vast majority of the FTA's 60-person staff in 1947 were Party members, while there was at least one Communist group among the FE's national officers.[14]

Second, there were large numbers of non-Party members who worked with CP members in these expelled unions. Their contemporaries and subsequent historians have not been kind to those who have been called, at best, "fellow travelers." These trade unionists, who quite freely and consciously worked with CP members, might better be called independent leftists.[15] John Watkins, an FE staff member, is a case in point. Several witnesses had identified him as CP member before a government committee, but he denied that he ever carried a card, accepted CP discipline, or participated in a meeting attended by only Communists; he, moreover, sometimes opposed CP policy. He had, however, "participated in Communist activities to such a degree that some persons may honestly believe I was a member of the party." He signed petitions for and gave money to "Communist causes" and attended caucus meetings at which CP members were present. Watkins, who irrevocably broke with the CP over the issue of Taft–Hartley compliance, was not duped: he worked with the CP because it "was in the interest of our membership and within the labor policies of the union and [of] the CIO."[16]

The CP, then, despite a small membership in the expelled unions, played a central role in them because of its leading political position, because it had members concentrated in staff positions, and because there were men and women like John Watkins in every expelled union.[17] Until we accept these independent leftists on their own terms and try to understand their willingness to work with the CP, we not only will never comprehend the Party's tremendous influence but also will not understand an important component of twentieth-century American radicalism.

What, then, was the working relationship of the Party with its CIO cadre from the CIO's formation to the end of World War II? Party leaders and its periodicals put out the current line—that is, its analysis of current political and economic developments—in speeches and publications. On many if not most issues, a Party member had only to read the *Daily Worker* to understand his/her political responsibilities. In virtually every case, the changing political positions of the expelled unions, especially concerning foreign affairs, paralleled those of the CP and the *Daily Worker.*

How CP members got the line adopted in their unions is more complicated. Until the late 1930s, there were CP "fractions" in each union; that is, CP members of a local met together, sometimes with a full-time Party official, before the local's regular meeting to agree on what positions to take and who would speak to them. There is strong evidence that the fractions continued to function after their abolition, albeit on a more informal basis, sometimes becoming premeetings of "progressives" with or without Party officials.[18]

In many cases it took little effort to implement the line, because the positions that the CP took often were in tune with a large segment of trade-union sentiment. The positions the CP advocated, moreover, in the main were adopted democratically. In other cases—for example, when CP cadre disagreed among themselves, or for particularly controversial aspects of the World War II line, or in the case of maintaining the CIO's center–left coalition—it was necessary for CP officials to intervene directly and/or provide coordinating direction. In some cases, certainly more than those for which we have adequate documentation, CP officials intervened directly to make personnel decisions or to place a cadre in a union.[19]

But there was a countervailing trend: bonds between Party trade unionists in the expelled unions and the apparatus weakened during this period. Some cadre drifted away from Party discipline while remaining within its orbit. Others dropped their registrations when the CP liquidated its shop and industrial branches in favor of community ones. Some leaders, no longer pariahs because of the congruence between the CP line and CIO policy and with confidence derived from an expanding wartime membership, increasingly saw themselves less as Communists and more as trade unionists. As the UE's Ruth Young put it, many became "Communist trade unionists" rather than "trade union Communists."[20]

This loosening of discipline within a context of continued intervention ended with the fall of Browder and with Foster's rise to power. Shop branches and fractions were rebuilt and trade-union cadre came under increased disciplinary surveillance as the Party reestablished its pre–Popular Front organizational forms and began functioning largely on the basis of "better fewer, but better." The accession of John Williamson, who had joined the Party in the early 1920s, symbolized the new regime.[21]

Classical Marxism–Leninism established the framework for the disastrous CP line in the period from 1945 to the mid-1950s. In a period marked by what the understated analysis of the unsucessful reformers of 1956 called "sectarian attitudes," the CP pushed hard against the CIO leadership, especially the "center" and "social democrats." The CP's cadre in the CIO, although increasingly isolated and attacked, showed to a surprising degree what good Communists they had remained by accepting the Party's decision to support Henry A. Wallace's third-party (Progressive) presidential campaign. There was much more trade-union support for Wallace than most historians have acknowledged, and his critique of the developing Cold War was accurate, but the decision was an enormously costly one, as it established one of the necessary conditions for the expulsions.[22]

The CIO Party cadre's acceptance of the decision to support Wallace marked the end of unilateral Party discipline within the CIO. The expelled unions supported the Progressive Party, but with varying degrees of commitment that often reflected the balance of forces within each union. The 1948 CIO convention witnessed a large-scale breakdown in CP discipline as the left-led unions largely deserted the cause of the Greater New York City Industrial Council, with some voting for majority resolutions or remaining silent in the face of vociferous attacks. In 1949, moreover, the UE–FE left the CIO despite the CP's wishes. The postexpulsion relationship between the expelled unions and the Party became increasingly farcical as the latter careened between ultraleftism—for example, in its campaign against white chauvinism and its shrill critiques of the former's petty bourgeois tendencies—and reformism, as in the decision to "reenter" the "mainstream" with the AFL–CIO merger in 1956.[23]

How to generalize about the CP's overall relationship to the expelled unions? First, much of the Party's influence originated in its leading political role and was earned democratically. Second, while it did sometimes intervene undemocratically, its sub-rosa maneuvering differed little from that of other groups, particularly the Catholic Church, which ran "conferences" parallel to the CP fractions that sought to influence CIO policy and personnel decisions. Third, the expelled unions were at least as democratic, if not more so, than other CIO unions.

There was one way—which made all the difference—in which the CP's relationship with the expelled unions diverged from that of other "outside groups": its subservience to the Soviet Union. This issue takes us into an evaluation of the strengths and weaknesses of the American CP.

The CPUSA exhibited, in Bruce Nelson's phrase, a "slavish loyalty to the Soviet Union." The role it played within the CIO and its political positions often were tied directly to what best defended the Soviet Union. This subordination often and effectively delegitimized every position the CP took.[24]

A good example—only one of many—is the CP labor policy during World War II. While in some ways simply a tougher version of the CIO's, it often subordinated everything to the struggle against the Axis and for the Soviet Union. Its defense of incentive pay; its sometimes draconian enforcement of the no-strike pledge; its lack of interest in civil liberties; its diminished advocacy of civil rights; its support for the National Service Act—all dearly cost not only the Party but also the working class.[25]

The issue here is not support for the war—except for pacifists, opposition was ludicrous—nor the no-strike pledge, which was inevitable. Nor was it any failure of CP labor cadre and those in alliance with them to produce material benefits for their members; current research suggests that the expelled unions "delivered the goods." It was rather the opportunistic manipulation of hyperpatriotism; the slandering and expulsion of honest militants; the sometimes cynical betrayal of the African-American quest for equality; the fervor with which CP trade unionists and those within its orbit advocated the alliance with "progressive capital"—these were some of the bankrupt aspects of the wartime labor policy. Perhaps most important, those who supported the CP line not only neglected to explore other avenues of struggle once strikes were banned but also failed to politically educate millions of "new" workers to the realities of capitalism. CP trade unionists, who were well aware of both failures, acknowledged them in 1945. "[W]e missed an opportunity," said "Bob S," the steelworker, "to educate thousands of workers in what our role in society is and what the role of the boss is. That is what we missed and that is a costly mistake."[26]

The commitment to the Soviet Union had even worse ramifications after the war. At the very moment anticommunism was gaining popular ground in America, it was providing daily lessons in its Eastern European classroom on how brutally authoritarian socialism could be. As Yuri Afanasyev, Director of the Soviet Institute of Historical Research, has noted: "For me it is obvious that Stalin and Stalinism have damaged the socialist project more than all the bourgeois ideologies in the world added together."[27]

The CP's second flaw was of a different order. As individuals, many if not most Party members and independent leftists were militantly secularist in a society that was extraordinarily religious. In this, they were the inheritors of Marxism's and the American left's hostility toward religion. This secularism most antagonized Catholic working people, who had good reasons to be anticommunist.[28]

A third flaw, related to this resolute secularism, was the left's inability to understand some of the most important aspects of anticommunism. For the left, anticommunism came from the large corporations, anticommunist government officials and/or agencies, or the bloc of racist Southern congressmen and senators. It would be foolish to ignore these sources and strengths of anticommunism, but it would be just as foolish, if not more so, to reduce anticommunism, as the left did, to these actors and motivations. Current research, including my own on the Catholic working class, suggests that one of the most important aspects of the domestic Cold War was its resolute antimodernism: the drive to reassert traditional values, especially those associated with gender, sexuality, and the family, that resonated deeply with many Americans.[29]

The most fundamental criticism to be made of the CP and its trade-union cadre is that it failed utterly in its professed mission to build a socialist movement. Communists in private and militant trade unionists in public, CIO Party cadre built good, in some cases excellent, unions. The membership of their unions, however, exhibited no more socialist consciousness in, say, 1950 than they had in 1938. This is not to argue, as some would have it, that Communists were nothing more than good trade unionists. They were political to the core, but their political perspective, drawn from the Soviet experience, was inherently incapable of providing the basis for the development of a socialist movement.[30]

Secrecy was an integral part of the CP's Marxist–Leninist perspective. While the Party often discussed this issue and considered bringing its cadre into the open, it never did so. Not only was secrecy central to the CP's revolutionary strategy, but it also had laid the basis for the political influence that in turn generated the necessity of remaining hidden. It, moreover, permitted CP trade unionists to escape responsibility for their organization's decisions. Clandestine membership was, however, a sadly mistaken strategy, for it laid the basis for the accusations of conspiracy that were so effective and made hidden members easy targets for the FBI. It was, moreover, just plain dishonest: the sense of betrayal that CIO members felt when hitherto secret members in leadership positions were exposed as card carriers still resonates from the printed page.[31]

What, then, were the strengths of Party cadre as trade unionists?

Most Communists in the CIO, as well the independent leftists who worked with them, were good trade unionists—at least as good as their opponents, in some cases much better. Not only did they systematically deliver the goods, but many of them did so in a spirit of self-sacrifice and commitment that borders on the saintly. James Matles's protection of the UE's treasury, which he never forgot came from the pockets of working people, is legendary. So, too, is his comment to UE organizers when they raised the issue of pensions: If you're doing a good job, you won't live long enough to collect one.

This spirit was not confined to the UE. Every expelled union fought for and won increased material benefits for its membership. The CIO leadership indirectly recognized this fact when they convicted the expelled unions of being Communist dominated, not of being ineffective labor unions. While many anti-Communists assumed these were one and the same thing, clearly they were not.

Did the left-led expelled unions have a distinct trade union policy? While many contemporaries and subsequent observers of both left and right have argued that they did not, Judith Stepan-Norris and Maurice Zeitlin persuasively argue the opposite. Based upon a sophisticated quantitative analysis of hundreds of CIO contracts, their study argues that the left-led unions' pursuit of explicitly anticapitalist goals in written contracts strongly differentiated them from other CIO unions. While there is evidence that the expelled unions' trade-union policy sometimes did parallel their opponents', Stepan-Norris and Zeitlin have cleared away much ideological rubbish and have considerably raised the intellectual level of the debate on this issue.[32]

Even if in some ways the leaders of the expelled unions were simply good trade unionists—and there is not enough research to be definitive here—in other ways they were much more: it was the FTA and the IFLWU, along with Packinghouse Workers, that came up with a successful organizing strategy for the South. It was the expelled unions, as we have seen, that organized people of color and women, and within which both rose to leadership positions. It was the UE who fought and won equal pay for equal work; it was Matles who continually stressed, in spite of a solidifying apathy, the necessity of organizing the unorganized.[33]

In several cases, most notably the FE, but also in some UE and IUMMSW locals, CP trade-union leaders not only accommodated themselves to but also nourished a brand of radicalism—though it always was in potential, and sometimes actual, conflict with the demands of a political party—that was antiauthoritarian and quasi-syndicalist. Party trade unionists worked best with this radicalism in areas most geo-graphically isolated from the heavy hand of CP headquarters.[34]

The leadership of the expelled unions, whether CP or independent leftist, understood capitalism: they were Marxists. This was no small thing, their refusal to accept what Charles Maier calls the "politics of productivity." It laid the basis, for example, for the FE's devastating critique of Walter Reuther's commitment to increasing productivity and the UE struggle against automation, speedup, and runaway shops in the 1950s. An important source of the left attack on the Marshall Plan was an understanding of its critical role in the stabilization of capitalism at home and abroad. Unions might have to adopt temporary truces with management, and capital might be forced to grant in-creased benefits to labor, but nothing obviated the class struggle that lay at the heart of capitalism. The destruction capital has wreaked upon working people in the past 20 years ought to suggest to both scholars and today's trade unionists that the expelled unions were on to something.[35]

The implications of the expulsions were devastating for both trade unionism and American working people. Some of the effects were immediate and obvious; others were long range and evident only decades later.

First, the expulsions helped establish the hegemony of the Cold War paradigm in American society and U.S. foreign policy. They effectively delegitimized serious criticism of the Cold War, ostracized those who engaged in that questioning, and dotted the i's and crossed the t's of the CIO's entry into the government's foreign-policy-implementing— *not -making*—apparatus. The CIO, in terms of personnel, money, and policy, became a junior partner in the United States' imperial efforts. Bipartisan congressional agreement on foreign policy found its labor equivalent well before the AFL–CIO merger. Michael Ross was not Jay Lovestone or Irving Brown, but no principled disagreements separated them.[36]

Second, the war against left unionism gutted a burgeoning north-ern and urban civil rights movement based in the working class. It also destroyed a growing Southern civil rights movement that was likewise grounded in the trade unions. Historians are only now begin-ning to sort out the implications of all this, but there is every reason to believe they were significant.[37]

Third, the drive against left unionists, both in the expelled unions and those in remaining CIO unions, eliminated and/or silenced a generation of shop-floor militants and helped solidify the developing "workplace rule of law" and trade-union reliance on the federal government. Militants' "discovery" in the early 1980s of "in-plant" organizing suggests the strength of the "workplace rule of law" paradigm, politically induced historical amnesia, and the impact of the missing activists.[38]

Fourth, the expulsions signified the slowing of serious efforts to organize industries dominated by people of color and women. UOPWA, FTA, and UPW achievements disintegrated under the pressures of an unholy trinity: the Cold War, CIO raiding, and an employer offensive. Some organizing efforts continued, of course, but under the auspices of a (white and male) leadership decidedly unsympathetic with—and in many cases outright hostile to—the independent initiatives of women and people of color.

The CIO missed a golden opportunity in its failure to make serious efforts to organize the white-collar sector. Mechanization and decreasing salaries, from the Great Depression on, had dramatically weakened the bonds between white-collar employees and management. The CIO, however, did not take advantage of this opening: its decision to leave what little white-collar organizing it did to its industrial unions effectively foreclosed any possibility of developing feminist organizing strategies. These industrial unions, moreover, according to an astute promanagement observer, pursued precisely the least productive approach to organizing. Management did take advantage of the space the CIO provided: by the late-1950s, it had largely recaptured the loyalty of its white-collar employees.[39]

But even more: the CIO simply stopped organizing the unorganized. Esconced in the nation's 2,000 largest factories, it, as Daniel Bell noted again and again in *Fortune,* was not up to expanding its membership. Although CIO convention delegates increasingly drew attention to this failure in their calls for a return to the crusading spirit that had invigorated the early days, it was not to be. It may overstate the case to say that the expulsions reinforced racial and sexual divisions within the American working class. It is no exaggeration, however, to say that they signified the CIO's wholesale retreat from a confrontation with these divisions. From the early 1950s, wage disparity and segmentation by sex and race within the working class, which had narrowed as a result of the CIO's organizing achievements, increased steadily.[40]

Fifth, the CIO carried out the expulsions a way that both integrated it into the state apparatus and strengthened that apparatus. CIO leadership often asserted that it had democratically and independently handled its "Communist" problem, but at least for James B. Carey and the IUE—the man and the union on whose behalf the national CIO office put everything on the line—nothing could be further from the truth. An article about the IUE and Carey might well be titled, "In Bed with the Feds: The Conception and Birth of a Bastard Union." There was scarcely a federal agency—the FBI, the presidency, the House Un-American Activities Committee (HUAC), the Atomic Energy Commission—that was not at Carey's service in the battle against the UE.[41]

The CIO offered at best pro forma opposition to the operations of surveillance agencies, particularly the FBI, and the industrial security program that was part and parcel of an increasingly militarized economy. In the case of the port security program, not only did the CIO acquiesce, but its affiliates helped initiate and administer what Murray's Report in 1950 promised would be the "most effective maritime security program ever devised."[42]

Sixth, the CIO leadership's acceptance of capitalism—or lack of understanding of it—stands in stark contrast to the expelled unions' comprehension of its dynamics. Nowhere can this be seen more clearly than in the case of capital mobility. In capitalism's continuing quest for what David Harvey calls a "spatial fix," shifting investment transferred job after job from one section of the country to another. But there is more. Capital mobility destroyed and destroys—for the process is an endless one—history: the working-class institutions, communities, and organizations that were the product of years of struggle.[43]

The CIO had, or should have had, a good sense of what capital mobility meant, for they only had to look at the impact of the textile industry's exit from New England. They also should have had a good sense of what the implications were, for they only had to look at the results for textile of Operation Dixie's dismal failure. Or they could have looked at the rubber industry, where decentralization and/or its threat significantly affected the evolution of the CIO affiliate.[44]

Capital mobility was an important part of the corporate postwar counteroffensive against the CIO and the class relations and institutions that it had produced. Between 1947 and 1954 alone, capital substantially transformed the United States' economic geography. Most of the capital-mobility issues the labor movement faced in the 1970s and 1980s—job destruction in center cities; bribery by job-hungry areas; government assistance to runaways; management consultant firms such as Fantus; companies' economic terrorism—were present in the postwar period.[45]

The CIO responded lamely to this capital mobility because it was trapped in a web of ideological and institutional commitments that closed off its options: to progress (which at least one expelled union shared); to capitalism; to economic expansion as the dissolvent of class struggle; to alliances with the Democratic Party; to an end to militance. Here and there, there were sporadic responses—for example, from the UE, FE, and the militant UAW local at Ford's River Rouge plant—that indicated a path of resistance to capital mobility. What predominated, however, were the solutions of Walter Reuther and the IUE. Inevitably, those chickens came home to roost in the 1970s and 1980s.[46]

At its baldest, the expulsions and their attendant consequences were essential to what some have called the postwar "capital–labor accord," but what might better be termed the postwar "negotiated class struggle." That agreement, in turn, was a necessary component of the "postwar corporate system," or the "postwar social structure of accumulation." No expulsions, no agreement, no U.S. corporate capitalist domination at home and abroad after World War II.[47]

What can we conclude about the expelled unions?

The CP's CIO cadre and the independent leftists in alliance with them not only made numerous real achievements but also placed several important organizing issues on the historical agenda. To ignore those accomplishments in the name of anticommunism produces bad history and bad politics. Fifteen years of capitalist assault on American working people suggests how dangerous such blindness, intended or unintended, is.

Yet to ignore, in the name of anti-anticommunism, the fundamentally flawed nature of the CP's political perspective for changing America—to disregard the problems (and that is much too mild a word here) inherent in the CP's commitment to the Soviet Union as a socialist "city on the hill"—produces similarly bad history and bad politics. Nothing shows more clearly the dangers of this position than the ongoing changes in the USSR and the mass upheavals in Eastern Europe.

ACKNOWLEDGMENTS

I delivered an earlier version of this essay at the State Historical Society of Wisconsin's conference, "Perspectives on Labor History: The Wisconsin School and Beyond," held in March 1990. Sharp comments from the following have led to several substantial revisions: Richard Altenbaugh, Susan Figliulo, Roger Horowitz, Bruce Nelson, Carl Parrini, Dave Roediger, Ellen Schrecker, and Seth Wigderson. I am thankful for travel grants from the Harry S. Truman Library Institute and the Henry J. Kaiser Family Foundation and a Beeke-Levy Research Fellowship (Franklin and Eleanor Roosevelt Institute). Because of space limitations, citations have been kept to a minimum.

CLASS AND RACE
IN THE CRESCENT CITY:
The ILWU, from
San Francisco to New Orleans

BRUCE NELSON

The International Longshoremen's and Warehousemen's Union
(ILWU) emerged out of two defining moments in the experience of
the U.S. working class in the 1930s. In 1934 a great strike wave
convulsed important segments of industrial America. Among longshoremen and other maritime workers on the Pacific coast, the legendary "Big Strike" of '34 ended 15 years of ironclad employer
domination and ushered in a sustained period of worker insurgency
at the "point of production." Then, in 1937, when the successful
campaigns of the Committee for Industrial Organization (CIO; fore-
runner of the Congress of Industrial Organizations) in auto and steel
seemed proof that labor was "on the march" as never before in U.S.
history, the west coast longshoremen abandoned the venerable
American Federation of Labor (AFL) and voted to affiliate with the
CIO. Confidently, they sought to uproot the AFL in port cities on the
Atlantic and Gulf coasts and to make the ILWU a genuinely national
organization of longshoremen and allied workers.[1]
    The key to this bold endeavor was the port of New Orleans, whose
dock work force seemed ripe for the plucking. In a waterfront community burdened with a vast oversupply of labor, flagrant abuses in hiring

methods, and autocratic unions, the ILWU program was simple but presumably compelling. The new CIO affiliate promised democratic unionism, the replacement of the notoriously corrupt "shape-up" with "the hiring-hall method of dispatching men without discrimination," and the "equalization of earnings." Its stunning defeat in a representation election that appeared to be "in the bag" meant the ILWU would remain essentially a west coast union. But beyond its significance for the ILWU, the outcome of this campaign provides important insights into the ferocity of jurisdictional rivalries, the ambiguous role of the state, the unevenness of working-class consciousness, and above all the complex character of racial accommodation and conflict during the turbulent 1930s.[2]

The ILWU members who arrived in New Orleans in the fall of 1937 were courageous and seasoned organizers, but their experience had been mainly on the west coast, where the overwhelming majority of the maritime work force was white. Apparently they were unaware that strong unions and a tradition of biracial unity had prevailed on the riverfront for nearly a quarter of a century before the return of the open shop in the 1920s. In confronting a labor force that was predominantly African-American, they lamented the "backwardness" of the Crescent City's black longshoremen and, in the wake of their bitter electoral defeat, complained that "the southern negro is only one step removed from the primitive superstitions of the African jungle tribes." In spite of their real commitment to militant working-class unity, the ILWU organizers failed to understand how the bitter legacy of racial competition for jobs on the riverfront had rendered black longshoremen suspicious of the motives of whites, even well-intentioned whites who—consciously or unconsciously—saw the unionism of the CIO as the means by which "the white man will lead the negro out of the pit and show him the light."[3]

The birth of the ILWU can be traced to the eruption that began on May 9, 1934, when members of the Pacific coast district of the International Longshoremen's Association (ILA) walked off the job in ports from San Diego to Seattle and points north. Within a week they were joined by seamen and other maritime workers; teamsters refused to handle scab-unloaded cargo; and in July a bloody confrontation between police and unionists triggered a general strike of more than 100,000 workers in San Francisco and Alameda counties. The 83-day waterfront strike became famous not only for these expressions of solidarity but also for the disciplined militancy of its rank-and-file participants and the left-wing political orientation of some of its key leaders. Especially in the San Francisco longshore local, a small core of Communists and CP sympathizers, led by Australian immigrant Harry Bridges, played a vital role in directing the strike locally and influencing its character up and down the coast.[4]

Soon after the longshoremen and seamen returned to work, a presidentially appointed arbitration board issued an award that offered major concessions to the ILA, including union recognition, de facto union control of hiring, and a six-hour day. The award was an attempt to right the injustices that had prevailed on the docks for many years, but it also came in the context of a continuing wave of job actions and "quickie" strikes at the point of production. Before long the shipowners were complaining that union stewards "establish the manner in which, and the speed at which, work is to be performed on the waterfronts of the Pacific Coast." To the employers' further dismay, the marine workers showed a remarkable propensity to incorporate politics as well as "porkchops" into their struggles, as they walked off the job to protest the aggression of Benito Mussolini's Italy against Ethiopia, demonstrate their solidarity with the embattled Spanish Republic, and express their outrage at the frame-up—and, in one case, the murder—of fellow maritime workers by local authorities.[5]

In the summer of 1937, the Pacific coast district of the ILA voted to leave the AFL and affiliate with the CIO, whose "tremendous march," Bridges declared, was "sweeping everything before it." A conference with John L. Lewis in early July resulted in the formation of the CIO Maritime Committee. Although Joseph P. Ryan, the corrupt, dictatorial, and narrowly self-serving president of the ILA, was conspicuously absent, representatives of most other maritime unions attended and many seemed ready to join forces with Lewis. The conferees decided that "[i]f possible" the entire ILA should affiliate with the CIO on the basis of a "complete reorganization along C.I.O. and democratic lines," and resolved that if Ryan should refuse their proposal (as he did a few days later), a CIO international charter would be issued to the Pacific coast district of the ILA and "all possible support [would] be afforded them in organizing Longshoremen on a National basis." On July 14, committee spokesman Mervyn Rathborne called for "an immediate drive to organize all Longshoremen into the C.I.O."[6]

The CIO Maritime Committee set up headquarters in New York City, the heart of Ryan's domain, and hired two capable organizers, Al Lannon and Ben Jones, both of whom were Communists and veteran maritime unionists. The initial focus of the committee's plans was the North Atlantic ports, and the far-flung port of New York in particular. Six additional organizers joined Lannon and Jones in New York, while individuals were dispatched to ports such as Boston, Philadelphia, and Baltimore. Significantly, the work in South Atlantic and Gulf ports was left largely to seafaring members of the National Maritime Union (NMU), acting in a voluntary capacity. Even though he and his associates were undertaking a daunting task with fewer organizers and far less money than they needed, Rathborne expressed great optimism. He told Lewis, "Our progress to date has convinced us that the International Longshoremen's Association on the Atlantic and Gulf Coasts can be moved into the C.I.O. as a result of two or three months intensive work."[7]

Of course, such sweeping predictions about the imminent demise of the AFL and ILA proved to be wishful thinking at best. The senior federation fought back vigorously, even viciously, and met the CIO's challenge with an aggressive organizing campaign of its own. At the national level, President William Green tirelessly reiterated the federation's long-standing claim to exclusive jurisdiction in virtually every contested arena and assured private employers and public officials that the AFL was a safe, "American" alternative to the subversive and violent CIO, which, he charged, was "tearing and ripping our movement asunder." But as the question of institutional survival became stark and immediate, AFL unionists quickly recognized that they could not rely on Green's rousing oratory or even on the good will of employers and local authorities. When all else failed, they unhesitatingly resorted to brute force to deter aggression. As one AFL official confided to Green, "organizing in the Gulf . . . is no picnic, due to the fact that all kinds of tactics are used, such as goon squads, gun-play [blackjacks], etc." It was, he acknowledged, "a strange way to organize, but . . . nowadays one must organize and deal with people as we find them—and according to circumstances."[8]

For the rest of the 1930s and beyond, jurisdictional warfare complicated and disrupted the development of unionism. Even on the west coast, the magnificent solidarity between seamen and longshoremen—embodied institutionally in the Maritime Federation of the Pacific—eroded and finally collapsed. In 1938, after a pitched battle with ILWU men on the San Francisco docks, the membership of the Sailors' Union of the Pacific voted to withdraw from the Maritime Federation and reaffiliate with the AFL.[9]

But the key to the AFL's continued presence on the waterfront was Ryan's ILA, which was deeply entrenched in New York and other North Atlantic ports. With the support of the shipowners, close ties to the New York Police Department, and a private army of goons and gangsters, Ryan had long demonstrated an unashamed willingness to spend, swindle, and bludgeon his way to victory. By October 1937, Rathborne was complaining that in the last month more than 25 CIO Maritime Committee organizers had been "brutally assaulted" on the New York waterfront by Ryan's goons. He charged that "several of the victims have been so badly slashed and gored by [steel cargo hooks] as to have required long hospitalization." Jones, who knew the terrain firsthand, came to believe that "the problem of overthrowing the Ryan dictatorship in New York is comparable to the problem of the German people, and the overthrow of Hitler in Germany."[10]

This realization led to a shift in the CIO Maritime Committee's focus from the North Atlantic to the Gulf of Mexico and the port of New Orleans in particular. With a population of nearly half a million in 1930, New Orleans was the largest city in the South and the second largest port in the nation. The CIO's advanced guard was convinced that a successful campaign there would have major ramifications far beyond the docks. The hope was that "if we succeed in organizing these workers into the CIO, we can easily organize the rest of this city," which would serve as a wedge for the CIO throughout the South. The fear was that failure in New Orleans would mean defeat on the Atlantic coast waterfront and increasing vulnerability on the Pacific coast. After the bloody confrontation with Sailors' Union members in San Francisco, Bridges warned that "continued lack of success on the East Coast will result in our whole structure here slipping out from under us at a few days notice." He became convinced that "get-[ting] the entire Gulf lined up," and then moving around the coast of Florida and up the South Atlantic, was "the only way" to crack New York and the North Atlantic.[11]

Penetrating the waterfronts of the Gulf meant confronting the problem of race relations on the docks. Historically, longshoremen's unions on the Pacific coast had relentlessly excluded African-Americans from their ranks. Bridges and the Communists had sought, with some success, to overturn this practice in 1934. Although the coastwide record would remain uneven for many years thereafter, the San Francisco longshore local elevated three black members to its executive board in 1937 and elected a black dockworker to the vitally important post of job dispatcher in 1938. Nevertheless, when ILWU organizers journeyed to the Gulf of Mexico, the long legacy of white supremacist unionism on the west coast and their own ignorance of the realities of unionism and labor market competition in the racially divided South would continue to shadow them no matter how sincere their commitment to racial equality.[12]

A quite different pattern of unionism had developed on the Atlantic and Gulf coasts. There the ILA had been forced to embrace a mosaic of nationality groups and above all to find a way of achieving an accommodation between blacks and whites. In some ports, the two races divided the work equally; in others African-Americans constituted an overwhelming majority of the dock labor force. In these circumstances, said Sterling Spero and Abram Harris, the black worker "probably plays a more important role [in the ILA] than he does in any other labor union." The organization had several black vice presidents, and scores of black delegates attended its national conventions. The key to this accommodation was not an ideology of interracial unionism but a narrow pragmatism based upon years of painful experience. "We are in the union today because the white man had to take us in for his own protection," said a black ILA official. "Outside the organization the Negro could scab on the white man. Inside he can't."[13]

ILWU organizers in the Gulf had to test their egalitarian creed in a new and alien environment where black workers predominated numerically on the docks but the ideology of white supremacy and the reality of racial separation remained pervasive. On this unfamiliar terrain, race proved to be a perplexing and volatile issue. "It is one that is loaded with lots of dynamite," said a representative of the Amalgamated Clothing Workers in New Orleans, "and can cause us much grief and misery." On what basis could an organization whose membership was overwhelmingly white appeal to a work force that was largely black? Could the ILWU survive the wrath of the South's rulers if it decided to challenge the norms of white supremacy? Above all, could "Communist" outsiders, whose very presence in New Orleans would generate controversy and even hysteria, win the trust of black workers who for more than a decade had had good reason to distrust the motives of white unionists? These were riddles the CIO unionists never solved. In the particular context, they may have been insoluble.[14]

New Orleans employers often had sought to play one race off against the other and especially to use lower paid black labor to weaken the position of white workers. White unionists, therefore, had begun to extend the hand of cooperation to blacks. The most advanced and innovative forms of cooperation developed among the screwmen, the aristocrats of the riverfront, whose name derived from the jackscrew they used to stow giant bales of cotton in a ship's hold. After a disastrous and violent period of competition in the 1890s, the white and black screwmen's unions decided to share the available work equally, with the same number of blacks and whites assigned to each hold. Although black union spokesmen publicly disavowed any aspiration to "social equality," the new method of operation represented a sharp challenge to the rigid segregation that was becoming normative throughout the South. The "half-and-half" principle, moreover, was applied to the unions as well as the workplace. Although organized in separate locals, whites and blacks from every waterfront craft joined together in a Dock and Cotton Council where, as of 1921, an equal number of delegates from each race represented 24 organizations with some twelve to fifteen thousand members. When the unions flexed their muscle, white supremacists charged that the Crescent City was "practically under negro government."[15]

Gradually, however, the combination of technological innovation, regional economic competition, and the spread of antiunion ideology created the basis for a conflict between labor and capital that would reduce the waterfront unions to an empty shell. The employers' principal concern was not interracial unionism but the stubborn control that the workers, especially the screwmen, exercised over the pace of work on the docks. And by 1923, according to historian Eric Arnesen, "steamship operators had the will, the power, and the allies to impose the reorganization of work that they had desired for decades." During a walkout that year they succeeded in breaking the strike—and the unions—by mobilizing large numbers of strikebreakers from rural sections of the state and then relying on the municipal and state governments and the federal courts to run interference for their open-shop offensive.[16]

With the defeat of the 1923 strike, a proud tradition of unionism in New Orleans came to an end. From 1923 until December 1935 none of the private operators signed a contract with a bona fide union. The notorious "shape-up" method of hiring, which seemed to be synonymous with favoritism, discrimination, and petty corruption, was initiated during this period. The employers delegated overall control of hiring to a black man named Alvin E. Harris, who instituted "a comprehensive fingerprinting and photo-identification system," with the result that no longshoreman suspected of union affiliation could find work. More than that, whether they were unionists or not, whites found it increasingly difficult to obtain employment. In 1927, a mayoralty candidate in the Crescent City charged that Harris had "Africanized the waterfront," and a veteran white longshoreman named Terrence J. Darcy sought to use the ILA as an instrument for restoring the position of whites on the docks. For the most part he failed, but he did succeed in convincing many black longshoremen that the return of the ILA would mean the end of their own access to relatively steady employment. For the next decade black workers would watch with apprehension as spokesmen for the white longshoremen campaigned openly as "The White Man's Friend" and promised a fight "to give more work to the white man on the river front."[17]

As blacks and whites once again fought—or at least sparred—with each other, conditions on the waterfront continued to deteriorate. A Bureau of Labor Statistics survey in 1930 determined that the Crescent City was the worst major port in the country with respect to average earnings and abuses of the hiring system. Of course, the situation became even worse as a result of the Great Depression; and as bad as the general condition was, blacks suffered far more than whites. By 1931, the unemployment rate among black males in the Crescent City was double that of whites. By the middle of the decade, African-Americans, who constituted 28 percent of New Orleans' population, accounted for 50 percent of the city's unemployed. Moreover, in the face of their own unprecedented deprivation, whites began demanding—and gaining—access to low-wage, low-status jobs that hitherto had been reserved for blacks.[18]

In 1933, the passage of the National Industrial Recovery Act provoked a flurry of organizing on the riverfront. The first move came from the shipowners who, in an effort to stave off bona fide unionism, "requested" the formation of "independent" unions. Thus, the Independent Colored Longshoremen's Association and the Independent White Longshoremen's Association were organized. At the same time, the old ILA locals, No. 231 (black) and No. 1226 (white), began showing signs of life. Although ILA President Ryan had encouraged the revival of these locals, he sought to charter the "independents" instead when he saw they had a larger membership. He was initially prevented from doing so by a court injunction blocking the move as a violation of the ILA constitution, but he would eventually circumvent the judiciary and have his way.[19]

In the meantime, many black (and some white) dockworkers continued to spurn the AFL union. New Orleans longshoremen, in particular, risked violent reprisals to cross ILA picket lines and handle cargo during a bitter strike that convulsed most of the Gulf ports in the fall of 1935. The Urban League's Robert Francis, a black economist who claimed to have developed "intimate contact" with the strikebreakers, apparently reflected the views of many black workers when he warned that "every move on the part of the New Orleans representatives of the I.L.A. has indicated their desire to drive the black man from the water-front." The black longshoremen, he concluded, "did not want to see . . . the ascendancy of the International Longshore-men's Association to absolute control of the labor market." But that's essentially what happened, by means of a complicated arrangement that involved collusion among the shipowners, the "independent" unions, and the ever-resourceful Ryan, who proved quite willing to accept an overwhelming majority of black workers on the docks so long as their leadership was amenable to his purposes. In the spring of 1936 he succeeded in scuttling the old ILA locals and chartering the "independents" as ILA Locals 1418 (white) and 1419 (black) in their place.[20]

In the fall of 1937, Jones and Bjorne Halling, another veteran marine worker, toured the South Atlantic and East Gulf ports, from Wilming-ton, North Carolina, to New Orleans, under the auspices of the CIO Maritime Committee. Jones, who marveled at the ferment that had developed in the Gulf in spite of the maritime committee's neglect, concluded that the area was "far ahead of the North Atlantic. . . . [W]e think that if a real knock 'em down slambang campaign is organ-ized, the Gulf is ours." But to accomplish that objective more organiz-ers would be necessary, and—like Halling and Jones—they would have to come from the committed and experienced ranks on the west coast. "Will you please not screw around[,] and send a good man here," he told Bridges. "We are declaring war—so get busy."[21]

Although New Orleans remained the keystone of the Gulf cam-paign, the most promising point of concentration was Mobile, where, according to Jones, the "overwhelming majority" of the longshoremen ("finks and all") appeared to favor the ILWU. When Jones and Halling arrived in Mobile in mid-October 1937, they found four ILA locals—of longshoremen, banana handlers, warehousemen, and checkers—with a combined membership of about two thousand men, at least 90 per-cent of whom were black. In spite of the presence of the four locals, however, there had been no autonomous and democratic union on the Mobile riverfront since 1923. When the ILA finally achieved recogni-tion again in 1936, it was through the incorporation of an employer-dominated benevolent association as Local 1410. Its leader was a veteran black longshoreman named Ed Rhone, whom the shipowners referred to as a "good nigger." He had worked hand in glove with the employers and the police to undermine the old ILA local when its members had voted to strike in 1934, and he vowed to maintain the new status quo on the riverfront "with the help of the good white people of Mobile."

Foremen and gang bosses apparently dominated Local 1410; one of them stated openly at a union meeting that the membership should accept the employers' contract proposals, "because the white folks got all the power." In the case of banana handlers' Local 1516, a National Labor Relations Board (NLRB) investigator reported that all five of its officers were foremen and gang bosses and that four of them had been appointed by a local representative of the United Fruit Company. Even George Googe, the AFL's director of organization in the South, acknowledged that locals 1410 and 1516 were "semi-company unions," but he defended them on the grounds that they were "the best that can possibly be had in this locality." However, a longshoreman with 35 years' experience on the riverfront would accept no such qualification or rationale. "1410 isn't anything but a company union," he declared. "Rhone can't move a pig without the stevedore saying so."[22]

The arrival of ILWU organizers provoked a good deal of ferment. On November 13, Mervyn Rathborne told CIO general counsel Lee Pressman that "we have decided to bring the movement out into the open and to organize an I.L.W.U. local in Mobile." Two weeks later Jones reported that "we now have about 85% of the men signed up. . . . All over the waterfront [they] are wearing C.I.O. buttons." Rathborne asked Pressman to file a petition for an NLRB election "as quickly as possible." But in spite of his sense of urgency, the election was not held until October 14, 1938, almost exactly 11 months after Rathborne's initial request.[23]

In New Orleans, where the CIO Maritime Committee finally began concentrating its relatively scarce resources in December 1937, waterfront workers were organized into separate ILA locals on the basis of craft and race. The key locals were No. 1418 (white longshoremen, with about 850 members) and No. 1419 (black longshoremen, numbering about 2,300). There was also a white checkers' local of about 200 members, and there were black locals of banana handlers, freight-car loaders, and warehousemen (although the great majority of warehousemen remained unorganized). These weak and compliant unions had done little to alleviate any of the problems facing workers on the Crescent City's riverfront. Indeed, the manner in which they had received their charters, and their continuing subordination to the shipowners, had rendered them virtually useless except as dues collection agencies. Every black dockworker was required to pay $2.25 in quarterly dues and 5 cents on every dollar earned to the ILA. (Whites paid $3.00 quarterly but no percentage.) The shipowners collected the money for the union, and men who protested the practice were threatened with loss of employment.[24]

Paul Hortman, the president of the black longshore local, appears to have been an articulate and aggressively self-confident individual. But according to the Crescent City's leading black newspaper, he "smack[ed] of company-ism." Like Ed Rhone in Mobile, he combined the attributes of employment agent, Tammany boss, waterfront goon, and—when necessary—professional strikebreaker. Hortman employed more than 60 men on the union's payroll, and they were the ones who attended meetings and ran the local's affairs. It was, said Jones, an "iron dictatorship." According to an ILWU report, "Every longshorem[a]n around the waterfront, no matter how ignorant he may be, knows that this is a Union which is Company dominated and run by the shipowners and absolutely refuses to have anything to do with it." Even the ILA district leadership acknowledged "the stigma of company domination" that permeated the black and white longshore locals in New Orleans.[25]

In these circumstances, how was the ILWU to proceed? In particular, how did the union's racially egalitarian cadre propose to structure their organization? Was it tactically necessary to acquiesce in the tradition of racial separation, or could they breach the walls of Jim Crow? In a parallel campaign by the CIO-affiliated Amalgamated Clothing Workers, the union organized separate meetings for black and white workers, and Jones himself had initially been convinced that "it is impossible to issue a general charter for negroes and whites at the present time." But after much discussion with black and white longshoremen, the workers themselves proposed that the ILWU should organize one interracial local. "This will be difficult in many ways," Jones admitted, "but we feel it is the best counter attack to the accusation that [the ILWU] is a white man's organization."[26]

In early January 1938, a dozen rank-and-filers announced the formation of a joint committee, consisting of black and white longshoremen, to organize a portwide ILWU local on the Crescent City docks. As a vital part of this process, several black workers were recruited as indigenous spokesmen for the CIO. One of them, Harvey Netter, later claimed to have done "practically all the talking" for the ILWU during the 1938 campaign. (In 1941, he would succeed the scandal-plagued Paul Hortman as president of ILA Local 1419.) But the most charismatic—and controversial—of the black organizers was Willie Dorsey, a veteran of more than 20 years on the riverfront. A lay preacher and spellbinding orator, Dorsey was also a physically powerful man who became an instant legend when he flattened a notorious AFL goon with a single punch and routed his gun-toting entourage. However, there were hints from the beginning that differences of culture and ideology would cause problems in the relationship between Dorsey and the white left-wingers in the CIO, who—as one of them acknowledged—found him "hard to handle." "It looks like he agrees with us," said Adrian Duffy of the NMU, but "when we pin him down . . . he goes off and develops counter arguments and is developing a technique of pointing to demands of the membership."[27]

Soon after its formation the ILWU organizing committee claimed that "over a thousand" new members had signed up; in fact, the number would quickly approach, and perhaps exceed, two thousand. But in spite of this hopeful development, the campaign was unable to develop any consistent momentum. Even a visit by Harry Bridges in late March did not fulfill the ILWU's expectations. At a poorly attended mass meeting—between 500 and 800 people in a hall that seated 1,800—Bridges declared that on the following payday longshoremen would repudiate the ILA and demand their full wage (including the 5 percent "check-off"), and that ships' officers and NMU seamen would tie up the port unless the ILA agreed to an immediate NLRB election. But according to NLRB regional director Charles Logan, on the appointed day "only four men on the river front declared themselves not to be members of the I.L.A. and asked for their full pay." "It looks like the whole thing has gone overboard on Harry," Logan reported. "I gave him credit for knowing what he was doing." Bridges apparently failed to understand that job action, the west coast's proven lever, remained out of the question for the New Orleans longshoremen, who could easily be replaced by the Crescent City's abundant reserve army of labor. Thus, in the absence of concrete victories, the ILWU was forced to wait and hope for vindication through an NLRB election. In early May Halling admitted, "The situation as it now stands, with nothing much happening, is good for the ILA but very bad for us."[28]

Halling's pessimism notwithstanding, the opposition perceived a threat that required a decisive response. Although Jones had once declared that the AFL was doing "absolutely nothing" in New Orleans, the federation began pouring men and money into the fray. Beginning in April, the CIO faced an escalating and multipronged counteroffensive—uniting the employers, the ILA and AFL, and the state and local governments—that would culminate in a reign of terror in New Orleans during the summer of 1938. The first major sign of the scale and character of the counteroffensive came at the Todd-Johnson Shipyard, where, according to Logan, "two lives were lost, and many men were injured, some to be disabled for life." The conflict erupted when craft unions associated with the New Orleans Metal Trades Council attempted to head off an organizing drive by the CIO-affiliated Industrial Union of Marine & Shipbuilding Workers of America (IUMSWA). On April 20, after an announcement that the NLRB would hold a hearing on the question of union representation at the shipyard, the Metal Trades Council voted to take strike action there the next day. AFL officials set up a picket line of several hundred men in front of the shipyard on the morning of April 21. Smith Erris, secretary of the IUMSWA local, charged that AFL and ILA officials had recruited most of the pickets from the waterfront, "promised the men five dollars a day and all they could drink and told them that they would have police protection in beating up shipyard workers."[29]

The ILA, meanwhile, held a special district convention in mid-May where it ruled that longshoremen who favored the CIO would be expelled from the union and that ILA locals demonstrating pro-CIO sympathies would have their charters revoked. Soon Halling was reporting the presence of a "big time beef squad" in New Orleans. "They have brought in about 50 outsiders to use goon tactics to force the longshoremen to remain in the ILA," he said. On Memorial Day, two notorious goons, Manny Moore and Santos Garcia, attacked a black longshoreman, "breaking a baseball bat over his head, beating him with the butts of their guns and then shooting him." Moore had already been involved in the beating of a shipyard organizer at Todd-Johnson and would soon be arrested and released on $2,500 bail for shooting two CIO members during a teamsters' strike. While out on bail, it was reported that he fired a sawed off shotgun at another CIO truck driver. Although witnesses informed the police, "no action was taken."[30]

In late June the sporadic violence gave way to a systematic reign of police terror. Apparently, the city administration had decided it was time to break the CIO once and for all. The fact that several of the companies targeted by CIO organizing drives belonged to powerful public officials or to their close friends and political allies no doubt raised the level of antagonism toward the new federation. But an even more important factor was the threat the CIO posed to the social peace, racial separation, and Babbittonian mood that the local elite regarded as an essential precondition for the restoration of economic growth. In a setting where some kind of unionism seemed inevitable, the AFL became the lesser of two evils; wittingly or unwittingly, its local affiliates increasingly played the role once reserved for company unions. In the midst of the bloody 1935 dock strike, an AFL leader had described the New Orleans police as "one of the most vicious strike breaking forces in the world." But the police now referred to AFL partisans as "our men" and worked hand in hand with the senior federation to destroy the CIO.[31]

The events that precipitated the reign of terror were the NLRB's holding of local hearings on the ILWU's claim to represent Crescent City longshoremen and a strike by a CIO-affiliated truck drivers' local. What better time than the NLRB hearings to demonstrate that even the federal government could not alter the status quo in New Orleans? But the main focal point of the violence was the teamsters' strike. To head off the challenge of an aggressive CIO organizing campaign in the city's trucking industry, the AFL Teamsters, with virtually no members among the drivers, had signed a closed-shop agreement with New Orleans drayage firms. In retaliation, the CIO declared a strike against ten companies on Wednesday, June 22. According to the ILWU's Bob Robertson, the AFL put "four truckloads of finks armed with baseball bats on the streets under police protection." Officers soon began arresting strikers in their homes, throwing them in jail overnight and beating them in an attempt to "make them report to work the following morning and sign an AFL card."[32]

On the first day of the strike, two CIO pickets were shot and 94 people were rounded up in police dragnets. Although the officers claimed to have arrested men of "both factions," the great majority of those detained were CIO members, most of them black. On the third day, the police arrested 58 CIO pickets at various points along the riverfront. Then they raided the CIO headquarters, which one detective characterized as "a [hangout] where negroes and whites mixed together," made 84 more arrests, confiscated numerous records (including all of the ILWU pledge cards signed by New Orleans dockworkers), and wrecked the office. Among those arrested were Halling; Paul Heide and Burt Nelson, who along with Robertson had been sent from the west coast to reinforce the Gulf campaign; and six women, including Heide's and Nelson's wives, who were charged with being "dangerous and suspicious characters." In explaining the mass arrests, Acting Police Superintendent John Grosch stated, "There's no room in New Orleans for C.I.O. Communists and Reds and if I can run them out of [town], I'm going to do it." He accused "the C.I.O.–Communist party" of sending "a lot of 'beef' men here from San Francisco to agitate among the negroes as to their rights."[33]

Undeterred by the wave of legal and extralegal persecution, Robertson reported that "the workers are ready to meet on the barricades," and a CIO shipyard worker declared that "if the teamsters win their strike the whole city is going C.I.O. 100%." But in fact the reign of terror was escalating and the "outsiders," all of them pegged as

"Communists," became its special targets. Felix Siren, of the Inland-boatmen's Union, was arrested while speaking at an NMU meeting attended by approximately a thousand seamen. Four detectives took him to a precinct station where they viciously beat him and then held him incommunicado. According to Siren, the detectives told him that "the police had always run New Orleans, and they would continue to do so, law or no law, and that I had no business coming down to New Orleans in the first place, telling the 'niggers' about their rights." The ILWU's Robertson and Nelson were also arrested, held incommunicado, and badly beaten while in police custody. Robertson had his spine fractured in two places, and Nelson suffered a ruptured liver. "They had me until 2 a.m.," Nelson recalled. "They moved me from one cell to another and beat on me some more. Then they took me out of town and heaved me in a ditch. I think they thought I was done for."[34]

The Louisiana legislature placed its stamp of approval on the actions of the New Orleans police in a unanimous resolution that called upon all agencies of government within the state to take "necessary steps to suppress, stamp out, and eradicate Communism and its attendant evils." In a clear reference to the activity of the CIO, the resolution declared that "the insidious propaganda disseminated by these alien imported radicals" had been directed at and taken root among Louisiana's black citizens, "and unless drastic steps are taken at once it will spread to the rural parts of this state and white supremacy will be endangered."[35]

Soon thereafter, raids on CIO halls and mass arrests began again. About 70 striking Yellow Cab drivers were picked up in a dragnet on July 7, while so many officers were assigned to provide individual protection for "loyal" drivers that the city was "almost without traffic policemen." The next day a raid on the NMU netted 86 people, most of them seamen waiting in the hiring hall for jobs. Heide reported that Halling, whose jaw had been broken by an AFL goon, "is in the hospital, and will be laid up for about 2 months. Robertson is flat on his back with a fractured spine, and will be laid up for some time to come. . . . Burt [Nelson] and I are still getting around, although the bulls are looking for us. They are going wild here trying everything to break us," he concluded defiantly, but "we are not broken yet."[36]

Formally, the jurisdictional conflict in the trucking industry was resolved by NLRB intervention, which allowed the AFL contracts to stand but stipulated that the CIO strikers would be returned to work without discrimination, would not be required to pay dues to the Teamsters, and would be allowed to choose their collective bargaining agent in a representation election following the longshoremen's vote. But the "employer–police–AFL combine" brazenly ignored the terms of this agreement. The police continued making false arrests of CIO organizers while allowing the AFL goon squad a free hand. On one occasion goons attacked a CIO driver and "[tore] out his eye with a cotton hook" because he refused to pay dues to the AFL. "Despite the fact that we have furnished the police with the name of the AFL 'organizer' who committed this act, along with six eye witnesses to the whole affair," said Heide, "the police have done absolutely nothing."[37]

The continuing harassment and intimidation made the CIO unionists more dependent than ever on the NLRB and the hope that timely elections would allow them to overcome the "employer–police–AFL combine." But at the same time CIO organizers in the Crescent City were virtually unanimous in their opinion that NLRB Regional Director Charles Logan was—as shipyard organizer Ben Harper put it—"the fly in the ointment." Halling declared that Logan was "playing right down the line with the employers and the AFL" and that the labor board in New Orleans was "not a friend of the workers, but an enemy, by the way it has been carrying on." Harper called upon the national leadership of the IUMSWA to "cooperate with the CIO in putting Logan where he belongs, out of the NLRB."[38]

At the national level, a key member of the NLRB criticized Logan for his "intimacy with Joe Ryan" and for going "altogether too far in identifying with the activities of [his] union." This charge may have had some merit. On at least one occasion, at a district convention of the union, Logan had shared the podium, and a hotel room, with the ILA president; and the appearance of the CIO and ILWU on the scene apparently made him even more partial to the ILA and its parent federation. (After several years of dealing with him, a CIO spokesman in Alabama would characterize Logan as "closer to the A. F. of L. than the shirts on their backs.") Certainly, the contrast between his friendly relations with ILA officials and other AFL representatives and the almost uniform suspicion and hostility he engendered among CIO spokesmen is striking. He called George Googe "one of my close friends" and Ryan "a good fellow." Ryan in turn flattered the regional director, whereas the irascible Bridges demonstrated little respect for the opinions of government administrators. Logan complained that when he had warned Bridges against striking the Gulf coast waterfronts, he "laughed at me."[39]

Another source of friction may have been the ILWU's limited but real challenge to the racial mores of the South. Logan took it for granted that waterfront unions in New Orleans should be organized on the basis of "the color line." In fact, although not a native Southerner, he was an unabashed racist who routinely referred to African-Americans as "niggers," even "goddamn niggers," in his correspondence and speech. On one occasion, in a letter to his mentor William Leiserson, he speculated that "there may soon come a day when . . . in many plants the nigger will either have to have a separate [bargaining] unit for himself, or leave the plant altogether." Why? Because "killing a nigger is still a meritorious act in many . . . small communities," he wrote without a trace of dissent. In a letter to the governor of Louisiana, he characterized black railroad workers as "jigaboos" and "jigs"; and he displayed an equally racist contempt for black longshoremen, dismissing their initial willingness to endorse the CIO with the statement that "those niggers will sign anything anybody hands them to sign. They have signed a lot of [pledge] cards but they have no knowledge of what they are doing nor any intention of doing anything about [it.]"[40]

A few days after making this statement, however, Logan informed members of the national board that an "immediate election" in New Orleans was possible and that "the men themselves" desired it. ILWU organizers continued to complain bitterly that Logan was "stalling," but given the NLRB's enormous caseload even the most aggressively pro-CIO member of its national staff did not believe that an election could be held immediately. Board Secretary Nathan Witt stated in May that "even if we were fortunate in concluding the [New Orleans] cases as soon as possible, no more than a month or two would remain under the present contracts" (which expired on September 30). As it turned out, the election did not take place until October 14.[41]

Whatever the cause of the delay, there can be no doubt that it was harmful to the CIO. As early as February an NLRB investigator had observed that the Mobile longshoremen were "swinging" to the ILWU ("no question about this"), but he had also speculated that "any delay" in holding the election could mean severe losses for the CIO, since its "present membership probably was obtained on the basis of immediate action for these men." Similarly, in New Orleans, a CIO organizer had reported in April that the longshoremen were asking, "Where are the improvements that Bridges and the CIO promised us and what are they doing now[?]" The long delay not only cast doubt on the ILWU's ability to deliver the goods, it also gave the employers and the ILA ample time to intimidate many of those who sympathized with the new union. The shipowners, moreover, were savvy enough to employ the "carrot" as well as the "stick." During the summer, they granted a wage increase and (temporarily) abolished the infamous precentage racket. The increase, from 80 to 95 cents an hour, meant that ILA members were making 15 cents more per hour than the men on the Morgan Line docks, where the ILWU had its only contract. It allowed AFL partisans to argue that supporting the CIO union would mean voting for a wage cut.[42]

On the eve of the elections, in both New Orleans and Mobile, the CIO held "huge mass meetings"; and even then, Heide recalled, "there was no indication . . . that our confidence was misplaced." But the next day the ILA won a stunning victory. For Crescent City long-shoremen, there were separate elections at 20 different companies. The ILA won 18 of them; the ILWU, one. In the twentieth election, the ILWU received one more vote than its rival but neither had a majority. Bridges reported that "the only companies we won were those with white longshoremen." The totals were 1,974 for the AFL union, 633 for its CIO challenger, and 50 for an independent union headed by Terrence J. Darcy. Out of 3,394 men whom the NLRB declared eligible to participate, there were 706 nonvoters. Even if all of them had cast their ballots for the ILWU, the CIO union still would have lost the election by more than six hundred votes, as the ILA piled up huge majorities at one company after another. The ILA also won elections among banana handlers at United Fruit and Standard Fruit. Among the clerks and checkers, where nearly as many workers voted for no union (68) as for the ILA (86), the ILWU received only 9 votes. In Mobile, the balloting was much closer but the outcome was essentially the same.[43]

Why the CIO's crushing defeat? Apart from the long delay in holding the election, there seem to be two main reasons. The first and most obvious is intimidation. "This intimidation took every conceivable form," said Siren, "but in general the employers, the administration, and the A. F. of L. joined in impressing on the workers that if the C.I.O. won, they would lose their jobs. The employers went to the length of writing to every individual longshoreman along these lines," and the foremen harped on the same theme "day in and day out." Moreover, the state and city administrations, which had encouraged and—in the case of the latter—even sponsored the reign of terror in June and July, continued to throw their considerable weight behind the status quo. According to Heide, Governor Richard Leche of Louisiana and Mayor Robert Maestri of New Orleans "were reported to have personally appeared on the docks on the day of the election and spoke[n] to groups of longshoremen, urging them to vote AFL, and telling them that every force in the State would be turned loose against them in the event that the CIO won the election."[44]

Although not all of these charges are verifiable, there can be no doubt that the shipowners, the AFL, and the city administration (acting mainly through the police) engaged in a sustained campaign of repression and intimidation that created a climate of fear along the riverfront. Attorney Richard Dowling, a New Orleans resident who at times represented the CIO, probably summed it up best when he stated, "The real cause of the defeat here was *FEAR*. The terrible fear of the POLICE. The fear of reprisals on the part of the City Administration. The fear of loss of jobs if the C.I.O. won. The fear that in some way the bosses would find out how they had voted and have them punished for it."[45]

With no living tradition of political or union democracy, and in the face of repressive measures that at times became a reign of terror, the majority of black workers were apparently unwilling to believe that a genuinely democratic union and a better system of industrial relations were really possible. The more secure among them, who constituted the core of the ILA supporters, seem to have feared that union control of hiring and a commitment to the equalization of employment opportunities would jeopardize their position vis-à-vis the less regularly employed. As for the insecure majority, most of whom had signed ILWU pledge cards, many of them simply did not vote. Among those who did, there were clearly some who were intimidated—directly or indirectly—into voting for the ILA.[46]

It would be wrong, however, to view black workers in New Orleans as uniformly distrustful of the CIO or to attribute their actions entirely to intimidation. The cotton compress labor force, for example was almost entirely black; and in a 1939 representation election they voted overwhelmingly for the ILWU. In five separate elections, Logan reported, "out of 800 possible votes, the AFL received a grand total of 12." Likewise, the New Orleans teamsters, the great majority of them African-American, suffered a good deal more violence and repression than the longshoremen. But in a 1939 representation election, they too voted for the CIO, by a ratio of 4:1. And while intimidation was clearly a major factor among the longshoremen, they seem to have been motivated also by a cautious pragmatism, by a sense of racial solidarity, and perhaps above all by a distrust of whites stemming from the legacy of racial competition for place on the docks.[47]

To what extent, then, was the ILWU's defeat in the longshore election inevitable? To what extent was it the union's fault? There is no simple, unambiguous answer to this question. In the midst of the reign of terror, the Louisiana legislature not only condemned the CIO as "Communistic" but warned that its organizing campaign was a threat to white supremacy; the detectives who beat Felix Siren cursed him for coming to New Orleans and "telling the 'niggers' about their rights"; the U.S. attorney in the Crescent City warned of a "very general fear . . . that the C.I.O. will encourage the negroes in every respect, beginning in the economic field." In response, the ILWU chose not to address the "racial question" and the larger system of white supremacy that kept blacks subordinate. Bob Robertson celebrated the fact that during the truckers' strike black and white workers had stood shoulder to shoulder on the picket line. However, he also came to believe that the "racial question" was "the most serious problem confronting us" and that the only way to handle it was by "keeping all the issues on a strictly trade union basis." The CIO's regional director in Alabama went even further and denied that the ILWU's organizing drive on the waterfront was aimed at achieving "social equality." "The only social equality I ever heard a negro ask about," he said, "is the same amount of money for the same amount of labor."[48]

Fighting against the special oppression of African-Americans had long been a hallmark of the CP. But although some of them were Communists, the ILWU organizers' principal objective was building their union, and they no doubt believed that mounting a multifaceted campaign for racial equality would only have intensified the already virulent antagonism of white supremacists toward the CIO. They were by no means alone in this calculation. In Alabama, where a sympathetic observer hailed "the splendid example of Negro and white co-operation" in the United Mine Workers (UMW), that organization's district president nonetheless warned that if the CIO were to "overdo it" on the "ticklish" issue of race, "there would be such a back-kick that organized labor would be the sufferer." Even the National Association for the Advancement of Colored People (NAACP) remained reluctant to launch a frontal assault on the citadels of white supremacy, and the Urban League chapter in New Orleans declared its intention to improve the condition of African-Americans without creating "any disturbance in the relations between the races."[49]

The caution of the ILWU organizers is understandable. But it may be that in one vitally important respect they misunderstood the terrain on which they were operating. Since 1923, most waterfront occupations in New Orleans had become "Negro" jobs and, as Heide acknowledged, black longshoremen had come to regard whites in the ILA as "scabs and finks" who were scheming to drive them from the docks. Even the ILWUers had to battle the perception that they were the envoys of "a white man's organization." Heide himself may have contributed to this perception when, after the election, his frustration with the results propelled him toward a stereotyped—and essentially racist—assessment of the black workers' vote. "The negro of the South is steeped in superstition and religion," he wrote. "In this respect, the southern negro is only one step removed from the primitive superstitions of the African jungle tribes."[50]

Quite apart from such a comment, however, the larger context of labor market competition only served to intensify black workers' suspicion of white unionists. As a singular—and fragile—enclave of black advantage, the riverfront stood in sharp contrast to the prevailing pattern throughout the South, where African-Americans had been losing ground for many years. While the number of Southern male workers in nonagricultural pursuits increased by more than 2.4 million from 1910 to 1930, the African-American percentage of the total dropped from 26.7 to 21.1. Unions such as the railroad brotherhoods that pursued racially exclusive policies contributed significantly to this trend. Between 1910 and 1930, for example, the percentage of black trainmen in ten southern states dropped from 29.8 to 16.3. But, even in a racially egalitarian union such as the UMW the black proportion of the coal mining labor force continued to drop precipitously: in Kentucky, from less than 25 percent in 1900 to 10 percent in 1940; in Tennessee, from 28 percent in 1900 to 2 percent in 1940; in Virginia, from 35 to 6 percent during the same time period. And in New Orleans, only a month before the longshore representation election, front-page headlines in the *Louisiana Weekly* announced that unionized black plasterers shut down a hospital construction site when four of their number were laid off and replaced by "out-of-town white men."[51]

In a context where whites were aggressively laying claim to jobs that historically had been reserved for blacks, the only way the ILWU's advocacy of "equality" on the riverfront could possibly have been persuasive to black longshoremen would have been to convince them that it would not be achieved at their expense—that is, by addressing rather than avoiding the issue of racial inequality. As one CIO unionist reflected nearly fifty years after the fact, "it is crucial to understand the distinction that should be made, and was not made, between the CIO's constitutional commitment to organize all workers, irrespective of race, creed, or color, and what discrimination means in terms of daily life."[52]

But how to make such a distinction in this particular setting? Was there, for the ILWU, a viable programmatic answer ready at hand? The experience of several other CIO unions that organized successfully in the Deep South provides instructive examples but no single blueprint for victory. In Alabama, the UMW held integrated union meetings in defiance of state and local segregation ordinances, waged a successful campaign to register its black members to vote, and won the admiration and active support of important elements within Birmingham's black middle class. But the political context in Alabama was—for a fleeting moment at least—far more favorable than in Louisiana and the venerable UMW was a far larger and more powerful organization than the fledgling ILWU. Even in the militantly interracial UMW, however, a black union spokesman felt compelled to disavow any aspiration to "social equality." "The broad-minded, better-thinking Negro," he said, "wants social equality no more than the same class of the white race."[53]

Closer to the ILWU's domain, the IUMSWA succeeded in organizing several shipyards in New Orleans and Mobile, where black workers, virtually all of them laborers, formed an important component of the industry's multilayered work force. Unlike the UMW, however, the IUMSWA locals followed a policy of racial separation—"just enough . . . ," as one official put it, "to satisfy the white men, and not enough to make the colored men feel they are being discriminated against." In New Orleans, IUMSWA spokesmen dismissed the charge that "there were both colored and white . . . together" at a dance sponsored by the CIO union as a "ridiculous" example of "the lying rumors circulated by the AFL and Company stooges." In spite of such exclusion in the social realm, black workers strongly supported the IUMSWA and may well have provided its margin of victory over the AFL in a 1940 representation election.[54]

It would be facile, and ahistorical, to suggest that the ILWU could or should have initiated a broad campaign for "integration"—the principal focus of the civil rights movement of the 1950s and 1960s—in 1938, although wartime conditions would lay the groundwork for such a campaign only a few years later. As black sociologist Charles S. Johnson said of the Jim Crow era, "practically all Southern Negroes *accept* racial segregation." If acceptance of such separation was often a matter of necessity, it was also in many instances "a matter of pride and preference." Thus, insofar as the ILWU organizers represented an attractive alternative to the ILA in New Orleans, it was less because they had formed an interracial union than because they promised an aggressive battle to improve working conditions on the riverfront. Had there been an early election, unaccompanied by massive intimidation, it seems likely that the ILWU would have won. But with the long delay, the contest grew much more complicated; and the white outsiders became the objects of a suspicion rooted in many years of racial competition and conflict, a suspicion that ILA leaders and some members of the black middle class in New Orleans were only too happy to exploit.[55]

While the increasingly beleaguered ILWU appealed to black long-shoremen on "a strictly trade union basis," its African-American opponents spoke the more familiar language of racial solidarity. In Mobile, Ed Rhone asserted on the eve of the NLRB election that "anyone voting for the C.I.O. tomorrow is a traitor to his race." And in New Orleans, a "Colored Citizens Committee" addressed a broadside to "My dear Longshoremen" declaring that "a vote for the C.I.O. will be a vote to drive the colored longshoremen from the highest paid jobs enjoyed by colored men of the United States and replace them by unemployed C.I.O. longshoremen and other unemployed radicals from the West Coast." (This became a common theme of the leaflets that circulated on the front. One scurrilous tract charged that "Stink-Mouth Bridges"—"a 100 percent Communist [who] gets his orders from Russia"—"wants to control the labor situation on the docks of New Orleans so that he can kick the Negro Longshoremen out of their jobs.") The citizens committee concluded, "It is your duty to your race, your family and your God to vote in this election and to vote for the I.L.A."[56]

Racial solidarity, in New Orleans and Mobile at least, had come to mean the achievement and maintenance of a black majority on the docks within a framework that reserved managerial and a few higher status working-class occupations for whites. Under this arrangement, there would be no challenge to the larger system of white supremacy. Indeed, the niche that the ILA leadership carved out for black long-shoremen would have been unthinkable without the continuing acquiescence of white elites in the private and public sectors. The ILA in some Southern ports would stubbornly adhere to the norms of racial separation not only during Jim Crow's waning years but until ordered to desegregate by a federal court in 1983! In this sense, the dock workers in the Crescent City seem to have constituted a somewhat self-contained world. Their union officials had a stake in segregation and in the continuation of the "shape-up," both of which provided the arena in which they could exercise a style of leadership reminiscent of the Tammany boss and the immigrant *padrone.*

In the final analysis, the fact that the ILA had long offered black workers a place on the waterfront at wages that were among the best available to African-Americans anywhere in the South was of no small consequence. Black workers in some ports, particularly in the West

Gulf, had carved out a relatively secure niche for themselves. They were, in the words of Gilbert Mers, "the aristocrat[s] of black southern labor," and they trusted—even revered—their union because, as a black leader in Port Arthur, Texas, told Mers, "we all know that the ILA got us where we are today."[57]

In New Orleans and Mobile, there was a good deal less security and trust than in the West Gulf. Indeed, it may be that the Crescent City's black longshoremen did not so much choose the ILA in 1938 as they opted—in the words of the Urban League's Robert Francis—to "bear those ills they have [rather] than to accept others which may be worse." After all, most New Orleans longshoremen had only been members of the AFL union since the spring of 1936. Up until that time, according to Francis, they had believed that "if in control [the ILA] would attempt to give the black man the bad end of the bargain." But once in place the AFL union represented a continuation of the relationship that had existed on the riverfront since the defeat of the Dock and Cotton Council in 1923—a relationship in which employer hegemony was mediated by aggressive albeit self-serving black leaders from the ranks who, in the face of a chronic oversupply of labor, played an important role in determining who worked and who didn't. The corruption and favoritism no doubt rankled, but the leadership was indigenous and committed to maintaining the black workers' advantage in the apportioning of jobs; eventually, the hourly wage rate increased significantly (largely in response to the CIO's challenge), and apparently a significant percentage of the men were able to make a better living on the riverfront than any alternative source of employment offered. Dowling admitted that "any condition here is far better than the dire poverty which they know in the Country. . . . those having jobs hang on to them for dear life." And Siren acknowledged in retrospect, "While conditions for long-shoremen [here] are bad in comparison with longshoremen on the West Coast, *in comparison with workers in other industries in Louisiana and Alabama they are excellent, particularly for the colored people* who constitute the majority."[58]

Beyond the stark reality of defeat for the ILWU and CIO, what conclusions can historians draw from this episode? There has been a laudable tendency in recent years to probe beneath the surface of events and examine the deeply rooted structural and ideological factors that constrained the development of working-class radicalism in the 1930s. To some extent the limited success of the CIO in the maritime industry bears out this perspective. But in the main the experience of the ILWU in the Gulf, and in New Orleans in particular, represents a challenge to those who view the growth of unionism in the 1930s in terms of an evolutionary development toward an outcome that was overdetermined by the structural characteristics of American industry.[59] To be sure, the maritime industry's complex structure—its decentralized, geographically dispersed character; its fierce institutional rivalries; and its bewildering array of separate crafts—confronted the advocates of industrial unionism with a formidable challenge. But the emergence of the ILWU, the Maritime Federation of the Pacific, and the NMU reveals, however imperfectly, the possibility of movements toward a more inclusive and militant unionism.

The principal factor that defeated the ILWU in the Gulf was neither the structure of the maritime industry nor the inertia of its work force. Rather it was the power of the CIO union's opponents and their ability to use the state as an instrument in defense of the status quo. It is true that in auto and steel CIO unionists were able to win major victories in spite of relentless and violent opposition from employers and local authorities. But at critical moments in Michigan and Pennsylvania the state served as an ally of insurgent unionism, and the CIO was able to mobilize massive reinforcements on behalf of its embattled legions. Even in Alabama, the heart of Dixie, militant coal miners played a role similar to that of the famed "flying squadrons" in Northern industrial states. As a Birmingham area steelworker recalled, "Those boys would come in here from Walker County with snuff running down their chins, both black and white. And they didn't take no stuff. If it wasn't for the [United] Mine Workers, we never would have got a union." In New Orleans, however, the CIO was isolated. Its ability to win the allegiance of significant numbers of longshoremen, shipyard workers, and teamsters only intensified the fury of its opponents. Increasingly, routine police harassment and intimidation was augmented by the state-sanctioned activity of AFL vigilantes who roamed the city brandishing weapons and beating CIO partisans almost at will.[60]

The one instrument that could have provided a counterweight to this phalanx of reaction was the federal government, acting through the NLRB and the Justice Department. But even though Bridges expressed the belief that "the N.L.R.B. took every precaution to have the election made a fair and democratic one," the board in New Orleans proved either unable or unwilling to prevent the employers and the ILA from interfering with lawful activity. Perhaps even more important was the failure of the federal government to intervene in the face of police terror and other state-sanctioned lawlessness, which reinforced the popular perception that local elites would impose their will at all costs, by fair means and foul. Attorney Dowling commented:

The people of this City have lived in constant fear of the authorities for so long that it is almost impossible to break this Dread which hangs over them. . . . The only time that this Dread was lifted was when the Labor Board threatened the Police in June for the interference with its work and the destruction of the Pledge Cards of the C.I.O. The population expected that at last the power of the Machine would be challenged by a greater power, the Federal Government. Everybody he[r]e was jubilant and expected the Government to act and to INDICT THE POLICE. When this failed to materialize the spirits of the people wilted and the old fear re-asserted itself. It seemed to everyone that even the [Federal] Government was afraid of this Gang here.[61]

The ILWU's defeat in the Crescent City reminds us of the state's vital role in influencing the outcome of events. In the South, the forces of reaction and white supremacy, including local and state governments, had routinely suppressed movements for social change, and they continued to do so, albeit with less than total success, during the heyday of CIO unionism in the late 1930s. But the special circumstances of World War II would create the basis for a more aggressive federal intervention that allowed CIO unions to develop and thrive in communities such as Gadsden, Alabama; Memphis, Tennessee; and Winston–Salem, North Carolina. In Winston–Salem, a left-led union, the Food, Tobacco, & Agricultural Workers (FTA), enjoyed remarkable economic success and also challenged Jim Crow with singular effect in the electoral arena until the protective hand of the state was withdrawn in the dramatically altered political climate of the postwar years. Even in New Orleans, the ILWU would succeed in building a racially integrated warehouse local that in 1947 would claim to have doubled the wages of its 1,700 members employed in 14 plants.[62]

Those who lament the suffocating effects of the federal government's supportive initiatives in the realm of industrial relations during the 1930s and World War II should perhaps contemplate the consequences of its ambivalent, temporizing stance in Mobile, New Orleans, and other Gulf ports during the first hopeful wave of the CIO's courageous but largely futile organizing campaign in the South. While acknowledging that even positive government initiatives have been a two-edged sword, and that they have usually come—belatedly and reluctantly—in response to intense pressure from below, it is also necessary to affirm that the protective intervention of the state has often been an essential precondition for the success of insurgent social movements.[63]

The experience of the ILWU in New Orleans also demonstrates the complexity of working-class consciousness and the complicated ways in which race has affected the social relations of production and the development of unionism. Although some black longshoremen displayed remarkable courage in the face of great adversity, and many dared to hope—however fleetingly—for a new deal on the docks, the majority proved to be cautious, pragmatic, even conservative. It may be ironic that the apparent racial solidarity of 1938 hardened into a continuing acceptance of segregation, even at a time when the winds of change were battering down the walls of Jim Crow throughout much of the South. But the familiar terrain of segregated unionism reflected the "strong preference for autonomy" that has always characterized black self-organization; and it no doubt provided an arena for the achievement of limited material security and for the development of black leadership in a society where formal integration has not fundamentally challenged the enduring reality of racial separation and inequality.[64]

As for the ILWU, it not only survived the purge of the CIO's left wing at the end of the 1940s but distinguished itself thereafter as a democratic, politically independent union that won impressive wages and conditions for its membership. Moreover, after much struggle, and in spite of some setbacks at the local level, it also became an outstanding example of racial integration and a pacesetter in the development of black leadership. Black workers, some of them migrants from the waterfronts of the Gulf, became a key component of the ILWU leadership's social base. Although these developments could not entirely erase the sting of defeat, they must have provided considerable comfort to the CIO organizers who had risked their lives in the attempt to build a democratic and racially egalitarian union on the docks of the Crescent City.[65]

ACKNOWLEDGMENTS

The author thanks the College of Urban, Labor, and Metropolitan Affairs at Wayne State University and the Class of 1962 Fellowship Committee at Dartmouth College for financial support; David Myers, Jeff Quam-Wickham, Eugene Vrana, and Ken Wenzer for archival assistance; Steve Rosswurm for editorial guidance; and Eric Arnesen, Alex Bontemps, Howard Kimeldorf, Dan Letwin, Gilbert Mers, and Judith Stein for critical comments on earlier drafts of this essay.

WHO CONTROLS THE HIRING HALL?
The Struggle for Job Control in the ILWU During World War II

NANCY QUAM-WICKHAM

For historians of the twentieth-century labor movement, one paradox centers on that fundamental question: did rank-and-file militancy in the new industrial unions of the 1930s diminish rapidly in the 1940s?[1] Many recent scholars have focused on the role some union leaders played in suppressing independent rank-and-file action during World War II. In particular, these labor leaders adopted the no-strike pledge and promised speedups in their attempts to maximize production during the war years. According to the critical interpretations, the inevitable consequences of these policies of class collaboration were "apathy toward the unions and disaffection with union leaders." Left-led unions have fared quite poorly in these accounts. Because radical unionists were among the most vociferous proponents of maximized production schemes, shop-floor militancy and rank-and-file independence are presumed to have languished in the war years, casualties of these same radical politics. Even in some of the most balanced accounts, the pro-Communist leaders of the International Longshoremen's and Warehousemen's Union (ILWU) have been characterized as administering the union's affairs during the war "in ways that best served the CP line," not the union's members.[2]

Difficult times, of course, demanded difficult decisions. Expanded union bureaucracies with their stronger disciplinary rules surely contained some rank-and-file dissent during the war years. Focusing on the alleged role productionist labor leaders had in smothering rank-and-file militancy does not fully explain workers' relative quiescence during the war. Union leaders' motivations for cooperating with the state in war production boards have been only partly explored by historians. In addition, as David Brody suggested several years ago, scholars must also turn to the rank-and-filers themselves to uncover "what was inherent in the labor militancy of the 1930s that gave it so short a life."[3]

For historians interested in the ILWU, labor's experience must be viewed with eyes alert to both the novelties of the war and the continuities of class struggle. Indeed, the continuity of industrial conflict forcefully shaped the pattern of wartime labor relations. The union did cooperate in attempts to increase production during the war, but it also protected significant gains made in the union struggles of the 1930s. Moreover, the ILWU's participation on the regional War Production Board and its subsidiary, the Pacific Coast Maritime Industry Board (PCMIB), did not disfranchise the rank and file.

Neither bureaucratic change within the union's structure nor the union's new relationship of formal accommodation to employers and the state upset many ILWU members. Instead, momentous changes in the larger society, especially the changing racial composition of the organized work force, challenged the prewar concept of rank-and-file "independence." A two-front battle within the ILWU revolved around the question of who would control the hiring hall. The union's leadership fought to maintain the integrity of the hiring system, defending the hall against attacks by boardroom bosses and the armed forces. On the other side, the leadership resisted, often unsuccessfully, the tendencies of some rank-and-filers to use the hall as an exclusionary device against African-American and Latino workers. In order to understand the character of rank-and-file militancy during the war years, we must briefly consider how the complexity of maritime workers' class and racial consciousness developed before the war.

The Generation of 1934
and the ILWU Before the War

After 1934, Pacific coast longshoremen and warehouse workers, under the leadership of Harry Bridges, fashioned one of the most democratic labor unions in the country. The cornerstones of that democracy were rank-and-file control of membership requirements, work rules, administrative structure of the union, and especially the hiring process. The longshore hiring halls were established by arbitration after the 1934 strikes; the hiring hall system in warehousing was instituted at the local level and then enforced by job action in 1935/36. Although the hiring halls were run jointly by employers and the union, unionists essentially controlled the hiring process through a variety of methods. By transferring the process of hiring workers from the employers' prerogative to the union's purview, workers and their union fundamentally transformed the structure of the labor market in Pacific coast longshoring and warehousing operations. No longer could *employers* arbitrarily refuse to hire individuals or certain groups of workers based on race, ethnic background, political orientation, or union beliefs. The ILWU's screening of applicants for jobs dispatched through the hiring hall vested tremendous power in the local union. As one ILWU publication put it, "the hiring hall *is* the ILWU."[4]

The ILWU gained a solid reputation in the 1930s as a left-wing union in which the rank-and-file activism supported the leadership's ideological commitment to radical politics.[5] This relationship between shared experience, radicalism, and rank-and-file militancy and independence fostered a fierce sense of community among west coast longshoremen. The generation of 1934, remembered dockworker Al Langley some five decades later, was "a fraternal outfit. . . . You felt that you had to protect one another. You know, that boss, you hated him so bad, you did anything to get even with him, even if you had to work your head off."[6]

Rank-and-file fraternalism, moreover, extended to union leadership, regardless of political differences, and continued in spite of increasing attacks on both the ILWU and Bridges. The press's criticism of both stepped up during the growing conservative national mood after the 1938 congressional elections. In that same year, the federal government began the first of four attempts to deport Bridges. To most of the ILWU's membership, though, he was indisputably still "for the working guy." One longshoreman even remembered that these attacks triggered greater aggressiveness among the rank and file: "*that* was when we became strong and militant."[7]

The Coming of War and the ILWU

The ILWU became aware of the power of the newly united force of industry and the federal government that occurred as a result of war preparedness even before the latter broke the North American Aviation strike with Army troops in June 1941. During the spring of 1941, the union began receiving reports of repeated attempts, often successful, by the military and private employers to subvert the union hiring process. In April, the union received notice from the U.S. Army and the Waterfront Employers Association that "certain stevedores" would henceforth be "denied admission to the Army Transport Docks" because "extreme care" had to be "exercised in selecting employees on national defense projects." When the union protested that its members were being discriminated against for political reasons and that this action breached established union hiring procedures, the Army replied tersely that its decision was "not subject to review by any organization outside the Government."[8]

By August, union officials also were expressing concern about the Army's plan to train a "Negro Battalion of 600" for longshore work at the Army's 14th Street dock in Oakland. Secretary of War Henry L. Stimson's response to the CIO and ILWU did little to allay their fears that union workers would soon be replaced by troops. The training and eventual use of troops on the docks, according to Stimson, was necessary "to insure the successful outcome of military operations"; citing safety concerns, he insisted that "military personnel must be used for this task."[9]

This was an alarming message to the union. In war, much of the cargo being loaded on vessels in Pacific coast ports would be military cargo destined for the South Pacific. Would the military eventually extend the use of Army longshoremen to other docks in the Bay area or to other ports on the Pacific coast? The challenge for the union was how to maintain its presence, especially its control over the hiring process, in the face of military demands.

One answer to these demands was the union's outright unwillingness to cooperate with the military. In August 1941, the dispatcher at Local 10's hiring hall received a call to provide six winch drivers for work on an Army transport ship at the Benecia Arsenal. Because winch drivers could neither load nor discharge a ship's cargo without longshoremen, and because no orders for dispatch of longshoremen to the job had been issued by the Army, the dispatcher refused to fill the order for the winch drivers. Later that day, an Army captain at the Benecia Arsenal admitted, after questioning by union officials, that "civil service employees would handle the cargo in the hold and on the dock." The union then refused to provide the six winch drivers to the Army.[10]

ILWU support for the establishment of a tripartite wartime production board constituted yet another response to the coming of war. In

November 1941, Bridges, who previously had proposed, then shelved, a similar plan, brought the issue of increasing production back to the ILWU membership. He appealed to union members to endorse the "Murray Plan," a scheme linking the "establishment of a joint labor relations committee for each basic industry in the United States" to increased production. He urged ILWU members to write their "respective Congressmen," recommending adoption of the Murray Plan, "in the interests of national defense, and as a step towards strengthening genuine collective bargaining and to offset passage of anti-strike and anti-labor legislation" then pending in Congress.[11]

Later that month, Bridges was in Washington promoting his version of a defense plan. On November 26 and 27, he met with U.S. Maritime Assistant Commissioner Edward Macauley, Sidney Hillman of the Office of Production Management, steamship company executive Roger Lapham, and labor arbitrator Wayne L. Morse, all of whom "expressed approval" of Bridges's plan. As then formulated, the plan would "establish an administrative council for the industry composed of union, employers and a government representative" that would "secure maximum production" and guaranteed no strikes by labor "for the duration."[12]

Bridges returned to San Francisco a few days after the attack on Pearl Harbor and presented his plan to the employers' association. The employers quickly accepted the provisions of the plan, but within a week they recanted their endorsement, intimating that the plan was but a "maneuver by [Bridges] under a patriotic mantle to confuse issues and with an eye to a favorable deportation decision." They insisted that "as a result of seven years of . . . almost deliberate sabotage in the industry through slowdowns, violations of agreements," they could not trust the union's "honesty or sincerity in presenting this plan." Management went on opposing the defense production plan, by now commonly called the "Bridges Plan," and the impasse between employers, the government, and the union over implementing it continued. The Bridges Plan did not become policy until mid-February 1942.[13]

Earlier, the ILWU rank and file had refused to abandon their commitment to nonintervention. Shortly after the Nazis invaded the Soviet Union on June 22, 1941, a Communist "club" within warehouse Local 6 introduced at a regular membership meeting a resolution advocating wholehearted support for the "war of liberation" against the Nazis. Yet without the support of the local leadership, the resolution suffered a stinging 10:1 electoral defeat. The membership clearly rejected CP-sponsored proposals on certain issues at certain times. But later developments also attest to the leadership Bridges provided: at the next membership meeting in July, Bridges, in an hour-long speech, introduced a similar resolution to the membership. This time the resolution passed nearly unanimously.[14]

In later months, the ILWU rank and file was more willing than business and government to endorse such provisions as the no-strike pledge and the oath to speed production. Several recent historical works quote at length the story of how Bridges, when he outlined the ILWU's official stance on the no-strike pledge and wartime speedup, was laughed at and nearly booed off the stage of the Wilmington Bowl in southern California by rank-and-file members of Local 13. As the account goes, after the union president outlined his plan, a rank-and-file member of the local chided Bridges: "Just because your pal Joe Stalin is in trouble, don't expect us to give up our conditions to help him out." This anecdote is meant to illustrate the depth of antagonism between a "class collaborationist" labor leader, who both cooperated with government and industry and was sympathetic to the CP, and militant rank-and-file unionists who were unwilling to swallow the Party line on wartime production increases.[15]

There was, of course, antagonism between some union members and their leader, but more happened at the meeting in Wilmington in 1942 than that oft-repeated tale indicates. As "Chick" Loveridge remembered it, Bridges was, in fact, "booed unmercifully" by the audience of dockworkers. But then, following a long wait in line, Bridges returned to the podium and "after he hit that [microphone] and talked for forty-five or fifty minutes, people wanted to polish his head and shine his shoes and bow to him and everything." Similarly, in an extensive series of oral histories of rank-and-file ILWU members, remarkably few recalled any opposition to the no-strike pledge. Bill T. Ward recollected that the no-strike pledge was "no big deal, really" to waterfront workers. Others concurred. Ruben Negrete, also a San Pedro longshoreman, remembered during the war, "[W]e worked our asses off [because] we were helping our country. . . . Now Harry made that promise that we wouldn't strike, and at the time, we all listened to Harry. We still do. . . . I don't think there was too much turmoil here, the guys were patriotic and all." Art Kaunisto, whose immigrant father had been blacklisted for radical union activities, put the issue within its historical context. "During them days," he said, "it was right after Pearl Harbor, there wasn't much said about it. You'd do your work and that was it."

Others remember more practical twists to the lack of criticism over the no-strike pledge. Elmer Gutierrez recalled that no matter what the membership thought, Bridges "was pretty well known for getting what he wanted." Loveridge thought the members understood that Bridges "had to take that [no-strike] position because . . . there was a war on. He was just about forced to do it, for philosophical reasons, for social reasons, and for contractual reasons." "Of course we couldn't say anything, 'cause a lot of us had brothers, uncles [in the service] and we had to go with the war effort," asserted Elmer Mevert; "there was no such thing as dissension." Al Langley remembered the reaction to the no-strike pledge was "generally favorable," although "a lot of people gave more consideration to the monetary gain [increased production would bring] than to the war effort that we were actually trying to accomplish. Ninety-eight percent of the membership coastwide supported Harry."[16]

Few members, by the same token, who were interviewed could recall any hostility toward the wartime speedup. Pete Grassi argued that work "was faster and everything; we wanted to win the war." Kathryn Young, remembering her days as a bottle labeler in a San Francisco warehouse, stated that "[I] worked like a son-of-a-gun" during the war. When questioned further, she could not recall any opposition to the speedup by women working in that bottling plant. Likewise, Charles Hackett reported that "no one [in Local 6] was opposed to the [speedup]. We even worked extra overtime, which was against our [union's] principles!"[17]

A general availability of work at the union's lucrative overtime rates of pay, hinted at in Hackett's testimony, suggests one possible reason why union members did not object strenuously to the speedup. Bill Castagnasso, a union member and supervising foreman on the waterfront, testified to the changes in the pace of work during the war. In the early years of the war, when "we started getting all these [new] guys out of the hall," he told an interviewer,

we started giving what we called "deals." We'd tell a gang, "OK, now look, for every [railroad] car of [200 oil] drums that you unload . . . you get one hour credit." So the gangs would come to work in the morning and . . . knock off their cars as fast as they could. . . . I have seen gangs go home at 12 o'clock with eight double-decked cars [unloaded] . . . and get paid for eight hours. Many, many times we'd have guys go home at four in the afternoon with twelve hours pay—eight straight and four hours over[time]. And this happened straight through the war. Guys were working hard.[18]

There are still other reasons why ILWU rank-and-filers remained relatively quiescent during the war. On the docks, some rank-and-file

ILWU members and employers made informal deals over work processes, in the evolution of the "four on, four off" system, where only half of the workers in an eight-man gang would be working at any given time. Few stevedoring companies objected to this system, as it padded the payroll, making cost-plus contracts all the more lucrative. For workers accustomed to the prewar frenzied pace of work on the docks and in the ships, cost-plus was a welcomed change. Longshoreman Frank Sunstedt explained that his fellow workers were well aware of the relationship between "four on, four off" and cost-plus contracts: "[The employer] would say, 'Hey, we don't need this many men down here. Why don't two or so of you guys go get a cup of coffee or something.' Well, you'd see that it would be readily acceptable to the men." Remembered Langley, "that was supposedly *our* privilege. . . . The employer never ever complained. He never insisted on all eight men working because it was cost-plus."[19]

Few employers or military officials interpreted workers taking advantage of "four on, four off" as slowdowns or work stoppages. On the other hand, the international leadership denounced the corruption inherent in the four on, four off system, equally blaming "labor hoarding" bosses and "deliberate shirkers" within the ranks for the continuing practice.[20] But local union officials often took the complaints as more nuisances than serious problems that should be addressed. John Mitchell remembered one such objection to the longshoremen's new wartime pace of work by a "goldbraid . . . a little old stinking ensign." As his local's president, Mitchell simply instructed the union members to get back "on their feet." Bridges could not stop the four on, four off system, given the reluctance of local union officials to end the practice. As two workers commented later, in the four on, four off system the employers "created a monster" that "they couldn't eliminate after the war"; longshoremen later paid the price in extensive employer surveillance of work processes on the postwar docks.[21]

The uses of this corrupt system reveal as much about the longshoreman's sense of community as they do his concepts of class conflict. John Martinez remarked that "all of us fellows had families, and during the war our sons were overseas. These fellows that worked for me, their sons would come home and I'd say, 'You go ahead and stay there. I'll take care of the job.' We would carry the guy." When regular gang members were sick, injured, or too drunk to work, fellow gang members would hide the facts—allowing the worker to collect wages. "Four on, four off" also allowed workers to complete chores that otherwise would have required a day off work: looking for an apartment, visiting the rationing board, shopping for scarce goods. In accepting this new work pace, longshoremen, in the words of one sociologist, "torn by the conflicting loyalties of nationalism and class, ultimately determined the proper mix of accommodation and resistance on the docks during the war."[22]

The union initiated its own forms of workers' control. With the International's help, ILWU warehousemen were able to consolidate gains made during the previous few years. The ILWU's great "March Inland" of the 1930s had been halted largely by the Teamsters; part of the truce from those jurisdictional battles stipulated that teamsters could not deposit their cargoes more than 20 feet from their trucks or inside ILWU warehouses. In the spirit of maximized production, ILWU leaders rescinded this agreement with the Teamsters. To "speed the war effort," Teamster truck drivers could cross well-defined jurisdictional boundaries to place their cargoes anywhere in ILWU warehouses or on ILWU docks as long as such cargoes were designated with a "T" (Teamster) ticket. ILWU warehousemen would then rebuild those "T-ticketed" cargoes, even if they were already palletized and ready and scheduled for immediate loading on board a ship. One Local 6 business agent later characterized the practice of "T-ticketing" as make-work that did nothing to increase production or speed the movement of cargo. The practice was adopted solely as a way of espousing productionist rhetoric while maintaining jurisdictional prerogatives.[23]

The Battle for the Hiring Hall:
Challenge from the Outside

Once war was declared, the prospects of employment in defense industries promised opportunities for economic prosperity to many people. "Buster" Hanspard, who had spent most of the previous two decades working on railroad and levee labor gangs in Mississippi and Louisiana, described the mood of cautious optimism in early 1942. "At that time," he remembered, "people was going everywhere then. People were scouting out everywhere." Yet paradoxically, as wartime employment in general began to increase in 1942, the ILWU became engaged in ever more serious battles to retain control over those jobs that it had before war was declared. On several fronts, the union's hiring system again was under attack by the military, which intended to use Army personnel and civil service employees as longshoremen and warehousemen all along the Pacific coast. In San Diego, the U.S.

Marines were, "in effect, being used as substitutes for longshore-men." In Seattle, longshoremen and warehousemen were being re-placed by civil service employees. Seattle unionists also worried that another "colored battalion" of Army longshore trainees would take over more civilian jobs then held by union members.[24]

Both private employers and the military sought to institute "pre-ferred" status for certain groups of workers in order to create "steady, specialty gangs that stay made up and work together all the time." The union's leadership responded by refusing to oblige both the mili-tary and private employers. As Bridges argued, "preferred gangs would disrupt the union, destroy morale and arouse bitterness" among men who worked rotated jobs out of the hiring hall.[25]

Opposition to the institution of "preferred status" workers was not limited to union leaders. In December 1942, the membership of ILWU Local 10 unanimously rejected a motion by its executive board to supply 20 steady longshoremen to the Army Transport Service (ATS) for loading ammunition at Richmond. A motion was then presented to supply the ATS with 50 gangs—of 18 men each—of steady long-shoremen for ammunition loading at the same terminal! That motion, too, was unanimously rejected. Instead, after a "lengthy discussion," another motion was proposed and carried "unanimously that Local 1-10 of the ILWU will positively dispatch safe and efficient gangs when requested by the Army and Navy Transportation Service," with no mention of steady, "preferred" status.[26]

Requests for "preferred" gangs was just one aspect of a continuing effort to supersede unions that grew into something of a bitter, run-ning battle between labor and industry throughout the war years. On Army docks up and down the Pacific coast, government clerks, who allegedly were "secured from the Veterans of Foreign Wars and blan-keted into civil service for the emergency, but without examination," replaced union clerks, who were laid off.[27]

Groups of "dock seamen," like civil service employees, replaced longshoremen on docks and warehouse workers in (railroad) car-loading operations over the protests of the ILWU. These "dock sea-men," the union protested, were hired by the Army via the "State Employment Office or off the street" to work at "longer hours, no overtime, [and] lesser rates of pay." The union's response was charac-teristic: organize these workers. These efforts, however, often were hampered by the military's bureaucratic "hostility and a determined effort to prevent union participation in the war effort." In mid-1942, for example, the union unsuccessfully proposed that "dock seamen" be permitted to register as permit longshoremen, a special permit longshoremen's hiring hall be set up, and that an ILWU member be hired as dispatcher for that hall.[28]

The military's outright hostility greeted ILWU efforts to organize dock and warehouse workers, as the armed services often hired non-union civil servants to replace union members.[29] Homer Dunlap was fired from his civil service job at an ATS dock in 1943 but returned to work at another military establishment as an ILWU warehouseman and union organizer. His "secret" task was to organize civil servants. One day while piling freight on the dock, he recalled, "here come the Captain and the Colonel and the Army. [It was] nothing but brass caps coming down. They took me across the road . . . and the Colonel did all the talking. [He] says, 'I got all these stripes around my arms and I don't want to lose them.' " Orders had come down from Washington to fire Dunlap for his organizing activities. When the union agreed to take him off the job, he was relieved. Fearful that his draft deferment would be canceled for his organizing activities, Dunlap later recalled that he "didn't want them to throw me in the army—you know, that's what they'd do to you." The ILWU also collected numerous affidavits from unionists who had been proselytized by military officials. An indignant union member resented the implication that patriotism and union affiliation were not compatible: "[I] was approached on three different occasions and it was suggested to me I drop my Union affiliations and join the Naval Supply Depot under civil service and a bright future was assured me by doing so. I am an ex-service man from the first World War and a CIO member."[30]

The patterns of wartime labor relations paralleled the prewar experience, at least in part, because of those recruited to perform the military's managerial functions. One high-ranking officer involved in San Francisco ATS operations was a former district manager for a steamship company who had, it was reported, recruited scabs during the 1934 strike. Additional reports indicated that other military officers were formerly superintendents and supervisors of local steamship and stevedoring companies. This antiunion bias extended to the top of the military as well. Rear Adm. Emory Land, head of the War Shipping Administration, once remarked that all union organizers during the war "ought to be shot at sunrise."[31]

A shortage of workers plagued the longshoring and warehousing industries on the Pacific coast by mid-1942. In San Pedro, the dearth of longshoremen was so acute that stevedoring companies resorted to calling the local high school in order to find enough workers to unload perishable and nonessential cargoes from vessels in the harbor. In ports up and down the coast, servicemen on leave were allowed to work temporarily as permit longshoremen and warehouse workers. By the summer of 1944, the War Manpower Commission endowed its top priority rating on longshore work in the San Francisco Bay area. As the eventual outcome of the war seemed assured by autumn of that year, moreover, war workers in search of peacetime jobs "fled" the Pacific coast at an astonishing rate.[32]

Employers, who conflated the general shortage of civilian workers in the latter years of the war with the allegedly inherent inability of the union, through its hiring hall, to provide enough competent workers, sought to solve labor shortages by recapturing the hiring process. They argued that civilian labor "pools" ought to replace inefficient union hiring halls. In reply, union leaders admonished locals to do better at fulfilling labor needs and requested longshoremen themselves to assist in recruiting new workers. Only concerted action by union members would "offset recruiting efforts by all public agencies." Despite the union's best efforts to recruit new workers, however, employers' threats did not cease. In June 1945, Henry Schmidt warned International Vice President Rosco Craycraft that "there have been some threats [from employers] . . . that they will be forced to set-up their own civilian longshore pools and thus circumvent the hiring hall or employ military labor battalions."[33]

Employer representatives on the PCMIB, as part of their campaign against the hiring halls, in 1943 took away the screening privileges formerly held by the union as part of its hiring procedure. In December 1942, the ILWU had initiated a recruiting and training program for new workers that functioned separately from the PCMIB. By mid-1943, however, Chairman Paul Eliel and employer members of the board seized control of this program and replaced its ILWU director with another "labor representative," John Kelly of the Web Pressman's Union, an AFL affiliate. The ILWU leadership, which vehemently opposed this move, argued that not only must experienced waterfront workers evaluate the fitness of prospective applicants for union work but that "new workers coming on the waterfront must be . . . educated in union organization principles by our union." The union, furthermore, insisted that only ILWU officials, in properly screening the applicants, could "keep an eye open to see that no undesirable elements opposed to the principles of labor may be fed into our union by employer interests." Finally, in a letter to the president of the Web Pressmen's Union, J. Vernon Burke, Bridges appealed to strictly traditional union concerns: "It would be very hard for us to understand, and possibly for your organization also, if under similar circumstances a longshoreman was put in charge of recruiting and training of apprentices for the industry over which your union has jurisdiction and contracts. We would think there was something very wrong underneath it all if such a situation occurred."[34]

By late 1944, the PCMIB had placed another official in charge of recruitment and training, but the union also found this arrangement unsatisfactory. The board stationed their recruiting officer at the U.S. Employment Service (USES). Laborers who came to the USES for jobs, many of whom had recently been laid off from work in shipyards, were screened by the board's agent. Once an applicant passed this review, he or she was sent upstairs to "four gentlemen representing employers of labor" who screened the applicant again. If the applicant passed this inquiry, only then was he or she sent to the union hiring hall to apply for work. Unionists were nearly powerless to prevent abuses of this system, even when prospective workers were openly discriminated against. Near the end of the war, the union members of the board protested when two job applicants were turned down because they were Chinese-Americans. But their objections were overruled because, as one employer representative stated flatly, "it developed that the work was too heavy," even though the men were not given the opportunity to try it. Not only was the union in jeopardy of losing total control over the hiring process, but the PCMIB and the state, through the USES, sanctioned racial discrimination in employment, despite Executive Order 8802 (prohibiting racial discrimination in employment) and the formation of the Fair Employment Practices Commission (FEPC).[35]

Finally, management also attempted to enlist the government's aid in winning their battle against the union. During the war, employers and their representatives continually tried to force a confrontation between the military and the union over hiring procedures. One such incident occurred when San Pedro longshoremen, members of Local 13, balked at increasing the sling-load limit of cement from 21 to 31 hundred-pound sacks while loading Navy vessels. Eliel, openly allied with employers on the board, threatened to order "U.S. troops . . . to work the ships."[36]

The Battle for the Hiring Hall: Challenge from Within

Wartime labor shortages figure prominently in the history of the ILWU. The union was waging the battle of its young life. For the leadership, the conflict was clearly framed in class terms: who would control hiring—workers or industry? Yet the rank and file fought the battle on two fronts. Workers fought capital on one side and other workers on the other side. ILWU leaders had to recruit new workers during the war in order to meet manpower requirements and thus stave off the bosses' attack on its hiring halls. In the warehouse division, at least one new worker in five was African-American or Mexican-American; in the longshore division, the percentage of minorities was even higher. Yet white workers often did not take kindly to this influx of nonwhites, especially after recruiting efforts intensified at the end of 1942. Many slowdowns and work stoppages came about as whites resisted the entry or promotion of minority workers on the job.

The ILWU's leadership drastically underestimated the extent and potency of racist beliefs among its rank-and-file members. A good example of this is a 1942 *Dispatcher* editorial in which Bridges chided members for "some incidents" of racism. Declaring that "discrimination against Negroes is anti-labor, anti-American and anti-white," Bridges attributed racist assaults on black workers to three things. First, the attacks were the "sabotage" actions of a few "appeasers, Trotskyites and other such Hitlerian fifth column elements" striving to "disrupt the whole war effort." Second, he asserted, in typical left-wing prose, that "Southern Bourbon labor-haters" were fomenting "Negro hatred and discrimination" in order to "create and keep a cheap labor market"; he continued, " 'Divide and make profits,' is their open slogan." Third, Bridges blamed African-Americans themselves: "Negro workers, lacking experience and discipline and nursing past wounds, have needlessly antagonized some older members of the union and have thus furnished fuel for the sabotage work of the deliberately disruptive minority elements."[37]

The ILWU leadership, however, made only limited efforts to enforce its dedication to the "economic and political equality" of all races. Officially, the ILWU's leadership openly denounced racist discrimination on the job, in the union, and in the larger society. In 1942, for example, Louis Goldblatt, an ILWU member, a Communist, and secretary-treasurer of the California State Industrial Union Council, CIO, illustrated this ideological commitment in his condemnation of the wartime internment of Japanese-Americans. Many ILWU leaders, furthermore, like other trade unionists, intellectuals, and political activists of the time, saw parallels between the race hatred of white Americans and the Aryan supremacist beliefs of the Nazis. But what distinguished the racist actions of many ILWU members and probably made those acts more tolerable to the international leadership is that it was often hard to distinguish between job consciousness, union pride, and flagrant racial discrimination.[38]

ILWU members looked to their own experiences in order to interpret racial antagonism on the docks and in the warehouses: the result was often a blurring of the distinctions between racism and class antagonism. Henry Gaitan, a Mexican-American who labored on the racially segregated lumber docks in San Pedro during the 1930s, recalled that waterfront employers had pitted one ethnic group against another in order to increase production in the prewar years. "What the company used to do," he remembered, was "to hire Italians over there, and then hire a group of Mexicans over here, and then a group of something else over there . . . and then say, 'Look, those guys can do a better job than you guys.' " Through this lens, he contended that it was the employers who, during the war, were "bringing these blacks from Texas. The idea was to break the union, weaken the union. . . . The [employers' association] was one of the instigators of it." Eugene Lasartemay, an African-American engineer, remembered how shipowners had traditionally used black workers as strikebreakers; Bridges constantly played upon this awareness to remind ILWU members that they should "learn how to work with [blacks] now" because employers had imported "blacks to break the strikes" of 1919 and 1934.[39]

The inability to draw a sharp distinction between job consciousness and racism was still apparent to Walter Williams over 40 years after the war. Williams, a CIO organizer who came to the waterfront after a bitter struggle over the training and upgrading of black tradesmen in a large shipyard, found the situation "almost confusing." "You had to wonder," he said, if whites resented black workers "because they considered us to be invaders, because we weren't there in large numbers when the union first organized . . . or whether it was just out-and-out racism.[40]

This "confusion" between race pride and union pride is superbly illustrated in an incident involving one of the first Mexican-American ILWU walking bosses and an all-African-American eight-man gang. Mexican-Americans had faced much prejudice on the docks before the war—so much so that several remembered the increased presence of blacks "took the pressure away from us Mexicans." Anti-Mexican-American sentiment did not, however, disappear, and John Martinez had "a lot of problems" with both white and African-American longshoremen. Martinez, who knew well the sting of white workers' bigotry through decades of experience as a dockworker, finally reached the breaking point. "One day," he recalled, "I had enough of it." He stopped all work on the ship after being insulted all morning by an all-black gang of longshoremen who were angry because Martinez had docked them an hour's pay apiece the previous day. The exchange that followed reveals much. The gang in the hold, recounted Martinez, said, "Hey there's that SOB. . . . What does [he] know about working? [He] never worked a day in [his] life!" Martinez stopped the winch and told them: "Now look, you mothers. You say I never worked a day in my life on this waterfront. I'll tell you, back in '33 and '34, and in 1936 and '37, [in] '40, I pounded the bricks for this union, when you all were still back in Africa!"[41] The fact was, however, that several of those African-Americans in the ship's hold that day were not "back in Africa" in 1934 when the ILWU was formed. They were experienced longshoremen who had come to San Pedro during the war from the Gulf coast, where, as members of segregated "Jim Crow" ILA locals, they had been relegated to only the most noxious work. Nor were they alone. A significant percentage of black dock-workers new to the ILWU during the war had been ILA longshoremen in the South before the war.[42]

In other cases, however, the source of discrimination was easily discerned: it was "out-and-out racism." One dockworker found himself in a gang with a black man who "nobody else wanted to work with," but learned to respect that man's skill while loading bales of cotton and wool with him in a ship's hold; they remained partners throughout the war. He later placed the blame for this hostility on the local union. "Corky" Wilson found that even though some blacks were "nice guys" and good, hardworking "old-time stevedores," he just "couldn't cope with the colored people." So he formed his own gang of eight men, no less than half of whom were family members. Walter Williams described one common response of "regular 'longies' " [long-shoremen] to black workers: some whites would say, " 'I'm going to call me a damn replacement' if they saw a black guy coming down into the hold. And they would call a replacement rather than work with us." Joe Stahl also remembered that many "old-timers wouldn't work with a black guy. [They] would turn around and call a replacement."[43]

Joseph H. Tipp, assistant to the PCMIB, noticed similar sentiments among long-time members of the union who felt threatened by the admission of black workers into longshore jobs. Tipp, in a series of reports to the board, observed widespread complaints on the San Francisco waterfront against "too many replacements, mostly colored, [who] have slowed down efficiency and production in most of the old-time, good gangs, according to the walking bosses." However, in his reports on declining production rates, Tipp never differentiated between inexperienced and experienced black dockworkers. Rather, he noted a general resistance among whites to all black workers. Henry Schmidt also remarked that many members of the generation of 1934 "were opposed to those people coming in. The typical, popular idea was that, 'We shouldn't start with this.' "[44]

Tipp further indicated that racism was sometimes masked by concerns about union conditions. "Many old-timers in regular gangs," Tipp wrote, objected to working with "colored boys, not because of their color, but because most of them are shiftless and lazy, folding up after a few hours . . . leaving most of the work in the hatch to the old-timers—but they draw the same pay." Like Williams and Stahl, Tipp also noted that many whites avoided working with blacks by calling replacements or dissolving their gangs. In 1942, the union, primarily in response to gang instability brought on by rampant racism, decreed that all gangs had to stay together for a minimum of 30 days. Shortly thereafter, Tipp observed that some old-timers subverted the new gang rule by deliberately "getting fired from a job for doing slow work in order to get rid of the gang."[45]

Incidents of racial antagonism were not limited to the docks. Before the war, the management of a Colgate plant in the East Bay, whose workers were organized in the ILWU warehouse division's Local 6, allegedly maintained a "gentlemen's agreement" with the union to limit African-Americans to a few poorly paid janitorial positions. These race barriers were broken in 1939—but only after one black man's bid to gain a better position in the plant was put to a vote of the union members at Colgate. The testimony of the vice president of the local, seven Colgate stewards, and the man bidding on the job, Eugene Lasartemay, was required before the membership voted to abolish the racial restrictions on job advancement. This action, however, did not eradicate race hatred in the plant during the war. Fannie Walker, a former domestic, was the "very first Negro colored girl at Colgate." She endured racial slurs, faced racial segregation in the lunchroom, was prevented from using the water fountain, and repeatedly had her lunch put on the floor, where "the dogs ate," by her fellow workers. Virginia Wysinger, another black worker at Colgate during the war, found that white workers harassed her by sabotaging the production process to make her look incompetent. Both women recalled that although some white workers supported them, racial harassment was only curtailed through the actions of the ILWU warehouse division's leadership.[46]

Yet what is important about these examples is not that racial prejudice existed, or that, as Bridges would have had it, the consequences of that bigotry were absenteeism and a slowdown of production, but that whites who did not want to work with African-American and Mexican-American workers could easily manipulate the union hiring system to their advantage. All a worker had to do was to return to the hiring hall where there were other jobs waiting to be had. This powerful instrument of workers' control—the hiring hall—clearly was misused by the reactionary and the racist to further job-conscious, not class-conscious, unionism.

Rank-and-filers often found themselves in direct opposition to international leaders, especially on racial issues. Many ILWU leaders supported the hiring of black workers through local union halls, but direct action by the International in settling racial disputes among the rank and file was often limited by other more practical considerations.[47] In December 1943, a longshore local in Portland, Oregon, refused to accept a black man as a full member "solely because he was a Negro." Yet, outside of a letter from Bridges asking the membership "to eliminate any form of racial discrimination from your ranks," the International took no action. Concerted direct action to prevent race discrimination would have necessitated a drastic modification in the operation of the hiring hall system, a measure the International was not prepared to take.[48]

The Portland incident contrasts sharply with another episode of racism nearly two years later where practicality led the leadership in a different direction. In June 1945, ILWU warehousemen in Stockton, California, refused to work with Japanese-Americans recently released from internment camps. This incident was not only a political and social embarrassment to the International leadership, but it also threatened the ILWU's organizing drive in Hawaii, where a substantial number of workers were Japanese-Americans. The International resolved the crisis by revoking the Stockton local's charter until the members accepted Nisei workers into their local. The hiring hall system, moreover, was not jeopardized by this action, as in the last days of the war the union was faced with a surplus, not a shortage, of workers.[49]

There is little evidence that the ILWU leadership actively contested racism within the rank and file. Instead, local autonomy prevailed. Locals screened applicants for membership through their "investigating committees." Even during the war, new applicants were quizzed about their backgrounds: What did they do during the 1934 strike? Had they ever been strikebreakers? What did they think about the union? What experience did they have? The answers to these and other questions were taken seriously; most applicants were required to document their claims. The investigating committee was, recalled Paul Ware, "a very important committee. It was the structure of the union." To Mickey Mahon, who applied for membership during the war, the investigating process posed some problems. The committee members, "all '34 guys, good, solid men," demanded of Mahon that he verify his whereabouts during the 1934 strike; after a delay the committee granted him union membership only after Mahon had somehow proven where he was in '34—unemployed, "living off the land: bumming water, food, panhandling, . . . washing dishes, [and] hang[ing] around Pershing Square" in Los Angeles. Few African-American workers made it to, let along through, the investigating committee process. Instead, remembered Williams, African-American dockworkers were offered the chance to work only after they had signed "a commitment to work there in a temporary status and to approve of being terminated after the war."[50]

The promotions committee was also a locus of rank-and-file control. Unlike many unionized workers, ILWU longshoremen were not promoted on a seniority basis alone. Instead, workers not only had to have both job seniority and job knowledge but also had to prove it to their peers before they were considered for promotions. Frank Sunstedt, chairman of the San Pedro longshore local's promotion committee during the war, noted that his local used the committee to deny African-Americans promotions: "No black member had ever been given a gang. . . . Every time a black man was about ready to get a gang, the [other] promotions committee members would go around and entice anyone else to get a gang, just to keep a black man out. . . . These guys used to . . . go through these files and any application of a black man, they'd throw it in the wastebasket." In an interview recorded almost 40 years after the war ended, Art Kaunisto expressed his enduring frustration about how his local's promotions committee functioned during the war. When African-Americans applied for gang boss ratings to the promotions committee, the committee members "would just kind of roust them around. A bunch of guys would ask them, 'Can you do this? Can you do that?' Christ, you're not supposed to be a college man to work on the waterfront."[51]

The wartime labor emergency compelled at least one promotions committee to revise its criteria for upgrading workers, in the direction of greater racial exclusivity. In 1945, Al Langley was the job dispatcher in Local 13's hiring hall, and, when he could not locate any available and qualified white longshoreman, he sent a black man, Rice Sims, out on a job as gang boss. When Sims arrived at the job site that evening, the gang of "white Navy kids" refused to work for him and walked off the job. The company fired Sims because his gang would not work, and Langley was reprimanded by the chief dispatcher for sending a black man out on a gang boss job. The union, afraid that it would be vulnerable to antidiscrimination lawsuits if it refused to dispatch other qualified black men to bosses' jobs, took the Sims case to arbitration. The resolution to this problem was "simple," and was extended coastwide as formal policy. "The employers and the union agreed that no man could be a boss unless he had five years in the industry [on the Pacific coast]. . . . We weren't ready for the blacks as a boss [sic]. They had to agree to something to keep down the fuss on the waterfront. . . . The blacks had then begun to get acclimated, and they knew their stuff. . . . They wanted to be part of the industry, too."[52] By establishing this rule, management and the union effectively restricted African-American and Mexican-American workers to lower paying hold and deck jobs, since most of these workers were hired during the war and thus did not have the requisite ILWU seniority to qualify for the more prestigious skilled jobs.

The hiring hall and the investigating and promotions committees unquestionably endowed longshoremen and warehouse workers in the ILWU with a high degree of workers' control over the social relations of production. As such, they were invaluable weapons in labor's arsenal for the class-based battle against industry. But they also were exceptionally effective exclusionary devices through which workers could determine which elements of the working class their union would represent.

Conclusion

Despite the ILWU's productionist orientation, the fundamental dynamics of interaction between employers and the union did not change after Pearl Harbor. What changed was not so much the essential conflict as the degree to which both the union and employers sought state intervention in resolving that conflict to their respective satisfaction.

There were work slowdowns and even occasional work stoppages, but these events, important indices of "shop-floor disaffection," seldom involved a direct confrontation between the leadership and the rank and file over either the no-strike pledge or a speedup in production. The ILWU leadership, motivated by both pro-Communist political considerations and the exigencies of more "traditional" unionism, enacted measures designed to maximize production but refused to sacrifice the real economic and contractual gains of the previous decade. The ILWU's wartime production record remains in dispute; most reports record a 10–15 percent rise in productivity over prewar levels, but others assert that little speedup actually occurred. It must be kept in mind, furthermore, that immediate prewar productivity levels, the standard against which wartime rates were measured, were far below pre-1934 levels.[53]

The real struggle within the ILWU revolved around the question of who would determine the vision and direction of the union in the war years. This process did not involve a clash between economic self-interest and patriotic support for the fight against fascism. It instead involved a struggle over the best way to protect the achievements of the 1930s. For the leadership, preserving the hiring hall system demanded some cooperation with the state. Yet many workers sought to protect the gains of the 1930s by preventing new workers from enjoying those very same benefits. In this context, rank-and-filism meant racism; if the leaders had more aggressively attacked racism, it would have meant attacking the rank-and-file members and control at the point of production. Many racial exclusionists in the union were not stereotypical "war babies"—young workers who "came from non-union, rural, conservative backgrounds"—but rather "old-timers," many of whom created that militant, left-wing union in the 1930s.[54] Does their behavior during the war say something about the character and limits of working-class militancy before the war? In considering the actions of the ILWU rank and file, we must ask: for whom, really, was the class struggle waged? Many rank-and-file members of the ILWU, acting contentiously to preserve job control and their sense of community during the war, placed real constraints on the leadership's ability to pursue a radical political agenda. In time, the ideological commitment to racial equality among left-wing ILWUers prevailed, but only after many highly contested and costly battles in the postwar period—battles that then, too, were fought over the hiring hall.

ACKNOWLEDGMENTS

The author would like to thank Jeff Quam-Wickham, Harvey Schwartz, Paula Fass, Bruce Nelson, Daniel Beagle, Lisa Rubens, James Gregory, and the editor of this volume for valuable comments on earlier versions of this essay.

BLACK AND WHITE TOGETHER:
Organizing in the South with the Food, Tobacco, Agricultural & Allied Workers Union (FTA–CIO), 1946–1952

KARL KORSTAD

Charleston, 1945/46

I had never been inside a union hall until the night that I spoke at the membership meeting of the Charleston, South Carolina, Central Trade Council. I discussed the problems Americans who had formed the Roosevelt coalition faced in the postwar period. About 15 white men attended, and midway through my remarks I knew I was in the wrong place. I had the feeling that I was holding up their monthly card game.

I was a staff sergeant in the U.S. Army Medical Corps, the noncom in Stark General Hospital's public relations office. Weekly, our office edited a tabloid and wrote a half-hour radio show; daily, we sent home pictures and stories about the troops brought to Charleston by the hospital ships, all intended to assure the readers of the hometown papers that their sons and daughters were on their way to the nearest Army general hospital.

By late spring in 1944, my wife, Frances, and I were living on a cobblestoned street around the corner from the Dock Street Theater. We had met in the fall of 1942 and married in February 1944. Frances's mother and father, decendants of old Charleston families, had moved to a 20-acre plot of land on James Island that they turned into a nursery, raising cut flowers, shrubs, and trees, as well as three daughters and five sons. Frances, the oldest of the daughters, had gone to the island's two-room grammar school, attended Charleston's Meminger High School for girls and the College of Charleston, become a caseworker in the county's welfare department, gone back for a year of graduate studies at Tulane, and returned to the child welfare department in the summer of 1943.

My mother was Scottish, Irish, and English; her father was a Presbyterian missionary. My father was the son of Norwegian immigrants. I grew up on the Red Lake Indian Reservation in northern Minnesota. When I entered the first grade, I was the only non-Indian in the class and thus on the losing end of a number of fist fights. I learned firsthand what being in a minority entailed. As they got used to me and I to them, I learned, too, what poverty meant. So it seemed only natural, as I went away to high school and then to college in the early 1930s, that I identified with the farmers and the working people and began reading the *Farmer Labor Leader,* which advocated state ownership of all natural resources. In high school I orated against capital punishment and chain grocery stores, and at Concordia College in Moorhead, Minnesota, in favor of the American Legion's "Universal Draft Act," which proposed to take the profit out of war by drafting corporations and business as well as citizens. I admired Floyd Olson, who had worked as a farm laborer and had been a member of the Industrial Workers of the World (IWW, or the Wobblies). Serving as county attorney for Hennepin County from 1920 to 1930, he made a name for himself investigating corruption in the Minneapolis City Council. As governor from 1931 to 1936, he helped the depression-ridden farmers and used the state militia to stop a trainload of scabs on their way from Chicago to Minneapolis to help break a teamster's strike. I can remember today just where I was the summer afternoon in 1936 when I heard that he had died.

During my senior year at Concordia I wrote a paper on Thorstein Veblen's *Theory of the Leisure Class.* Veblen's concept of "conspicuous consumption" gave me new insights into the roles upper-class and upper-middle-class persons played in our society and how they had created a value system that justified and defended their positions as leaders.

In 1937, after teaching high school English for two years in Ulen, Minnesota, a small farming town in the Red River Valley, I entered graduate school in English at Syracuse University. Along with some 10 or 12 other graduate students, also searching for answers, I was fortunate enough to study under Leonard Brown. Leonard explored the ideas of Charles Darwin, Karl Marx and Friedrich Engels, Sigmund Freud, and Oswald Spengler in his search for a better understanding of the function of literature in our times and in history. Such contemporary writers as Kenneth Burke, Malcolm Cowley, Edmund Wilson, W. T. Auden, Stephen Spender, C. Day Lewis, Archibald MacLeish, E. E. Cummings, and Kenneth Fearing each in his own way was looking to the "left" and to the new breed of social scientists for answers. As instructors in English 101, we taught these writers and others like them. I went into the armed forces in 1942, a Minnesota populist, who had, in the five years at Syracuse, "joined" the New Left Renaissance, which had grown and flourished in France and Britain and here at home during those years, dedicated to winning the war and ready to help build a more humane world in the years after.

It was a long way from Minnesota and Syracuse and the values of the left intellectuals to the world views of Charleston, South Carolina. There was a big difference between Norwegian immigrants and old Charlestonians, too. But from the beginning, Frances and I were kindred spirits; we felt at home together. We had lived through the Depression. We had worked to help pay our way through college. We shared common concerns about the postwar world and wanted to do something about them at the same time that we built a life for ourselves.

Becoming part of a Southern family involved me in an entirely new experience. I had never really known any black person well. Like all Northerners, I had been influenced by the media's caricatures of Southern whites and blacks. It took considerable time to begin to understand the complexities of race relations in the South. It was exciting. I saw that despite the legacy of slavery and Jim Crow, interactions between blacks and whites in Charleston were common. Moreover, many relationships were warm and personal. In their daily lives, blacks and whites often worked closely together, helped each other, laughed and cried together, and knew each other as individuals. In the hospital, too, I saw the returned soldiers, black and white, pushing each other in wheelchairs to the PX, ribbing each other and commiserating with each other in a ward of 40 amputees, and defying the Jim Crow laws in the public buses when the ambulatory patients came back to the hospital after a night on the town. Both Frances and I thought it possible for the members of the black community and the workers in the trade unions to become allies in the struggle against those who would replace Franklin D. Roosevelt's "Four Freedoms" with what they were touting as the coming "American Century."

Those of us in the hospital's public relations office talked constantly about our hopes for the postwar world. There was a WAAC from Michigan, a former sportswriter from New Jersey, a language specialist from Columbia University, and a student from New York University named Sidney Fishman. We supported Henry A. Wallace and the progressive wing of the Democratic Party even after the city bosses and the labor leaders blocked Wallace's renomination for vice president in favor of the safer Harry S. Truman. Sidney and I had become close friends. In the summer of 1945 Sidney and I prepared a manifesto for progressives.[1] Its introduction read:

The general direction which conservative strategy will take in the ensuing months and years is now quite clear. As a matter of fact, it has been since long before the victory. We have long known that they would foster a stream-lined imperialism abroad in connection with their free enterprise campaign at home. Since North Africa it has been obvious that they [i.e., the corporate leaders] would attempt to insure the return of conservative leaders in the liberated countries. The only new element in the pattern has been the revivified "fear Russia" campaign which they began immediately after V-E Day.

We did not underestimate the strength of the corporate sector, which had emerged at the war's end with more financial clout than any group in the history of the world, while our Allies and our enemies were bankrupt, their populations decimated, their infrastructures destroyed. Yet we remained confident that the progressive agenda could be realized. If the unions could continue to increase their numbers, if they could forge a stronger unity between blacks and whites, between men and women, among all religious and nationality groups, they could be crucial in moving America down the road that we envisioned: the fulfillment of the social programs of the New Deal, an end to colonialism, and a beginning of free independent nations worldwide. Moreover, if the workers in the South could build this kind of unity in their unions and in their community struggles, they would be able to free themselves from the poverty and the deprivations forced upon them by the Southern elites. We wanted to be a part of that effort.

That was why I had begun working with the AFL's Trade Union Council, and the reason that Sid Fishman and I searched out the two CIO locals in Charleston: Local 15 of the FTA(Food, Tobacco, Agricultural & Allied Workers Union)–CIO and the local of the NMU(National Maritime Union)–CIO. In the summer of 1945 we began working with Local 15 as volunteers, preparing leaflets, teaching reading and writing skills, and releasing stories about the union to the press.

The Local 15 members worked at a cigar plant owned by the American Tobacco Company. The long, dark redbrick factory stretched along the river, directly under the Charleston side of the Cooper River Bridge. Most of the workers were women, about half of them black and half white.

I first met the leaders in an office over a shop on North King Street. They had just returned from a War Labor Board hearing. That had been the first time, they said, that a group of workers had gone together, white and black as a committee, to represent a union in Charleston.

Membership meetings consisted mostly of the black workers and the few white leaders. But workers told us that more and more whites were getting involved, working with the blacks on union committees. More of them were beginning to come to the membership meetings.

At the center of it all was Reuel Stanfield, a Midwesterner, too old to have been in the service. Among the leaders of the maritime strike in Los Angeles in 1934, he had been arrested at the docks in San Pedro, allegedly for carrying dynamite in the trunk of a car (dynamite, which Reuel said had been planted while they were on the picket line). He drew a five-year sentence in San Quentin; there he met Tom Mooney, who convinced him to spend his time learning how to read and write so that he could be more useful to labor's cause.[2]

Sid Fishman and I also organized "The New South" lecture series through the local CIO Political Action Committee. The lectures were held in a large African Methodist Episcopal church on a nonsegregated basis during the winter of 1945/46. The speakers included Aubrey Williams, former director of the National Youth Administration and then the editor of the *Southern Farmer;* Dr. Charles S. Johnson, the famous sociologist from Fisk University; and the Rev. Kelley Barnett from Chapel Hill. Attendance by white Charlestonians averaged over a hundred each night, with workers, church people, and professionals—even a banker—in attendance. Four to five hundred blacks, representing every section of the community attended each meeting. Blacks and whites stood at the door each night to welcome those who came.

I left Charleston soon after the series began to earn three more months of service needed for a discharge and was out of the army and back in Charleston by February. That October the Charleston workers had joined with other FTA members in Philadelphia and Trenton in a strike against the American Tobacco Company. They were asking for joint negotiations, trying to break the historic North–South wage differentials. In Charleston all of the black workers had gone out, joined by about a hundred white workers. The strikers in Trenton and Philadelphia had pledged not to return to work until contracts had been signed in every plant.

In January 1946, one of the antiunion white mechanics spit on the leg of a black woman on the picket line. She wiped off her leg and swore at him. The police arrested her for disturbing the peace. Before the municipal judge the next morning, two of the white women pickets testified. One of them said, "That scab spit on this sister's leg and she swore only once. If it had been me, I'd have done a whole lot more than just swear." The judge dismissed the charges. To the white women, the white mechanic had become a scab and the black woman a sister. For some, changes were taking place in Charleston's vocabulary and understanding.

By mid-February, the Charleston workers needed help to pay for rent and utilities. At the request of the FTA leaders, I went to Washington, D.C., to raise needed funds. Elizabeth Sasuly, FTA's Washington representative, started me off. I received a desk at the Washington office of the Southern Conference for Human Welfare and, with the help of Clark Foreman and the rest of their staff, organized the Emergency Committee to Aid the Families of American Tobacco Company Strikers. Virginia Durr, wife of Clifford Durr of the Federal Communications Commission, offered to chair our committee. She was the sister-in-law of Supreme Court Justice Hugo Black, and she has continued to be a voice for progress and democracy in the South. We soon had the support of Senator Claude Pepper, Aubrey Williams, Representative Helen Gahagan Douglas, Frank Porter Graham, Mary McLeod Bethune, Leon Henderson, and others.

I went to New York City to meet Dr. Willard Uphaus, executive director of the Religion and Labor Foundation. I found an alert, soft-spoken man who listened carefully to my story. Without hesitation he offered our committee the use of his mailing list. "Many of them are Southern preachers," he said. The single mailing garnered more than $3,000.

In hundreds of factories, CIO unions asked the companies to take the American Tobacco Company's Lucky Strikes out of the cigarette machines. In Charleston that winter, mornings and afternoons, the hundreds of pickets sang their song, a song that they had adapted from the spiritual "I Will Overcome Someday." They taught it to Zilphia Horton at Highlander Folk School, and later she and Guy

Carawan revised it and taught it to a new generation of civil rights activists. "We Shall Overcome" became an anthem of struggle all over the world. The boycott and the solidarity of the workers brought the company back to the bargaining table, and the strike was settled in April.[3]

My work helping Local 15 had come to an end. Frances left the welfare department and came to Washington. We talked about whether I should go back to graduate school at Syracuse. A letter from Leonard Brown offered little encouragement. "I've lost any feeling for the place," he wrote. "I doubt that much we are interested in will be possible. . . . We've reached the big imperial days when the country will button rigidly down, and one of the first things to be buttoned fast will be the educational system." Meanwhile, Donald Henderson, FTA's president, asked me to go to Memphis, Tennessee, to serve as business agent for FTA Local 19. I opted for the labor movement.[4]

In Charleston it had become evident that the workers would fight to keep their unions. White and black FTA members appeared able to overcome the prejudices of their social environment and work together as equals. Furthermore, the lecture series seemed to point to the fact that there were middle-class whites who were willing to explore the possibilities of a new South in joint meetings with the black community. Memphis would present different problems, but it would also present new opportunities.

Memphis, 1946/47

We hit the road running after the long and tiring train trip from Washington to Memphis. Today, some 45 years later, it is difficult to convey how exciting and fulfilling those days in 1946/47 were. American workers were on the move. Veterans were anxious to get home. Black men were trying to keep the jobs the war had brought them, as were white and black women.

Like thousands of others, we couldn't find a furnished house or apartment, but then Frances got a job as a supervisor at the Shelby County Department of Public Welfare. Boss Ed Crump, Memphis's long-time mayor and political leader, took care of the city and county workers, and within a week we were comfortably settled in a two-bedroom furnished house southeast of the city off Lamar Avenue near a streetcar line.

The Memphis CIO Council tied together the 30,000 CIO members in the city, workers in rubber, hosiery, textiles, paper, steel, communications, newspapers, maritime, food and agricultural products, and wood. W. A. Copeland, a former newspaper man, had been appointed the council's chairman. Copeland, short, heavy, partly bald, usually with a cigar in his mouth, stood in good favor with John Brophy, who directed all of the CIO councils across the country. Confident of his position, Copeland let it be known that he disapproved of the mixing of black and white workers.[5]

The CIO, Local 19, and most of the national unions, with the exception of the rubber workers, had offices on the second floor of 66 South Third Street, two blocks to the north of Beale Street, which was famous for the "blues," and two blocks east of Main Street, which was lined with the offices of the bankers and cotton brokers. So we were conveniently located, betwixt and between.

Local 19, one of the first of the CIO locals in Memphis, began meeting in a hall down by the river in the early 1940s. Its members had slowly organized and won adherents among the workers in Memphis Compress (the city's cotton compress plants) and the cottonseed plants, feed mills, and wholesale groceries. Black men made up most of Local 19's members, which also included some women and perhaps 200 white men.[6]

John Mack Dyson, a tall, spare, quiet man, pioneered the early organizing. In 1946, he served as the president of Local 19 and as a member of the FTA executive board. Born black at the end of the nineteenth century in the South, working at an early age when he should have been in school, Mack Dyson was rightly proud of Local 19—in what they had won—and of the leading role he had played in the struggle. Sometimes I became impatient and wanted to move more quickly, but I learned to admire Mack Dyson for his strength and the position of trust he held among his fellow workers. I did what I could do, and he did what he could do. Neither of us felt he was "helping" the other.

He and I would go to meet a plant committee to negotiate on a contract or a wage reopener, both dressed in suits and ties, each of us carrying a briefcase. We would enter the segregated buses, usually almost empty at that time of day, and go about half way back, where Mack Dyson would take a seat. I would take one directly in front of him. We would talk all the way out about the negotiations. Occasionally, the bus drivers would look back at us through their rear view windows, trying, I guess, to figure out just who we were. We didn't try to test the segregation laws. We understood each other, and that wasn't what we were out to do just then.

Local 19 membership meetings presented a wonderful mix of prayer and business. Each group had its own chaplain. Mack Dyson, who chaired the meetings, always cautioned the chaplain against a long prayer, "since all of us, and mainly the sisters here who are already tired, have yet to go home to cook and do the housework." Usually his admonition was heeded. If the chaplain was an elderly man, however, the calling down of the blessings of the Lord upon all of those who were sick, or hungry, or tired, or sad could go on and on. Mack Dyson, who sat next to me, would turn and whisper, "Oh, shit." When the reverend finally finished, Mack Dyson would thank him for his helpful words and in a brotherly way suggest to him that perhaps we could do just as well with fewer words the next time. A union hymn always preceded the prayer. Almost every night of the week in the summer when all of the windows were open, the strains of "We Shall Not Be Moved" floated out the union hall windows down to Beale Street and three blocks up to the Peabody Hotel. Maybe the rich, full sounds of those voices carried up to Boss Crump's building, the Southern regional office of the Metropolitan Life Insurance Company of America.

We had been in Memphis only a month when the Southern staff of FTA, its national officers, and its Southern local leaders met at the Highlander Folk School in Monteagle, Tennessee, to work out FTA's role in the CIO's Southern Organizing Drive ("Operation Dixie"). Donald Henderson, Harold Lane, FTA's secretary-treasurer, Elizabeth Sasuly, and Joseph Califf, FTA's research director, as well as the regional directors, organizers, business agents, and rank-and-file officers of most of the Southern locals were there.[7]

I had never attended a meeting of FTA officers and rank-and-file leaders. Furthermore, although I hadn't known it when we began working with Local 15, I had learned by then that many of the leaders and staff of FTA were members of the Communist Party. I looked forward to the conference at Highlander and to see how these individuals, from widely diverse backgrounds and cultures, Communists and non-Communists, would act and react as they sought solutions for their pressing common problems.

Working with Communists presented no problem to me. At Syracuse I regularly read *The New Masses*. The application of Marxism to literary criticism, sociology, and history was commonplace in academic circles in the 1930s. Although I could empathize with T. S. Eliot's "This is the way the world ends, not with a bang but a whimper," I, with most of my graduate school colleagues, was not ready to settle for such an ending. Too young to have been influenced by the betrayal of those who had promised "a war to make the world safe for democracy," we were open to new ideas and new economic theories, including Marxism.

This was the first time, too, that I had taken part in a leadership meeting led by Donald Henderson, who had a history of working as a Communist on the problems of the agricultural and food-processing workers that dated back to the mid-1930s. He was impressive. He knew how to listen. He made everyone feel free to participate in the discussion. No one was "put down." When he did speak at length, he drew from the consensus that was developing in the meeting as well as from the depth of understanding he had acquired through the years.

The discussions were long and heated. There were sharp differences. After the meeting concluded I felt that we agreed perhaps on only one thing: the existence of a "class struggle." Some of us had come to this understanding through reading; others had come to it through long and bitter experience. By the "class struggle" we meant that the relationship between the workers and those who led the corporations was adversarial. The workers' strength lay in their solidarity, in their ability to act together. Furthermore, we saw the necessity of bringing the workers' struggles out of the plants and into their communities in order to make their voices heard on the social issues that affected them and their families. In the South, in particular, the workers could make no headway unless they were able to wipe out the use of the poll tax and the power of the registrars to disenfranchise poor whites and virtually all blacks.

Early in the meeting, two organizers, both white, one from Alabama and one from North Carolina, strongly recommended that FTA concentrate its energies in the South, organizing the poorest of the poor, black and white sharecroppers, tenant farmers, and agricultural laborers. Without a doubt the plight of these workers stirred deep emotions in everyone there. I never did find out where this seemingly organized advocacy of such a position came from, whether from the Communist Party or a section of the Party. Henderson spoke to the point quite sharply. He recalled the failures of the 1930s, when FTA, then the United Cannery, Agricultural, Packinghouse & Allied Workers Union of America, had tried to organize and maintain viable local unions among the seasonal agricultural workers. He contended that the decision made at the 1940 FTA convention to concentrate on workers in the plants that processed agricultural products had led to the growth of a stabler and stronger union. From these bases we would eventually reach out to the field workers.

During the formal discussions and the conversations before and after the meetings, many of the delegates referred to a growing tension between the staff members of the CIO and the FTA. There were differences over the FTA policy of building unity and holding nonsegregated meetings between the black and white workers. Furthermore, the CIO organizers would have preferred that we concentrate on trade unionism and not on developing programs that challenged the social problems that faced both the white and black workers in the South. One of the tobacco workers from North Carolina urged that we organize the leafhouse workers on our own, apart from the CIO. Since the elections sponsored by the Southern Organizing Committee would be held in the name of the CIO, he contended that we couldn't be certain the committee would turn the newly organized tobacco workers' locals over to FTA.

Most of the tobacco workers argued that if the leafhouse workers were going to be organized, the job would have to be done by FTA and not by full time representatives of the CIO, becaue it would take a crusade to organize these workers, a struggle not only for a union but also for a mobilization of the entire black community to put an end to second-class citizenship, for better housing, for the right to register and vote. They argued that there would be no question about where unions so organized would be assigned.

Henderson acknowledged that there were forces in the CIO that were bent on isolating FTA and other left unions. But he said that the large majority of the CIO unions and their leaders were determined to maintain the kind of unity that had made the CIO the strong force that it was. FTA stood for unity among the international unions. We should stand side by side with the Southern Organizing Committee, building the kind of unions we thought it would take to win. We left the meeting confidently looking forward to whatever the future held.

When we returned to Memphis, Mack Dyson and I concentrated on the negotiations that were pending in the cotton compresses and the cottonseed oil mills. Insofar as possible, we arranged for the contracts to expire in September or October, when hundreds of trucks descended upon Memphis, filled with cotton bales and cottonseeds. The companies were more vulnerable then. They had to compress the bales before they were stored or shipped so that each bale took less space. Storing the green seeds where they would not self-combust was critical.

The FTA had strong locals in the compresses and the cottonseed oil mills. The eight men who ran the press that compacted the 500-pound bales into half or a quarter of their volume and the eight or ten men who operated the presses that squeezed the oil out of the boiling hot seeds were highly skilled, usually working as a team, relying on each other to ensure that no bales or pans of oil were dropped or spilled. They were the core of the unions.

The union committee at Memphis Compress was particularly experienced and vocal. We met at the plant, amid acres of long sheds that were open on each side along the wooden platforms that ran the length of each building, each topped with a galvanized roof. The office sat in the middle of the buildings, a square tower; the manager's office was on the third floor. There was no air conditioning, but there were windows on each wall and all of them were open. The manager sat behind his desk, usually with a cigar in his mouth and his hat on the back of his head. Beside him sat the company's attorney. In a semicircle in front of the desk sat the six of us, the plant chairman at the far end nearest an open window.

Wages were never an active issue. But at Memphis Compress, working conditions were hotly debated. At times we would sit in this cooker continuously for two or three hours. The manager constantly chewed on his unlit cigar. To show us what kind of a man he was, he would occasionally spit and hit the brass spittoon about 5 or 6 feet from his desk. It would ring like a bell. Brother Johnson, the plant chairman, chewed tobacco. After a minute or two had passed, he would turn his head and spit out of the open window. We all waited quietly for the spit to splash and sizzle as it hit the hot tin roof. The manager would look at Brother Johnson; Brother Johnson would look back at the manager. Each respected the other. No one said anything. We just picked up the discussion where we had left off. We almost lost a new young attorney with a tender stomach one afternoon.

The Memphis CIO Council met once a month. Delegates from each of the locals attended. The meeting was chaired by Brother Copeland. For the most part the gatherings were segregated, the whites in the front and the blacks in the back, except for FTA Local 19 and the NMU delegates, who sat together.

In November 1946 the federal government eliminated price controls, despite protests from the CIO, and the immediate jump in the cost of living that resulted led to the need for substantial increases in wages. Earlier that year, the strikes of the Railroad Brotherhoods and the United Mine Workers (UMW) in the summer and President Truman's use of the courts and the available antiunion legislation to head these workers off generated an increased interest in unions. In Local 19 plants, those who had not joined became union members and began attending meetings. This was true, too, of the white workers in the large Buckeye plant in Memphis. And workers in unorganized plants began approaching our office and our members, wanting to join Local 19.

In July 1946 a man who identified himself as a worker in the Buckeye mill in Corinth, Mississippi, called to say that he and the rest of the workers wanted a union. He asked if I could drive over and meet with them. The next week I drove to Corinth and parked in front of the hotel. A car soon pulled in next to me. The driver motioned for me to follow him. We drove south, across the railroad tracks into what was obviously the "black" part of town, and soon stopped in front of a small, weather-beaten church. Crowded inside sat almost a hundred workers, about half white and half black, mostly men but some women. Seating was segregated, but not entirely so.

There was no need for me to belabor the FTA policy of one union for all of the workers, with both blacks and whites sharing the leadership positions. The Corinth workers understood that the only way they could build a union and win a contract was by trusting each other and sticking together. They asked good, down-to-earth questions about how the union worked, what the contract covered, and how they could make the company live up to the terms of the agreement. The next week they brought the signed cards and the dollars to Memphis. We won an election, but the company hesitated about negotiating. The workers were forced to strike. The managers tried to send a truck through the picket lines into the plant. The highway patrol contended that the action was provocative and refused to let them in. Buckeye shortly signed a contract. Later that fall the leaders asked us to send them more membership cards, because the workers in the brick plant wanted a union. The plant was owned by the mayor. The Buckeye workers organized that as well as a cotton compress. This was happening in the backyard of such notorious racists and anti-Semites as Senator Theodore Bilbo and Representative John Rankin.

In August 1946, we began preparing to negotiate the contracts in the cottonseed oil plants. At our meetings during the fall the leaders and the members decided that they wouldn't accept another 5 cents per hour increase. They needed more than that. The contracts in the oil plants expired on September 1, 1946. The largest plant, the Jackson Avenue Buckeye plant, where most of the white workers were employed, had consolidated its membership that summer. The white workers not only joined the union but many became active members. Most of the workers in the Hollywood Avenue Buckeye plant were black, and they were also strongly organized. We decided to concentrate on these two plants and began meeting with the company in

August. The company never offered more than a 5 cents per hour raise.

October 1 came and nothing much had changed. We had set up picket captains, welfare committees, hot food committees, all of them with black and white cochairmen, a union practice, as well as a special committee of some 20 young veterans, most of them white, who offered to patrol the areas around the plants (the two plants were about a mile apart). The veterans argued that the police would think twice before they jailed them. After a fruitless negotiation session, we finally informed the company representatives that the workers had decided that they would close the plant down that night.

By nightfall the day workers had driven a flatbed truck to a vacant lot across from the Jackson plant entrance and rigged up some lighting and a speaker system. They all gathered there at closing time to cheer as workers from both plants came out at midnight. The committee leaders went over the assignments. The picket cochairmen suggested that there should be both black and white workers at each gate so that if any workers tried to go to work, one of their own would be there to talk with them. For the first time in Memphis, as far as we could learn, black and white workers picketed together. At first, the black workers stayed together, as did the whites. Within a few hours they were completely integrated. They had things they wanted to say to each other.

Some 70 empty railroad freight cars had been left in the yard at the Jackson plant. When a switch engine turned to the spur that led to the plant gate, the veterans began picketing on the public road. The engineer stopped and slowly backed out. His contract allowed him to refuse to enter an area that he might consider hazardous. The Buckeye management had had plenty of time to move the cars the afternoon before the strike, but they waited to move them through the picket line to show the workers' weakness; the workers wanted them kept inside the fence as a symbol of their strength. The cars stayed until the strike ended.

We began to meet with the managers at Armour, Cudahy, Swift, DeSoto, and Perkins, the plants we had not struck, during the second week. The meeting with Armour had been set for Thursday morning. Unfortunately, on Tuesday and Wednesday afternoon, Mack Dyson and I had to spend valuable hours meeting with Paul Christopher, president of the Tennessee CIO Council, Earl Crowder, regional representative of the United Steel Workers, and W. A. Copeland. They wanted to question us about a meeting we had organized a number of weeks earlier at which black and white workers considered working with the National Negro Labor Council (NNLC). The NNLC was on the attorney general's list of "subversive" organizations, and membership had been prohibited by the national CIO office, we were told. We contended that the NNLC, organized by black workers in Detroit to protect their jobs and their positions in their unions and headed by Coleman Young, now mayor of Detroit, was no more subversive than the Association of Catholic Trade Unionists. There was no question of a "secret agenda" or "dual unionism" involved. Our discussions were not heated, merely time consuming and diversionary. But the meeting signaled the growing efforts of the conservative elements in the CIO to curtail any political activity not approved by the national CIO office, particularly actions in the South that might challenge the status quo on race relations.

We did meet with Armour's management on Thursday morning. They offered a 15 cents an hour wage increase and improved vacation and holiday provisions. The management of the Cudahy plant made the same offer.

We arranged to negotiate with the Buckeye management the next morning. They offered to match the vacation and holiday pay offers of Armour and to raise the minimum wage to 70 cents an hour. This meant only a 10 cent per hour increase across the board, since Buckeye had been paying 5 cents an hour more than the industry. While there was some disappointment among the Buckeye workers, a large majority voted to accept the offer. They all went back to work the following Monday. Soon the workers in the other cottonseed plants had negotiated new contracts.

In January 1947, we attended FTA's sixth national convention in Philadelphia. It was the kind of meeting that all of the delegates needed, worried as they were about the rising cost of living and the steadily increasing campaign of antiunionism that was filling the newspapers and receiving the attention of Congress.

Henderson's report as FTA president didn't say it was going to be easy. He warned that we would probably have to do more than we had been doing. But he also pointed to the drive among the leafhouse workers in Virginia and North Carolina, carried out according to the plan developed at the Highlander meeting as a part of the Southern Organizing Drive. "We have had outstanding success," he said. "Up to December 1946 we have been involved in 62 elections covering our industries and have won 52 of them. The elections won represent bargaining rights for 12,616 workers according to the records. The elections lost represent 990 workers."[8] He also told the delegates of FTA's campaign among the more than 30,000 cannery workers in

California. Despite tremendous pressure by the owners, the Catholic Church, the Teamsters, and the vigilantes, a majority of the workers had voted for FTA. The companies and the Teamsters had contested the elections, and the National Labor Relations Board (NLRB) had set them aside, calling for new elections the coming season.[9]

The convention was not given over only to the speeches from the officers. The rank-and-file leaders were in the majority. These local leaders chaired the many committees. I sat in on the Constitution Committee. We each had a copy of the constitution. We had a list of suggested changes, but the committee members insisted upon reading the document, paragraph by paragraph, to suggest changes of their own and to weigh the changes that had been proposed. The chairman began reading the title: "The Constitution of the International Food, Tobacco, Agricultural & Allied Workers of America, CIO." A brother from one of the New York cigar maker locals rose to his feet immediately. "Comrade Chairman, Comrade Chairman," he said. "I am from Puerto Rico and I have an objection to the name of the union." The chairman, who was obviously embarrassed by the use of the word "comrade," spoke up and suggested to the delegate from New York that it was the practice in the union to address the chair as "Brother Chairman or Sister Chairman." The delegate from New York answered, "That may be all right, but to me all of the workers in this room are my comrades. And, Comrade Chairman, I rise to protest the use of the words 'International Union.' This union has no jurisdiction over the workers in Puerto Rico. That sounds like Yankee imperialism to me. I hope that we will do away with the word 'international' here this afternoon."

When the convention was called to order the second morning, Connie Anderson, the education director, asked for the floor. "I suggest that at such an important meeting it would be more fitting for the officers not to sit up late into the night playing poker, but rather to get some rest after they have completed their work, so that they would be better able to give the kind of leadership they can give." She didn't make a motion. She left the platform and went back to her seat. Henderson said they would take heed of her concern and turned to the day's agenda. Her point had been made.

That was the kind of convention it was. Everyone who had something to say had the opportunity to say it. There were disagreements, of course, but the program that was developed and the feeling of commitment the delegates took home with them prepared them for the antiunion attack that was in the making.

By the time we returned to Memphis, the workers needed another round of substantial wage increases if they were to stay even with inflation. The corporations refused to make any reasonable offers. Consequently, as they had in 1946, a wave of nationwide strikes began. These strikes, like those of the preceding year, served to increase further the workers' unity and militancy, but as the corporate leaders planned, they also gave the rabid antiunion forces fuel to heat up support for their programs among the American people. In March 1947, the Truman Doctrine virtually put the nation back on a war footing. And in April, Congress passed the Taft–Hartley Act, among the most restrictive pieces of labor legislation in our country's history.

In May 1947, the thousands of FTA members at the R. J. Reynolds Tobacco Company in Winston–Salem, North Carolina, struck. After the war, the company had begun mechanizing the stemmeries where as many as 2,000 of the black women who were the core of the union's strength were employed. At the same time management had begun replacing the older white workers who were retiring from the cigarette-making departments with returning white veterans and their wives. Because the union had never been able to force a company-wide seniority system, which would have entailed completely desegregating their work force, the company was able to lay off black women in the stemmery division who had long years of seniority, at the same time as they were employing newly hired white workers in the cigarette-making and -packing divisions. The result was that, unlike the strike in 1943, when the striking black workers rapidly closed down the entire operation since the hard jobs of preparing the tobacco for the cigarettes were filled exclusively by black workers, in 1947 the company was able to move white workers into these departments, now mechanized and employing thousands of fewer workers, and continue to keep the plants operating.[10] Nevertheless, the support of the national CIO, which cooperated by asking their members to join in boycotting Camels, RJR's major brand, added to the disciplined militancy and constancy of the striking Reynolds' workers, brought a settlement to the strike in July 1947.

Later in July, the FTA executive board, meeting in its Philadelphia offices, decided after considerable debate to follow the policy of most of the CIO Internationals by refusing to register with the new Taft–Hartley National Labor Board. They chose the option of going it alone, using their organized strength to bring the companies in their industry to the bargaining table and to win contract agreements.

On Labor Day of 1947 the Memphis CIO sponsored a parade. There were thousands of us, organized by locals, carrying banners. The Local 19 delegation, many hundred strong, black and white together, marched down the main street singing, "We're Going to Roll the Union On."

In October, Henderson asked me to go to Raleigh, North Carolina, to become the director of the Southeastern Region and to work with Moranda Smith, an outstanding rank-and-file leader from Local 22 in Winston–Salem, with the understanding that after a year or so she would become the regional director, the first black woman to hold such a position in the trade union movement.

The Southeastern States,
November 1947–December 1951

The Southeastern Region, the largest in FTA membership, stretched from Dade City, Florida, to Richmond, Virginia. Most of the members were concentrated in eight centers. Local 22 in Winston–Salem, with some 10,000 members in R. J. Reynolds and the city's independent leafhouses, was the largest. Local 10's 7,000 members worked in independent leafhouses in Virginia and North Carolina. There were about 1,000 members each in Richmond, working in tobacco-processing plants and at the FFV Cookie Company, and 1,000 more in Suffolk, working in the Planters Peanuts factory. Charleston's 1,200 members were employed by the American Tobacco Company making cigars. Dade City's 800 members labored in a citrus-processing plant. Two hundred members in Apopka worked in a factory that made boxes for the citrus industry.

Moranda and I visited all of the locals except those in Florida, beginning in February 1948. The majority of the members in the region were black women, struggling not only for higher wages and vacation and holidays with pay, but also for "respect" as human beings on the job and in the community. It soon became obvious that if ever there were workers who needed a black woman as their regional director, they were the food and tobacco workers in Virginia, North and South Carolina, and Florida.

We went first to Suffolk, Virginia, where FTA represented the workers in the Planters Peanuts factory. Robbie Mae Riddick, a strong, decisive black woman in her forties who had come out of the plant, was the president of Local 26 and the local's business agent. She had asked Moranda to join her in a meeting with Suffolk's black ministers. The ministers had requested that an officer meet with them to discuss the charges of "communism" that had been directed at FTA.

Sisters Smith and Riddick found themselves meeting with friends, blacks who, like them, were among the leaders of their people. The ministers understood from their own experience and from what they knew of their people's history that those who spoke up for their people's rights had been and still were being penalized for their beliefs, sometimes driven from their communities, sometimes lynched. Most of the men seemed to accept FTA's position that although there were Communists in the leadership and the membership of the union, no one in the union was about to join in the game of "naming names" or conducting a purge. To start down that road, FTA contended, was to join those who wanted to put the drive against Communists at the top of organized labor's agenda. Moreover, Moranda could assure them that the Communists in the union were not, as they were caricatured, bomb-throwing, antireligious radicals. And FTA's efforts to build black–white understanding and unity in the South was not a Communist plot to stir up violence. In February 1947, this position on Communists in the union was widely accepted in the black community. Later, by 1950, after three more years of intensified Cold War pressures, it became more controversial, although Local 22 in Winston–Salem maintained close working relations with the Ministerial Alliance through 1952.

Local 53, in Richmond, represented the workers in the company that made FFV cookies. The majority of the members were white women, although there were many black women and a few men in the local, too. The leader was Adelle Ellis, a short, fiery white woman in her forties. In March, we were there for the meeting with the company's representatives and the state's mediator in the Capitol.

The meeting was held in a room just off the Capitol's main lobby. The three company representatives sat on one side of the table, the union's committee on the other, and the "colonel" who represented the mediation service sat at the head of the table. Adelle Ellis and Max Sussman, the business agent, presented the union's position. There were many minor provisions in the contract that needed to be ironed out. We were proceeding quietly and efficiently when we were interrupted by Governor William Tuck.

The colonel introduced the governor to the company representatives and then turned to introduce him to Ellis. As the Governor approached her with his outstretched hand, she stepped back, put her hands on her hips, and said, "I'm particular about who I shake hands with, Governor, and I won't shake the hand of the man who signed the Right-to-Work bill." The governor hesitated a moment, recovered, and then strode on out, his white Stetson on his head. He stopped at the doors, turned and said, "I hope you will work out your problems as good citizens of Virginia." The colonel just stood there. Ellis sat down and suggested that they go back to work.

Moranda Smith and I spent April, May, and June 1948 in Charleston. The AFL Tobacco Workers International Union had petitioned for a new election in the American Tobacco plant. Because FTA was not using the Taft–Hartley Board and could not have its name on the ballot, the AFL mistakenly assumed that it could win hands down. The workers would vote "yes" or "no" to the question "Do you wish to be represented by the AFL–TWIU?" FTA asked the workers to vote "no," signifying that they did not want to be represented by the AFL. Which is what happened. "FTA Whips AFL Raid by 704 to 474" the *FTA News* headline declared. The American Tobacco Company agreed to negotiate a new contract with Local 15.

We returned to Winston–Salem in July 1948 to concentrate our energies on the intensive drive to organize the white workers in the Reynolds plants. The company had refused to bargain when the 1947 contract expired, and the 1947 strike had made it plain that winning over more than the few hundred white workers who were members of Local 22 was necessary for the survival of the local. Jack Frye, an organizer for FTA in Houston, was brought in to lead the drive. Mary Lou Koger came over from Nashville, and Fred Less from the cannery struggles in California. They worked mostly with the young white veterans who, often with their new wives, were hired in the cigarette-making and -packing departments. Frye set up a small canteen in a storefront shop near the plants. Soon many of the younger workers stopped in to chat and relax before and after the shifts began. The organizers spent afternoons and late evenings visiting the workers in their homes, most of which were located in small towns and rural areas some 10–30 miles from Winston–Salem.

Frye told me that after a few months he began to feel that they were making significant headway. Almost a hundred workers attended a dance in the union hall on a Saturday night. And while the dancers were all white, the black leaders of Local 22 were there, too, introducing themselves and mixing with the crowd. Soon more than a hundred whites had signed membership cards and began to pay their dues in cash to Frye. Somehow or other these names were turned over to the company with a request that their union dues be checked off. Frye reported that when these names were revealed to the company it began an intensified harassment of these workers. Workers were spread to other departments when a group was found in one department. Husbands and wives had their shifts changed so that they no longer coincided. And the company overseers began a campaign of verbal abuse. The hundred new white members spread among the six thousand other white workers found themselves completely isolated. Many of them came to Frye to let him know that they and their wives couldn't stand the pressure. They asked that their membership be canceled. Others came to tell him that they were leaving Winston–Salem to find work elsewhere. Despite this setback, Frye and his group continued with their organizing efforts.

Since April, even though without a contract, the Local 22 workers were able to maintain most of their strong organization in the plant. Department meetings, plant meetings, and stewards' council meetings went on as usual. The company continued to settle grievances, for the most part abiding by the provisions of the contract.

The Local 22 members continued their work in the community, too. Housing in Winston–Salem in 1948 was deplorable. The union members made it an issue. They collected more than 2,000 signatures, about half from whites and half from blacks, on a petition that demanded that the city take advantage of the available federal public housing funds to wipe out the disgraceful slums. In the city hall hundreds of workers watched the city council act favorably on the petition, and soon an application to construct 1,200 units was approved.

In 1948 Local 22 helped carry the presidential campaign of Henry A. Wallace to the people—as did most of the FTA locals. Thousands of Winston–Salem workers gathered in the local baseball stadium to hear Wallace present his program for peace abroad, full employment at home, and an end to segregation. Even though many of the workers supported such a program, they did not want to "waste" their vote. Impressed by Truman's last-minute whistle-stop populist campaign, they voted Democratic.

In August 1948, the state CIO had brought the UTSE(United Transport Service Employees)–CIO to Winston–Salem to organize the workers in Reynolds. FTA's regional office publicly deplored their decision and proposed that even though there were political differences between the two unions they should be working together to organize the unorganized.

Meanwhile Moranda Smith and I had to continue working with the other locals in the region along with Robert Lathan, himself a leaf-house worker and an FTA vice president directly responsible for Local 10. We had attended meetings and aided in negotiations for new contracts. In the summer of 1948 the Local 10 workers had fought for and won new contracts with wage increases and improvements in their benefit packages. And they continued to confront local and state practices that affected their standard of living. The Employment

Commission, for example, was able to deny unemployment compensation to workers who had not worked more than 14 weeks during the season, provided their employer had applied for this "seasonal exemption" for companies processing agricultural products. For years the companies had been working overtime trying to get the season's work done in less than 14 weeks. Finally, in the 1949 negotiations, all of the companies except R. J. Reynolds agreed to waive their rights to the exemption. The companies' action was equivalent to granting the thousands of workers a 20 cents per hour raise. Even more dramatic was the leafhouse workers' successful effort to overturn the Employment Commission's practice of denying unemployment compensation to women who refused to work as maids for the going rate of $7.00 a week. Not only did the victory mean that the women could collect their rightfully earned unemployment compensation, it also had the effect of raising the pay for household service to the level of their compensation payments, in itself not enough, yet much more than the dollar a day they had been receiving.

Moranda Smith was named regional director in 1949. I joined the Local 22 staff to help in the organizing efforts among the white workers. Moranda had worked with all of the locals in the region except those in Apopka and Dade City, Florida. Consequently, we took a week away from Winston–Salem to go to Florida. The members of Local 23 in Apopka had removed the husband and wife who had been running their union for a number of years. Even though half of the local's members were black, this white couple had built a small union hall on the "white side" of town, off limits to blacks after dark. The workers had elected new officers and requested help in their upcoming negotiations.

Joseph Califf, FTA's research director, led a week-long education program for the members of the "new" union, and Moranda and I drove down from Charleston on a Sunday. We had been driving around the region since 1947, day and night, on long drives and short ones. Finding a restroom was difficult on long drives, and eating was always a problem. Oftentimes we would stop at a bus station, where restrooms were available and we could eat the same food, "separate but equal." On the way to Apopka we stopped at the railroad station in St. Augustine. The kitchen was large. One elderly white man was both cook and waiter. The station was empty except for us. He served Moranda first on "her side." Then he turned to me and asked, "Didn't you two come in together?" I nodded yes. He asked me if I would mind coming around to the counter where Moranda was being served. "My feet are killing me. All this walking." We agreed that that was one way of eliminating Jim Crow, but we couldn't wait that long.

When we reached Apopka we drove to the union hall where Joe Califf had been holding classes. Joe and I went back to the hotel, and one of the members took Moranda to a house in the black section of town. I didn't know where she was staying, nor did anyone else except a black leader of the union. That night we met with the members of the local in a large church in the black part of town. Half white, half black, they received Moranda as their regional director, with intense enthusiasm. The new local secretary-treasurer, a white woman, made arrangements for Moranda to stay with her and her family Tuesday night, so that Moranda could teach her how to handle the accounting. The members discussed the contract proposals they had been working on all week, which we were to present to the company attorneys the next morning in Orlando.

The attorney's office was over a plush retail clothing store in the downtown area of the Orlando of 40 years ago. Moranda led the negotiations for the union. The attorneys did their best to get used to such an arrangement. That night we presented an account of the meeting to the workers in the church and worked out a position to present to the company on Wednesday.

Tuesday, Moranda and I drove over to Dade City to meet with the business agent. Cars filled with the union leaders were waiting for us next to the hotel when we got back. They told us that a carload of white men had taken one of the black members, an elderly man, out in the country where they had roughed him up, demanding that he tell them where Moranda was staying. When they realized that he wasn't going to talk, they left him. He had walked back and told his story to the union leaders. They knew they could protect Moranda, but they couldn't stop further attacks on their members. The local leaders suggested that Moranda and I go back to Charleston. They and Joe Califf would take over the negotiations the next morning. The new secretary-treasurer was the last to say good-bye. There were tears in her eyes. She was ashamed of her town, she said.

A few weeks later, Moranda went to Charleston to a Saturday night chicken dinner at the home of a white woman, along with four black women and four other white women. Things weren't going right in Local 15, and they had asked Moranda to come down. Once they began talking about the growing factionalism in Local 15, they discovered that most of the misinformation that had begun to divide them was coming from the business agent. Keeping the leadership divided, settling the grievances himself, becoming therefore the center of the union were all recognizable tactics used by those who wanted to establish a sinecure. The business agent was dismissed. Another was found. The women discovered that merely by "breaking bread together" they had been able to solve their problem.

Beginning in the late summer of 1949 and continuing through 1951, FTA's work was concentrated on the struggle to regain its bargaining position in Winston–Salem, opposed as we now were not only by the UTSE–CIO but also by the TWIU(Tobacco Workers International Union)–AFL and the company's Reynolds' Employees' Association, each of whom was attempting to win enough support among the workers in Reynolds to petition for an election.

In the interest of mere survival, it became necessary for FTA to reassess its position on the use of the new Taft–Hartley National Labor Relations Board. The strategy of claiming the "no union" votes as support for FTA, as we had successfully done in Charleston, obviously was not going to work in the Winston–Salem situation. In the summer of 1949, the FTA executive board voted to change its policy toward the NLRB. Henderson resigned as president, to comply with the provision of the Taft–Hartley Act that prohibited members of the Communist Party from serving as union officers. John Tisa, the organization director, took his place. Henderson was appointed national administrator. In April of 1947, when the Taft–Hartley Act was passed, national leaders like John L. Lewis and Philip Murray denounced the law and announced that they would boycott its provisions, that they would continue to represent their members as usual, without the benefit of the NLRB. By 1949, most of the unions, including Philip Murray's United Steel Workers of America, who originally had defied the new board and refused to use its services, had agreed to comply with the Act.

The CIO Southern Organizing Committee continued to support UTSE–CIO, an all-black union. The AFL, on the other hand, continued its usual tactics of trying to win the whites first, hoping that the blacks would follow. The company used every weapon in its arsenal: its control of city and county political power, its strong influence over state and national politics, its ownership of the newspapers and radio stations, its cultivation of the black and white middle class, its appeal to anti-Communist hysteria, and its portrayal of the union as a threat to white supremacy.

The election in March 1950 resulted in Local 22 getting 3,323 votes; the AFL, 1,514; the CIO, 541; and "no union," 3,426. The AFL and the CIO were surprised: they never seemed to understand just why the workers in Reynolds would reject any all-white or all-black union.

The company, too, was surprised. They couldn't believe that the workers would continue to vote for Local 22, given the pressure that management had applied.

During the next two weeks Reynolds stepped up its attacks on Local 22. The morning of the runoff election Mayor Marshall Kurfees (originally elected with the help of Local 22 against a machine-picked candidate) was on the radio urging the Reynolds workers to "drive Stalin's songbirds from the streets of Winston–Salem." Neither the AFL nor the CIO asked their members to support Local 22. The runoff resulted in 4,428 votes for Local 22; "no union," 4,381; challenged ballots, 134. In August all of the contested ballots were added to the "no union" vote, giving it a 60-vote majority over Local 22. Had all of the workers who voted for unionism in the first election voted for Local 22 two weeks later, Local 22 would have registered a strong majority.

Moranda Smith, trying to do all she could to help with the campaign in Winston–Salem, continued to organize regional council meetings and to do justice to her obligations to all of the locals in the region. She traveled by bus, losing sleep, eating as best she could in the Jim Crow South. In April 1950, she died from a massive cerebral hemorrhage. Paul Robeson spoke at her funeral. And he filled the large Baptist church downtown under the shadow of the Reynolds Building with the resonant, rich sound of his voice singing "Swing Low, Sweet Chariot, Coming for to Carry Me Home." The streets were crowded for blocks. The cortege following the funeral party to the cemetery was hundreds of cars long. The thousands of workers, mostly black, followed by leaders of the union and the black community, attended the largest funeral in the history of Winston–Salem.

Local 22 continued its efforts until November 1951. FTA, along with the United Office & Professional Workers of America (UOPWA), each of whom had by then been seriously weakened by the raiding efforts of the CIO, had merged with strong District 65 to form the Distributive, Processing & Office Workers (DPO). James Durkin and John Stanley, president and secretary-treasurer of UOPWA, came in to lead a new campaign. I continued to work as an organizer with the union, concentrating my efforts on the white workers. The white workers were now in the majority, and we knew that no progress could be made until we had won over a considerable number of them to the union. Like the others I would go out into the country to meet with night workers in the early afternoon and again after supper to find day workers. Reynolds was hiring workers who lived as far west of Winston–Salem as Elkin and Yadkinville, North Carolina. In many instances both husband and wife worked in the factory, harvested a few acres of tobacco, took care of farm animals, and raised food for their animals and themselves. I seldom met with strong antagonism. Talked to alone, most of the Reynold's workers thought FTA had helped them, even if they weren't members. They still needed more money and better conditions, and if they thought that there was any possibility of the white workers organizing and staying together, like the "colored workers," they said they would join. But they didn't believe that would happen, and they needed their jobs. I was never race-baited nor red-baited in white workers' homes or on the street in front of the plant gates when I was handing out leaflets. Some said, "Stay with it. It's a lot easier inside with you out here." After a year-long effort, however, we had not made enough progress in organizing the white workers for DPO to feel justified in continuing. The Local 22 office was closed in November 1951.

DPO offered me a job in New York City. But Frances and I felt it was more important to stay in the South, to put down roots, and to work for change in other ways. We still believed that the cure for the crippling disease of racism that infected our nation would be found in the South, where blacks and whites were not separated in the ghettos of the Northern cities. With help from her father and brothers, we started a garden center and landscape business in Greensboro that we still operate today.

By 1952, it was apparent that the goals we had set for ourselves in the heady days after the war's end would not be realized. In fact, in 1952 it looked like the world might be heading toward World War III. At home anticommunist hysteria made progressive political action all but impossible.

I couldn't help but feel that the leaders of the CIO were partly to blame, abandoning, as they did, their role as the leader of the progressive postwar coalition and seeking security as a minor partner in the Cold War coalition of Democrats and Republicans. As a result, today's unions have become, for the most part, harmless ghosts of the living organizations they once were.

The failure of the CIO's Southern Organizing Drive was particularly tragic. My experience with FTA suggests that a "Crusade for Freedom" that exposed the class inequalities in the South and attacked the economic and social structures that separated the region's workers by race offered a real possibility for bringing blacks and whites together. Such a strategy was never easy and not always successful. But without a realistic program of building strong fighting unions upon the foundation of racial unity, organizing the workers in the South stood little chance.

WILLIAM SENTNER, THE UE, AND CIVIC UNIONISM IN ST. LOUIS

ROSEMARY FEURER

Recent studies have challenged the distorted view of Communists as illegitimate trade unionists who sacrificed workers' interests to Moscow's. Instead, some historians now argue that members of the Communist Party (CP) in the CIO usually acted as spirited but "conventional" trade unionists. Fearing loss of support if they revealed their politics and unable to envision a transition to socialism other than cataclysmic, they failed to connect their socialist beliefs to their trade-union behavior.[1] For trade-union policies that concretely linked unions to the goal of social transformation, scholars point to Philip Murray and Walter Reuther, not the Communists, for innovative proposals such as the Industry Council Plan or the 1945 "Open the Books" campaign against General Motors.[2]

This essay will address the relationship between socialist beliefs and trade-union practice through an examination of William Sentner's career through World War II. Sentner, president of District 8 of the United Electrical, Radio & Machine Workers of America (UE) from 1937 to 1948, was a Communist, but an open Communist. Partly because of that openness, partly because of the marginal status of the industry with which he dealt, partly because of his intellectual immersion in the historical struggles of American working people, Sentner confronted head-on the tenacious realities of capitalism. In so doing, he tried to bridge the gap between his commitment to socialism and the concrete possibilities he faced in a way that most Communist trade unionists avoided when they kept private their socialism. Before red-baiting attacks caused the decline of the UE in St. Louis, Sentner was a leading proponent of a *left* trade union perspective that made connections between the community and the union in what might be called "civic unionism."

Sentner's roots were working class, but his introduction to radicalism was intellectual. His father, a Russian Jewish immigrant, helped organize St. Louis's first International Ladies Garment Workers cloak union local in 1909. "When I was a kid, I used to break windows in strikes for two bits apiece," Sentner later recalled. He enrolled in a local university's school of architecture in 1924 at age 16, eager for middle-class success. He soon felt alienated from campus social life because of his status, and so was drawn to a radical intellectual who introduced him to Marx. When Sentner's money ran out after two and a half years, they hit the road, traveling together until Sentner joined the merchant marine on the west coast in 1928. He occasionally came back to St. Louis, but for the next four years signed out on merchant ships as a laborer and fireman (stoker), traveling to Europe and the Near East. On board, he studied Marx and U.S. labor history within the radical milieu of the merchant seamen; at port, he studied the architecture. Although he returned to St. Louis in 1932 to work as a draftsman, Sentner considered himself an intellectual and mixed with the leftist crowd at Bohemian Tavern. By early 1933, he had joined the local John Reed Club.[3]

Events in early 1933 propelled Sentner into a life of trade-union activism and a commitment to the CP. The St. Louis branch, with only 90 members, was then emerging from its small isolated enclave. Its limited contact with national leaders was an afterthought of the Chicago office's efforts to organize southern Illinois mine workers. "We always looked upon St. Louis as if nothing happened there" attested Chicago CP organizer Bill Gebert. But in July 1932 the St. Louis Unemployed Council, energized by a core of young activists and African-American recruits, led mass demonstrations that prevented the removal of 15,000 people from the city's relief rolls. This successful relief work provided contacts with the working poor, including a group of black women at Funsten Nut Company, among the 2,000 mostly black women in St. Louis' nutshelling sweatshops. The CP sent Ralph Shaw, a veteran mine workers organizer from Illinois to St. Louis to establish the Trade Union Unity League (TUUL) unions. Shaw built a core leadership among the women at Funsten and, when the company refused to negotiate, the workers struck in May 1933.

Sentner initially supported the Funsten strikers as a volunteer but quickly became their popular leader and helped to frame the character of the strike. The strikers drew up their own demands, such as equal pay for black women, and sought allies and intermediaries, including black churches, white clergy, the American Civil Liberties Union, and the Urban League. The TUUL strategy to spread the strike was successful; one shop after another struck in sympathy. After eight days, 1,500 demonstrating nutpickers and their supporters marched from CP headquarters to city hall to ask the new mayor to arbitrate the strike. The mayor contended the strike was a "private matter" outside his purview, but Sentner countered that since almost half of the nutpickers received city relief because of their low pay, it was "a municipal matter." The company, pressured from above and below to settle, then unsuccessfully tried to get Sentner excluded from negotiations. In announcing the settlement, which included all demands except union recognition, the mayor was forced to follow the strikers to CP headquarters, whereupon the strike leaders thanked him "for his interest and assistance."[4]

The strike not only forged Sentner's commitment to labor activism and his identity as a Communist but laid an experiential basis for the strategies he would pursue in the CIO. Although in the mid-1940s Sentner referred to the period in which he joined the Party as the "first Communist Party movement"—and remembered that when he joined he thought "we would have a revolution"—what marked the nutpickers' strike was not the revolutionary rhetoric of the Third Period (1927–1935).[5] Rather, well before the turn to the Popular Front in 1935, Sentner, in consonance with workers, emphasized building community alliances, even with liberal groups, and presenting particular workers' struggles as community concerns. Perhaps Shaw's long experience in coal mining towns, where the connections in the political economy between work and community were strong, and where the community was usually deeply involved in strikes, also affected the development of this approach.

Sentner was unable to build the same kind of community and workplace movement that the nutpickers strike suggested in his new role as TUUL organizer. This was partly due to the CP's liabilities, but also because his adversaries were now better prepared. The mayor was determined not to find himself marching to CP headquarters again, and the Urban League, recognizing the appeal of the TUUL, organized a competitor, the Negro Workers Council. The nutpickers locals survived for over a year, but only because of the pressure the women and Sentner continually placed on city relief offices for aid to blacklisted and laid-off workers. Sentner, though, did have more organizing and strike successes, mainly among excluded black workers, in the next few years. The marginality of the industries and the isolation caused by their racial composition hampered organizational stability as much as their association with the TUUL. Yet four locals survived to make the transition to the AFL when the CP disbanded the TUUL unions. In the AFL, Sentner helped organize a core left grouping that became the basis for the local CIO.[6]

By the beginning of the CIO drive, Sentner had a wealth of organizing experience, many contacts in the area, and an understanding of the local political economy interpreted through his own political perspective. He was hired for the Steel Workers Organizing Committee (SWOC) drive, but in a mid-1936 letter to John Brophy outlining the potential for organization in St. Louis, Sentner urged the CIO to concentrate on organizing the electrical industry: "It is my opinion that this industry, if organized . . . would revitalize the entire St. Louis labor movement."[7] Sentner proved correct, but that was the result of the local left influence, not the national CIO.

Sentner's thoughts about the critical role of the St. Louis electrical industry were based on an recognition of the interactions among industrialists on a local level. First, though the electrical companies were not the main firms of St. Louis's economy through the first three decades of the century, their managers had been the key drivers of the local open-shop victory. Second, the local companies' relationship to the oligopolistic electrical manufacturers and to the regional labor market forged the character of the industry. St. Louis was the center of the "independents"—those companies which competed with General Electric and Westinghouse on products such as certain motors, electric fans, and transformers. To manufacturers such as Wagner, Emerson, and Century, the "Big Three" of the independents, low wages were the key to competing with the larger firms, as they relied more on them than on modern mass production techniques for their profit margins. Their needs, in turn, dovetailed with those of St. Louis businessmen whose labor strategies in the 1920s and 1930s emphasized the cultivation of the "community wage," a euphemism for the unskilled pay rate. As businessmen became consumed with attracting industry to the city, a low "community wage" had become an essential part of their civic boosterism.

The regional labor market of the 1920s enabled business to draw on a large pool of young labor and hence keep the "community wage" low. The agricultural and mining depressions of the 1920s increased the flow of young rural migrants to the city from the Flat River region of Missouri, Arkansas, and southern Illinois. The city, moreover, was geographically well situated on the main railroad lines connecting north and south, and there was no major manufacturing city directly south of St. Louis on either side of the Mississippi. St. Louis, therefore, was essentially becoming more of a Southern city in the 1920s and 1930s, both in the character of its manufacturing work force and in its wage structure.[8]

There had been many attempts to organize the St. Louis electrical industry before the CIO. In 1934 Century Electric workers had organized 100 percent into the International Association of Machinists (IAM) and walked out spontaneously. During that strike, the TUUL had urged workers to spread it to other plants, which the IAM would not and could not do. The most powerful drive for self-organization, however, occurred at Emerson Electric. Radical shop floor changes, as the company launched a modernization drive, and continued low wages for younger workers combined with Section 7a (of the National Industrial Recovery Act) and Wagner Act organizing to produce a continual dynamic for worker self-organization. As they were disillusioned with the IAM for its 1934 failures, the organizers' efforts had focused on the company union, which attempted to declare its independence in late 1935 but was stifled by both co-optive and repressive company policies.[9]

The strategic role of the left must be viewed against this background. As the company union was floundering, a leftist core began to form. Robert Manewitz, a second-generation Party member, hired on at Emerson in February 1936 at the urging of district Young Communist League (YCL) director Clara Warnick. He contacted two Emerson paint shop workers he knew from previous relief work, Lou and George Kimmel. The Kimmel brothers, already socialists, joined the Party during the course of organizing. Bob Logsdon, the other key organizer, was a Socialist Party member on the assembly line. Manewitz invited Sentner, now known as the "CIO's orator," to the first meeting, and he advised them how to proceed: the UE drive was on.[10]

By the fall of 1936, this left group had clearly become the leaders of the unskilled, had won over a goodly number of company union representatives, and was making inroads among the machinists and toolmakers. As the UE core grew larger and stronger, they pleaded with the UE national office to send an organizer to St. Louis to spur on the other shops. "Please tell us what is holding this up. Do you want us to have a certain amount of members . . . ? Do you want any financial guarantee?" Manewitz wrote in exasperation in November 1936.[11] The UE, however, was too concerned with organizing the large General Electric and Westinghouse plants elsewhere to give St. Louis top priority.

The local left, instead, assisted the drive. Sentner served as unofficial coordinator while still on SWOC's payroll, and Warnick hired into Century. After she was "discovered" and fired, YCL activist Henry Fiering quit his SWOC organizing job in late 1936 to replace her. Finally, in January 1937, the Emerson workers got Sentner appointed as a part-time UE organizer.[12] By February, the pro-UE workers had taken over the company union. In response to a mass layoff they called a well-orchestrated sit-down on March 8, 1937.

The core left group around Sentner solidified workers' support through their strategic role in the successful Emerson sit-down strike and subsequent CIO organizing. George Kimmel led 35 strikers in a two-day sit-down in the city relief offices to secure relief for strikers— and, for the first time in St. Louis history, community funds were used to help organize unions. Fiering's small organized core at Century Electric was strategic in spreading the Emerson strike. By April 1937, they had shut down that plant after a veritable war at the plant gates.[13] The Emerson strike, which lasted 53 days (the second longest such occupation in the United States) launched the first real mass movement of workers of the CIO period in St. Louis. As Sentner reported: "It is my opinion and this has been confirmed by others . . . that OUR STRIKE at EMERSON, has aroused the workers in the other Electrical plants as well as in other plants in about the same manner as Flint aroused the auto workers." UE officer Earl McGrew relayed the national office's new respect by declaring that the strike was the "best organized and smoothest functioning ever staged by our union." By its end there were 6,000 UE members in St. Louis, and by autumn 1937 there were 16,500 in District 8. To Lloyd Austin, an Emerson punch press operator who had tried to organize a union several times since 1926 and who became a picket captain during the strike, Sentner and the CP were "the light at the end of the tunnel, come to show you the way out."[14]

Sentner framed the issues of the Emerson sit-down in much the same terms he had the nutpickers' strike four years earlier. "We have been able to make the whole issue a civic one involving the mayor and forcing him to demand a settlement," Sentner informed the UE national office. It was for Sentner, moreover, not just a "civic" *issue* but a "civic strike." He reminded the strikers: "You are not striking for yourselves alone. . . . This is a civic strike because if everybody in this town received the pay scale you get[,] St. Louis would be a shanty town." "It is this low wage scale," Sentner further declared, "which has given St. Louis the black name of an open shop Southern labor town. It is against these conditions which our organization and the CIO is fighting." Such statements held resonance with Southern migrants.[15]

The connections Sentner drew between workplace and community placed labor at the center of the city's welfare. "Our organization," he argued, "which is primarily interested in the economic welfare of the working people, is however also interested in the effects of their economic status on our community." Scholars often have separated bread-and-butter issues from those of "workers' control," but Sentner posed the wage issue as a way for labor to gain community control as well as to ensure that geographic differences not determine wage rates. As he explained: the Emerson sit-down strike "is important because it represents the first effort to organize electrical workers of the St. Louis area to prevent employers from using St. Louis as a low-wage field, thereby cutting down wage standards which have been established by the CIO in other areas." This was a "workers' rationalization" of standards, an effort to gain control over conditions by joining with others across the nation in establishing those standards. The strikers, moreover, aimed to control the distribution of wages within the plant, in solidaristic, not hierarchical, fashion.[16]

Sentner's frank declaration of his Party membership probably influenced others in the UE to also disclose their politics. Manewitz and the Kimmels, as well as many others recruited during the Emerson strike, declared their affiliation and held open Party meetings. Shortly after the end of the Century strike, Fiering made his "politics public" at a meeting of 50 Century shop stewards and asked them to vote on whether he should remain the only paid officer of the local on that basis. After "considerable uproar and debate," he recalls, all but one, who afterward punched him in the nose, voted yes.[17]

The St. Louis UE's openness gave added effectiveness to the electrical companies' charges of Communist domination and led Sentner to enunciate explicitly his beliefs in the relationship between socialism and democracy. The accusations began to have an impact when dramatic layoffs occurred in late 1937. At Emerson, for example, an anti-Communist club formed to drive the Party members from the local's leading positions on the grounds that the company otherwise would not deal with the union. To head off arguments about "Communist control," Sentner asked that the District 8 president's position be elected by referendum ballot through each local, instead of at the district convention as was the case in other UE districts.[18] From this change in District 8's constitution in 1937, the UE membership directly elected Sentner president every year until his resignation in 1948. In a 1939 speech, probably given at a CP meeting, Sentner clarified his unwavering commitment to democracy and socialism:

> Communists make their program known—they do not fly under false colors—they openly state they feel that socialism, the highest form of democracy is the only solution to the economic and political ills of our nation . . . and that this will be achieved when and only when the vast majority of the American people want socialism. . . . I am a member of the CP. My office in my union is an elective post, and for the past two years the 8500 members have reelected me. . . . When the time comes that I no longer serve the best interest of the membership of my union, I am sure that they will exercise their democratic prerogative and elect someone else.[19]

Sentner, then, used the UE, not the Soviet Union, as an example of what he meant by democracy and paralleled that with his vision of socialism. District 8's officers, moreover, became the leading proponents of rank-and-file democracy in the Missouri Industrial Union Council and led efforts against the executive board control of that group; they argued instead for leadership by shop stewards.[20]

Being open about Party membership was most rare in the CIO. In fact, in so doing Sentner defied the Party's own "discretionary" arrangement with John L. Lewis. Why? In the first place, Sentner had never used a Party name, and his ties to the Party were well known in St. Louis by the time he became a CIO official. "When I joined, I told everybody in town," he recounted to *Fortune* in 1943. Second, he said that he had "enough faith in the average intelligence" of the UE's membership that it would accept him as an open Communist. Third, he argued that to hide his membership was to accept and promote the "lie" of the party as a "conspiracy."[21]

Sentner was under no illusion that workers might convert to socialism overnight. While many Communist trade unionists might remain committed to a Soviet revolutionary model even while engaged in the Popular Front, Sentner foresaw a whittling away at capitalism, not a cataclysmic change, and he voiced this position throughout his CIO career and beyond. Before Sentner's Smith Act trial in 1954, he wrote to District 8's officers and shop stewards: "Because of my deep feeling that socialism will be achieved in America only when a majority of the people want it, my life's work has been devoted to building unions and helping them obtain the best wages and working conditions possible under existing conditions." Communists were to play the role of giving constructive leadership to workers, just as they had in organizing unions, meanwhile gaining their trust and building class consciousness. The tensions between building class consciousness and engaging in class conflict while attempting to bring more security to workers within capitalism was one never fully resolved by Sentner. His desire to operate openly, his search for legitimacy, however, became even more critical to him given this position.[22]

Sentner fundamentally believed that the Party's approach should be derived from daily contact with workers. "Whatever else they may say about my husband, they cannot say that he just followed the Party line," argues Toni Sentner. "My husband was an intellectual but he was also practical. He disagreed with the Party on many occasions. On [some of] the decisions they would set down, he didn't agree with them because his experiences taught him different." What did he do when he disagreed? "Well, he had his union activities." Sentner, in other words, used the constraints of trade unionism as an excuse to reject unrealistic Party dictates. When Alfred Wagenknecht, head of the St. Louis CP, chastised Sentner for selecting Logsdon as chief organizer for District 8 rather than a Party member, Sentner retorted, "You run your organization and I'll run mine."[23]

Historians have noted that the Party's trade unionists operated more autonomously than those without that base. Manewitz, moreover, characterized Sentner as a "rugged individualist" who felt he could define what the Party was in St. Louis. "The C.P. never ran Bill Sentner," Sentner told the *Fortune* reporter in 1943. "No one fools around with what I believe . . . and I don't fool around with what they believe." Sentner always had acted somewhat independently, a task much easier in St. Louis than in New York. As one expelled member, referring to Sentner and Shaw in 1935, remarked, "They are not true Communists. . . . They try to follow their own minds instead of the teachings of the great leaders of the Party."[24] Sentner's experience as a trade-union leader, then, exaggerated his already somewhat independent relationship with the Party.

Indeed, in place of a typical CP fraction, Sentner built a left-leaning coalition in the UE. Those workers from electrical shops who joined the Party were in almost all respects a reflection of working-class formation in the 1920s. They were not heavily weighted toward skilled workers and, except for Sentner, Manewitz, and Fiering, all were "indigenous" to the shops. Many had been rural migrants with little union or radical background. "There was a guy fresh out of the hill country," recalls Fiering. "He didn't know how to spell communism, but I was one, and if it was good enough for me it was good enough for him!" The leftist cadre in the St. Louis UE, however, was composed not only of those who joined the Party but also those committed to the kind of social unionism that Sentner articulated. Logsdon represented the outlook of this group best. He understood that Sentner's "whole theory was based on the fact of having a bunch of people who would work with him, you know, who didn't have the same deal against them." But it would be wrong to view people like Logsdon through the lens of "dupe" or even "fellow traveller." Logsdon, a rural migrant who had come to a socialist viewpoint through his work and Depression experiences, remained an independent, though fervent, supporter of Sentner. This, then, was a contingent relationship.[25]

Sentner's relationship with this group of Communist and non-Communist radical cadre became a benchmark of Sentner's articulation of socialist beliefs and was as important as his relationship to the CP hierarchy. It was through them that he could be effective and propound some of his ideas. Sentner sometimes had to delicately traverse the gap between the CP line and the desires of the membership. But through the years, he tested ideas and approaches as well as foreign policy resolutions on this radical group before presenting them to the membership. "He knew if it didn't fly with us, it wouldn't go through with the membership." Logsdon added. If a choice was to be made, he made it in the direction of the membership, not the Party.[26]

Sentner framed socialist concepts in the American idiom. In education classes for the UE and the CIO, the American legacy of radicalism in connection with unionism—of 1877, 1886, and the Wobblies—was emphasized. The UE persuaded the local CIO to celebrate May Day as the CIO holiday in 1937. The rally was held near the site of the first AFL May Day hours protest. Sentner proclaimed to the crowd of 3,000 that the CIO was engaged in "not just another labor campaign" but a "crusade to free the American working people from wage bondage and to open the way to industrial democracy guaranteeing a more abundant and happy life to the working people of our great nation."[27]

The use of the term "wage bondage" came from Sentner's emphasis of the legacy of the Knights of Labor. He liked to recount the local Knights' struggles against Jay Gould and its coincidence with the "tradition of the 8 hour struggle of 1886." Shorter hours was the modern means to the long-term goal of overcoming "wage bondage." Through modern technology and mass production—"a benefit of American productive ingenuity"—workers could enjoy both "abundance," that is, consumer goods, and less wage labor. Older, more utopian aspects of the concept, moreover, remained. As he told 500 shop stewards in 1944, "We will have a 30 hour week as a policy because when we increase the American standard of living, it does not just mean buying so much, as more time for study, development of family life, more time for recreation, physical development of American men and women.[28]

In Sentner's usage, the term "industrial democracy" was a dynamic concept synonymous with socialism. Bandied about since after World War I, the term benefited from its elasticity. It was used by radicals as well as Catholic social theorists, who drew different conclusions about its relationship to capitalism and management rights. For Sentner, it was useful as a way both to show that corporate power undermined American democracy and to express socialist ideas and concepts within an accepted American idiom. It also dovetailed nicely with republican citizenship themes Sentner often articulated.[29]

Labor as an institution, Sentner believed, would be the leading force behind social transformation if it fought for the entire working class, not just the organized segment of it. Labor's power would grow by making connections between labor and community groups, with labor as the prime mover on community issues. This was the essence of civic unionism. At the first District 8 board meeting, he reminded the delegates, "It is our duty to . . . the working class to turn the[ir] special interests into the broad interests of the citizens of our country." Throughout his career, Sentner worked at building links between labor and community groups. The St. Louis UE built coalitions with civic, church, and black groups in that city and helped bring the CIO into those coalitions.[30]

The civic-minded approach that was created in District 8 encouraged the generation of tactics that linked the community and the union. While this approach did not put socialism on the agenda, it certainly went beyond the bounds of conventional trade unionism and in Sentner's mind paved the way for workers to see the links in political economic terms. Fiering's radical cadre at Century, for instance, picketed the homes of workers who hadn't signed up in the union in early 1939 with leaflets that argued that the workers' actions were hurting the community. In 1945, one of District 8's locals picketed the residences of an employer and the company's attorney.[31]

It was on the terrain of both shop-floor and community struggles that District 8 survived from 1937 to 1939. By late 1937, layoffs threatened to decimate the union. Sentner summarized the situation as "damned bad. . . . Unemployment has just about wrecked us morally and financially." In response, the UE launched a tremendous effort to mobilize its members as well as the St. Louis CIO to fight for the expansion of relief and WPA (Works Progress Administration) jobs. Sentner led the first citywide mass meeting for relief under the CIO, and Logsdon chaired the local CIO efforts. These demands tied the local community to the union movement and brought unemployed workers to the union; in turn, it positioned the local labor movement as the sparkplug for all the unemployed.[32]

These unemployment struggles had a critical impact on collective bargaining and shop-floor politics. Fiering and the radical cadre he had organized at Century, for instance, sustained 700 laid-off members of Local 1108 for almost two years through militant demands on the local relief and WPA agencies. Consequently the Century local was strengthened for their 1938 contract negotiations. Sentner bragged to the national office that these efforts "smacked them all between the eyes." Century managers "had hoped to some degree that they would have by this time gotten inner control of the organization and . . . soften the whole tune of the union, and through mass layoffs undermine the prestige and morale of the organizations. Prior to WPA it did have that effect. Century was surprised we could give them a solid licking."[33]

At Emerson, despite dramatically reduced work force levels, Local 1102 used the arbitration provision in the contract to challenge wage rates and piecework rates established on new jobs. For the first time in the St. Louis electrical industry's history, an economic downturn had not been used to reduce workers' paychecks. "Our arbitration feature was the club over their head which held reductions to a minimum during the past year," Logsdon reported in summer 1938. When the union demanded the right to codetermine the wage rate for a new motor line, management saw it as the final straw. Claiming that those matters were "the sole function of management to decide," Emerson made elimination of the arbitration provision its top priority. Taking advantage of the layoffs, they refused to arbitrate issues and submitted an employees' "book of rules" which contradicted the union contract. The union took the case to the National Labor Relations Board (NLRB). While the September 1938 trial examiner's report ruled that the company was entitled to fix the rate of pay on new assembly operations, it declared against the book of rules. "This is the first decision of the Labor Board against the management clause," Sentner excitedly told the District 8 convention.[34]

In summer 1938, District 8 fought the nation's most militant campaign against the Mohawk Valley Formula in the company town of Newton, Iowa. Under Sentner's guidance, striking union members at

Maytag fought a "back to work" movement by marching back into the plant with the scabs and then staging a sit-down. Forced to evacuate, they conducted a community and labor campaign that lasted until September, when they were forced back without a contract under state pressure. Back in the plant, they continued to stage short sit-downs, pressuring Maytag to bargain even without a contract. The "pet cock of labor production flows as labor wants it to flow" at Maytag, Sentner crowed.[35]

Sentner's position as an open Communist trade unionist came under attack in 1939 from both within and without the UE and the CIO. He was indicted in Iowa on criminal syndicalism charges for his role in the Maytag sit-down. For over a year, while the case was pending, he solicited support from the local trade union movement for his defense and organized civil liberties committees in St. Louis and Iowa. These efforts, however, coincided with the St. Louis CIO's attempt to disassociate itself from radicalism and communism. Arguing that charges of communism had "taken its toll on our own members," the St. Louis CIO passed a resolution condemning "isms" to be submitted by the delegates to the national CIO convention. Sentner spoke against the resolution on the grounds that it would look as "though my own union repudiated me when I go on trial Monday at Newton." He also argued that while he knew the "overwhelming majority" of workers were against fascism, Nazism, socialism, and communism, they were against each for "different reasons" and so it was wrong "to lump the so called isms together and say we're agin it, . . . like an ostrick (sic) hiding its head in the sand and refusing to examine what makes the sand storm."[36]

Before the trial, Sentner still thrilled to the challenge of the criminal syndicalism fight, but when convicted on October 7, 1939, he was a little less sanguine, especially when arrested while on bail for appeal, in an obvious setup involving a small electrical corporation and the red squad of the St. Louis Police Department. "It seems that this attack against us will never end. The heat is really on," Sentner wrote, "and aimed at our organization here as the focal point, with reaction knowing that if they can get us then they will be able to move in on all fronts with ease."[37]

Sentner's fight against his conviction met with success—the Iowa Supreme Court overturned it in 1941—but pressures on him regarding his open CP affiliation mounted. At the 1939 CIO convention, James Carey, UE president, argued for a strongly worded resolution in support of Sentner that carried unanimously. On October 18, however, the UE's organizational director, James Matles, upon returning from the convention, wrote to Sentner urging him to resign from the Party in view of "the present attacks on the labor movement" of which "our organization is carrying its share." Reminding Sentner that he and the other officers had supported him despite his insistence on openness, Matles advised: "I am sure that if you give this matter serious consideration you will agree, as a loyal member of our union, that the interests of our organization and many thousands of its members would be better served by such action on your part." After the December UE executive board meeting, where the issue was again discussed, Sentner wrote to Matles that he had resigned from the Party. "My decision on this matter was prompted by the realization that my undivided attention and service could be best spent in serving the thousands of members of our Union and the CIO."[38]

It is not possible to fully account for Sentner's resignation after having gone through so much for his right to affiliation. Whatever his reasoning, he did not loudly proclaim that disassociation and was still widely considered a "red" by the membership; few, including Logsdon, remember his resignation. He attended no CP meetings for at least two years. But by 1942 he had renewed his affiliation. The formal break with the CP in 1940 and 1941 did not really alter Sentner's views vis-à-vis the Party or his belief in the association of socialism and trade unionism. While his foreign policy positions generally were consistent with the CP's, he did not make them prominent in District 8, especially after mid-1940.[39]

Sentner's legitimacy crisis as an open Communist coincided with both a trade union crisis and the arrival of W. Stuart Symington as president of Emerson. By early 1939, District 8 was in dire financial straits, unable to mount organizing drives because of low dues payments owing to layoffs; dues-paying members had not numbered more than 3,000 per month for almost a year. When employment began to pick up in early 1939, Sentner became fixated on the drive for the dues checkoff or closed shop. The primary target was Century, but the first offer of a checkoff came from Symington. Symington was on friendly terms with Carey and a liberal, but neither of these was the main reason he offered the dues checkoff. Rather, he wanted to rapidly modernize production since Emerson had lost many of its contracts and most of its workers had been employed only sporadically for over a year. Given the record of shop-floor resistance at Emerson, however, there was little chance he could do so without some incentive to the union.[40]

Symington therefore offered the union a dues checkoff in exchange for "cooperation" on production issues. He also "opened the books" to demonstrate the company's poor financial condition. Sentner saw the offer as a way to divide the reactionary employers who had not as yet accepted the union as permanent. As he related it to the UE national office, "They need breathing space for several years, or go under, & we need UNION SHOPS. And this is the deal we are attempting." District 8, Sentner argued, should "make hay while the sun shines for the consolidation of the union, and attempt to enter into a different form of relations then the heretofore dog eat dog variety." Eight hundred members of District 8 apparently agreed with Sentner's assessment, for they endorsed a resolution that accepted the closed shop as the compromise for "cooperative relations" in solving the local industry's problems: labor relations predicated on bringing the local electrical manufacturers up to the production standards of the larger companies as long as wages were increased "in proportion to" improvements in production.[41]

Why this deal? What are we to make of it? First, it did not represent the union leadership's "sellout" of the membership, but rather the activist rank and file's recognition of the necessity of compromise. Hard facts accumulated by the union had brought geographic and productive disparities into sharp relief. GE's plant in Fort Wayne, Indiana, where most of GE's motors were produced, paid workers 30 cents more per hour than Emerson, but GE's production methods also were far more advanced than Emerson's. The limits of shop-floor struggle at the point of production within a national capitalist economy had become evident. Second, since Sentner found himself in the position long faced by garment trade union leaders—the necessity of bringing marginal employers up to accepted industry production standards—he, like them, thought that "cooperation" on production issues also might also bring opportunity to participate more fully in roles designated as management prerogatives.[42] For Sentner, there was a connection between this development and his vision of socialism. Within the limitations of capitalism, Sentner and the union leadership were building the idea that modernization was to be judged against labor and community needs.

Progress at Emerson in what the union called "cooperative relations" did not go smoothly, however. The bargain between the UE and Emerson placed two union stewards in the time-study department. This meant, from the union's perspective, that piecework rates were to be determined jointly: "This establishes the principle that the establishment of new pay rates is subject to the mutual agreement of the company and the union." Symington, who obviously thought the union would sanction management's decisions, angrily withdrew the checkoff offer when the union did not do so. Rates were lowered unilaterally with the new timings set by the engineers Symington had brought with him, but continued resistance brought some concessions. By mid-July 1939, the union, with Logsdon's help, had established a joint union–management committee to deal with future wage rate changes and had gained access to time studies.[43]

Contention over the meaning of labor–management cooperation on rationalization issues continued into the fall of 1939. In a special resolution in August 1939, Local 1102 declared the company was "promoting an old tactic of speed-up and lower wages concealed behind the rhetoric of cooperation. . . . The union has concientiously (sic) attempted to work out production problems faced by the company to the mutual benefit of all. The Union hopes to continue toward this end. Likewise Local 1102 expects all possible and reasonable cooperation from the management of the Emerson Electric Company." With the authorization of a strike and concerted shop-floor actions, the company again conceded some points, but after September 1 negotiations stalled. Logsdon concluded that "the new management differs from the old only in that they try to soft soap the local people while putting cuts into effect, while the old management went about it openly."[44]

In October, however, the UE local learned that Emerson was considering a move to Evansville, Indiana, where, free of charge, plant equipment and modern production facilities would be provided. Symington formally denied that this move was connected with efforts to get the union to accept his terms of cooperation, but the union was not fooled. Realizing the significance of the threat, the membership quickly approved the stalemated contract. Symington soon was hinting that employees might want to match the Evansville offer through payroll deductions.[45]

Symington clearly had seen an opportunity in Sentner's ongoing crisis of legitimacy as an open Communist and his criminal syndicalism trial. Sentner understood the position he was in: he not only needed to demonstrate "constructive" leadership in the face of continuing attacks but also to face up squarely to the realities his membership faced. He condemned the threatened move to Evansville—"a competition of bartering hardships and sufferings—a competition which at best merely relieves unemployment, hunger and human suffering, of one community at the expense of another"—but also asserted that the union had to be realistic: "With factors far beyond the control of the workers and those directly affected at this time, I believe it our sacred duty to protect those who are closest and dearest to us."[46]

Symington, who remained, despite everything, the most progressive employer with which District 8 bargained, played his final card. After the membership approved the 1939 contract, he granted a voluntary checkoff and apparently consented to advocate remaining in St. Louis if the union could match the other offers for the company. The Emerson local, in turn, launched a "civic campaign" from December 1939 to March 1940 designed to raise funds from business and real estate groups to keep the company in town. While it is doubtful that Sentner really believed that it was wise to set this sort of precedent, he and the union made great political use of it; they charged that the city's somnolent business leaders were sitting back and letting Emerson depart without an effort while the union was trying to figure out a realistic way to keep the company in town. When no offers were made, the union's executive board drew up plans for a $140,000 employees' loan from payroll deductions, reimbursable through a profit-sharing plan.[47] Sentner was secretly happy that the vote on the loan was very close (with as many workers refusing to vote as voting for the plan): "The meeting was healthy and full of fire—which also was alright as far as I was concerned. . . . It is an object lesson on the fact that the people in the plant still have much against the company and the top people in management can't expect us to give them any blank checks." In the end, Symington refused the workers' offer and decided to build a new plant in St. Louis County, but kept the profit-sharing plans. He declared that the union's expression of cooperation "augurs well for the future" and lauded Sentner for his efforts.[48]

One might be critical of Sentner's moderate style in the campaign to keep Emerson in St. Louis, but his approach was neither a bureaucratic response nor a complete capitulation to capitalism. As always, Sentner got the union leadership to mobilize the membership for the civic campaign, thereby building their involvement and participation. Just as workers had defined cooperation and rationalization of the workplace in different terms than the company, Sentner placed the union's aid to the company in a different light: "Workers, if they expect a voice in the management of industry—industrial democracy—must be willing to help solve the problems of management." Sentner claimed that anything that strengthens organized labor—and he said he thought it was strengthened by the company's decision—"paves the way for an ultimate transition to an industrial democracy that is complete—some form of socialism."[49] Sentner, then, placed in a situation not of his choosing, still tried to relate his trade-union practice to his socialist beliefs.

The legitimacy that the UE and Sentner derived from the "civic campaign," moreover, aided them in other areas. A five-month strike against Century Electric in 1940 in conjunction with a tremendous community campaign produced a mandate for settlement and ended with an "open the books" demand and victory for the union. Two newspapers wrote favorable editorials on the UE, including the *Post-Dispatch*, which recorded its "achievements" for the community. By September 1940, Sentner told the District 8 convention, "We can proudly say that our organization has become an accepted civic organization in the communities in which we live."[50] In the midst of the Nazi–Soviet Pact, when the CP and left-led unions had lost much support, Sentner and the UE had gained a certain measure of credibility in St. Louis.

While the CP was denouncing "bourgeois democracy" in accord with of its new foreign policy line, Sentner continued to frame issues to union members in terms of industrial democracy. The 1940 Century strike was fought ideologically in terms of "Americanism." Strikers pledged a "credo for Americans," vowing to remain on strike because "America is my country. I believe in its ideals, its democracy and its future. I want to preserve the American way of life for myself and for citizens." In March 1941, Sentner spoke to the District 8 convention regarding the threat to outlaw strikes: "If big business is successful in eliminating strikes, American Democracy in my opinion will disappear as a National institution and some form of totalitarianism will take its place. . . . If labor is successful in defending and extending American economic, industrial and political democracy—American democracy as the national institution of our great Republic will grow in strength and prosperity."[51]

The American CP has been judged harshly for quickly positioning working people's welfare behind the "win the war" effort after Hitler invaded the Soviet Union, and it has been argued that they gained acceptance only when they were on the right of the rest of the labor movement. But this scenario is not fairly applicable to Sentner. It is true that Sentner's influence and prominence crested during the war. But that was only because of the work of the local leadership he had helped to build along the way, a leadership that was the key to District 8's organizing success. The UE became the largest CIO affiliate in St. Louis, representing 54,000 workers at its largest. Consequently, Logsdon was elected president of the local Industrial Union Council (IUC), where he attempted to strengthen shop steward leadership of that organization.[52]

While Sentner generally followed the CP line on the war, especially regarding the no-strike pledge, he endorsed Logsdon's argument to the national UE that the union should not "lose sight" of the "defense of democracy here" in UE shops.[53] Despite his stance on the no-strike pledge, Sentner aimed to connect the immediate interests of workers with attacks on management rights. Thus while he vigorously attacked the War Labor Board's Little Steel Formula, he argued that the WLB was an inroad into managerial power and a way for labor to "up the bottom people—the people most in need" and thus "affect the whole wage structure in this area." The WLB, Sentner argued early in the war, "has shattered the so-called management prerogative and has done a service to this country and has extended the democratic rights that labor was given under the Labor Act. . . . They have severed and eliminated management prerogative that has sort of had a hold on us since we won our rights under the NLRA."[54]

Sentner's wartime position that labor should receive its share of increased productivity was congruent with his earlier position. The most publicized examples of increased production involved showing how slowing down machines enhanced quality and eliminated waste. At several plants in St. Louis, District 8 worked with the WLB to write contract provisions ensuring that, if operations were broken down, workers would receive the same wage for the subdivided parts. Sentner, moreover, complained to John Brophy in 1943 about Brophy's approval of a South Carolina WLB case that allowed a wage reduction when new machinery was installed. "It seems to me," Sentner argued, "that this is an important decision which in fact agrees with industry that they may reduce the earnings of workers through the introduction of new machinery or the rationalization of operations."[55]

Although some CP trade unionists lost rank-and-file support during the war because of their overzealous advocacy of incentive pay and the no-strike pledge, there is no evidence this was true in Sentner's case. Part of the complex relationship between Sentner and workers during the war can be seen in Thomas Knowles's assessment. Knowles, one of the most militant unionists in District 8, was a key instigator of an Emerson wildcat strike in 1944 to protest a backlog of grievances. During an interview, it was suggested to him that since Sentner opposed strikes he must have opposed Sentner. But Knowles replied: "No! I thought Sentner was great! He was proud of his political affiliations and was breaking his neck for the workers. Oh, he was absolutely against wildcat strikes during the war because of his political beliefs, they were 100% with the company on that, but he believed right as far as working people were concerned."[56] It is true that the Emerson local produced the strongest anti-Sentner contingent in District 8 after the war, but the reason lies outside Sentner's wartime record.

If, as Howell John Harris has argued, the "main function of managerial ideology is to justify continued possession of power and autonomy by the business elite," Sentner clearly made his greatest attack on this ideology during the war. Support for the Industry Council Plan (ICP), which proposed labor's intimate and equal participation in decisions relating to war production, encapsulated Sentner's approach to the war. Committed to the ICP before the UE's endorsement of the war and amid the CIO's wavering support for it, Sentner vigorously argued for democratic planning that included a commanding role for labor. In union and convention halls, in press releases, in discussions of the labor–management committees, at rallies, and to myriad liberal groups, Sentner argued that labor could democratically manage the wartime economy better than corporations, and for the public interest. Further, in conjunction with District 8 leadership, he presented concrete proposals for alternative methods of war production that would benefit workers and stave off decline of communities because of wartime production, beginning with an ambitious national retraining program designed to prevent layoffs during plant retooling.[57]

Sentner argued that the postwar economy could only be just if labor had a major role in planning it. When the mayor appointed 25 members to a reconversion committee in 1943, Sentner and Logsdon successfully appealed for labor representation and Logsdon organized the shop steward council in the local CIO to discuss the postwar economy. District 8 brought together 650 UE shop delegates (elected from each plant department) in a reconversion conference to discuss workers concerns about the postwar world. District 8's most ambitious proposal was for a Missouri Valley Authority as a means for achieving full employment in the postwar regional economy. While this scheme was based on the TVA model, Sentner hoped to fashion a strategic role for labor in the creation of what he called decentralized planning for "civic production." District 8 became the de facto organizer for the MVA, and aimed to keep "liberals" and "business" from "total control of the policy planning." Instead, Sentner hoped the proposal would be the catalyst for a grass-roots political mobilization of workers, farmers, and small businessmen under CIO leadership. Meeting the enthusiastic support of Missouri IUC delegates, it was endorsed by the 1944 CIO convention, possibly the last CIO policy proposal to genuinely come from below. Sentner later told District 8 delegates that while the MVA "really isn't" socialistic, "I think it is a step in the direction of . . . the people . . . having more say so in the government."[58]

District 8 gave racial and sexual equality a high priority during the war as an extension of the vision of civic unionism. Its vigorous call for the end to the area's reserve labor force of blacks and women was its solution to both the wartime labor shortage and a just economy in the postwar period. The UE launched a campaign calling for the full utilization of black and women workers on an equal basis in conjunction with its successful drive to organize the largest war production plant in the city. Sentner was instrumental in getting the mayor to establish a Race Relations Commission that dealt with employment as well as segregation issues in St. Louis. This varied activity obliged the *St. Louis American,* the city's black newspaper, to say the UE was at the "forefront of racial issues" there. It was the UE that launched the drive in St. Louis for child care facilities. Sentner, moreover, was most vigorous in his condemnation of leading businessmen's assumption that blacks and women would be shunted back to prewar positions. Instead he vigorously advocated planning for an economy that would create more skilled and interesting jobs and reduction of working hours after the war.[59]

Sentner's efforts to implement civic unionism were at their peak during the war. A St. Louis FBI agent accurately assessed Sentner's activities toward the end of the war: "He manifests . . . a belligerent aggressive offense on behalf of labor which is designed to take the part of labor in all its controversies in the St. Louis area. Subject strenuously endeavors to inject himself, as well as the U.E., into any social problem which touches the labor field. It is estimated that the local St. Louis papers carry news stories concerning him on an average of one story or more each week." Sentner could have chosen to conceal his renewed membership in the CP, but he became even more convinced of the necessity of openness and more confident than ever that he could maintain his legitimacy as a Communist trade unionist. "He even at one point said there would be no more red-baiting after the war," Logsdon recalls, and adds, "I just laughed."[60]

Nevertheless, Sentner grew frustrated with the Party's position well before the French Communist leader Jacques Duclos wrote American Communists to denounce their leaders' "class collaborationist" line, especially as it became evident that the leadership was offering no solution to worker unrest beyond renouncing strikes. In early 1945, he upbraided those CP unionists whose solution to the Party's position was to "run away from strikes" and refused to join Herbert

Benjamin, the new head of the Missouri CP, in condemning the union involved in the most heated labor conflict of the St. Louis war period, the streetcar strike of 1944. In commenting on the draft resolution surrounding the Duclos letter, he scored the CP national committee as harshly as did Earl Browder for preventing "the fullest discussion of policy questions" and argued that the Party's problems "reflects a lack of confidence in working people and must be cut out of the work of our organization." Further, he called for a thorough replacement of leadership in the Party with "workers actively associated with the [mainstream] of American labor . . . capable of understanding and solving realistically the complex problems" that confront American workers.[61]

Sentner's openness made him a prime target for red-baiters in the UE who gathered momentum as the war wound down. In October 1945, he defeated James Click, who ran on a platform of anti-Communism, by a 3:1 margin in the referendum vote for district president, but he was forced to decline to run for the district presidency in 1948. That defeat, however, is not nearly as remarkable as his continual election until then despite the wide array of forces aligned against him. When Sentner stepped down, moreover, the membership voted for his so-called hand-picked leftist candidates, not the Click faction.[62] Yet the supreme irony, one appropriate to the tangled history of the CP, is that during part of the time that Sentner was defending his right to his political beliefs before the membership, he was suspended from the CP because of a "doubt as to his loyalty to the organization," a fact he learned only years later.[63]

The "conventional" tag applied to CP trade unionists encourages the notion that outside of foreign policy positions not much was changed when the CIO purged the left unions. It is true that capitalism precluded significant differences in contracts and the firm-level strategies of unions. In District 8 it is as regards extracontractual factors that distinctions can be seen. Sentner, in trying to make connections between socialism and trade unionism, sustained the idea that it was "an error to maintain that a union is nothing but a pure and simple economic organization."[64] Despite the twists and turns of the CP line, in District 8 an explicit challenge to management prerogative and the notion that production should be geared to community and labor needs rather than for profits, as well as the emphasis that labor unions should be at the center of social change in the community, were constant themes. On that score, the leadership and a significant portion of the membership sustained Sentner. District 8's unionism was, if nothing else, beyond the bounds of conventional unionism.

Of course, it is well to remember that Sentner was not exactly a representative CP trade unionist. His openness distinguished him considerably and, as I have argued, led him to try to show how his politics related to his unionism and to the American tradition of democracy. This is what caused his enemies consternation, because he did not seem to be a "typical" Communist. The words of a CIO opponent years later are apt: "Bill Sentner was a heck of a guy. I always hated to think of Bill as a Communist."[65]

Sentner spent the rest of his life defending himself against persecution and prosecution in the anticommunist fever of the 1950s. His prominence as a labor leader made him the leading target in the St. Louis Smith Act prosecutions, in which he was convicted in 1954. His wife Toni, moreover, was probably prosecuted under the McCarran Act solely because of her relationship to him. Despite Sentner's continued grave misgivings about the CP's direction, he did not officially resign, according to the FBI, until early 1957. He remained committed to the idea of "civic unionism" until his death, in 1958, from heart failure.

THE CATHOLIC CHURCH AND THE LEFT-LED UNIONS:
Labor Priests, Labor Schools, and the ACTU

STEVE ROSSWURM

Few labor historians would deny that the Catholic Church played a significant role in the history of the CIO. Likewise, few historians of American Catholicism would dispute the importance of the CIO and working-class issues to the Church. Most of the former, however, have written within a secularist framework that brushes aside the significance of religious influence, and most of the latter have written within a framework that all but ignores the importance of class. There is, therefore, little sustained and systematic scholarship on the relationship between Catholicism and the history of the CIO or on the importance of the Church's working-class membership to its development during the CIO period.[1]

This essay will address these serious scholarly deficiences in its focus on relationship between social Catholicism and CIO Communism, particularly the left-wing unions that were expelled. It briefly will discuss both the origins of the Church's firm commitment to industrial unionism and the institutions that arose out of that undertaking. It then will examine the Church's multifaceted laborist activities and its handling of the Communist issue during the CIO's first decade. In 1944 and 1945—in a change in focus that most historians have overlooked in their assumption of a continuous, all-encompassing anticommunism—the Catholic Church dropped the positive approach that had characterized its anticommunist program, turning to an entirely negative one as its CIO activity became synonymous with the effort to destroy communism. From 1945 on, then, Catholic laborites waged a relentless war against CIO Communists and those who worked with them. This successful struggle not only changed the CIO but also profoundly transformed the Catholic Church as it deserted its vision, as outlined in Paul Weber's writings on what he called "economic democracy," of an anticapitalist reconstruction of American society. As purely negative anticommunism became all consuming to Catholic laborites, radicalism of any sort became increasingly suspect and procapitalism became a political and religious litmus test. Working-class Catholics, as we shall see, were left to cope with the vagaries of American capitalism on their own.

Five general concerns produced widespread and serious Catholic support for the CIO. First, not just operating within the framework of the social encyclicals, but also inspired by the pioneering efforts of Monsignor John A. Ryan, the Catholic hierarchy strongly supported both unionization and social justice. It did so both in word, with numerous official and unofficial statements, and in deed, by permitting and often encouraging the work of labor priests and the establishment of labor schools. Second, Catholic clerics were increasingly worried that the Church was losing its working-class male membership. This concern was not a new one—Ryan had asserted a similar position 20 years earlier—but by the 1930s key labor priests were arguing that only an intimate Church involvement in working-class struggles for dignity would retain working-class men. Third, the Church aimed to respiritualize an increasingly secular world. Convinced that secularism, "the practical exclusion of God from human thinking and living," lay at the "root of the world's travail," the Church—labor priests as well as the hierarchy, committed Catholic trade unionists as well as the most pious devotee of novenas and the rosary—sought to reintegrate the supernatural with the material. Fourth, Catholics sought to defeat the Communism that was much more than merely an aspect of secularism. Militant, organized, and coherent, the Communist movement appealed to the same instincts upon which Catholicism ought to have been drawing.[2]

Finally, as well as most profoundly, the goal of Catholic laborism was to "restore all things in Christ": to (re-)create an organic society in which conflict was absent and human solidarity supreme. "Now this is the primary duty," as *Quadragesimo Anno* noted, "of the state and of all good citizens; to abolish conflict between classes with divergent interests and thus foster and promote harmony between the various ranks of society."[3] For many Catholic activists, by the mid-1940s, the means to this goal—which they increasingly called "economic democracy"—had become identified with a radical version of the Industry Council Plan.

To address these motivations and goals, the Catholic Church developed a wide-ranging set of laborist activities: social action schools for priests; national social action conferences for both clerics and laity; labor schools; labor priests; and chapters of the Association of Catholic Trade Unionists (ACTU). We will discuss each of these in turn.

First, social action schools for priests. The Catholic Conference on Industrial Problems had been meeting since the early 1920s, but with the birth of the CIO it was obvious that priests were ill trained to deal with labor issues. In November 1936, the bishops' annual meeting approved Ryan's plan to hold a series of "Priests' Social Action Schools." Popular and well attended, the four schools held in 1937, as well as those held for the next three years, educated participants in both theory and practice. Much time was devoted to the exegesis of the social encyclicals, but both clergy and lay experts also informed participants about the nitty-gritty of economic life and working-class organization. Although employers made presentations at these schools, in keeping with Catholic social theory, the tone and content was strongly pro–industrial unionism. The veteran laborite Father Peter Dietz complained that those at one school acted as if "there never had been a labor movement until the CIO appeared on the scene."[4]

The issue of communism was an important topic of these schools. The participants discussed left-wing activism, and local committees were instructed to do surveys "of local Communist and 'third party' activities" and send these to the Social Action Department (SAD) of the National Catholic Welfare Conference (NCWC). Out of these reports, as well as questionnaires, came the first Catholic survey of Communism in the United States. This report suggested a "Program of Action" that established the positive aspects of the Church's anticommunist program for the next 20 years. While not denigrating "direct attacks on Communism or direct exposition of its evils," it argued that only a positive program could "strengthen and guide the whole reform program towards a sound new social order and keep it from Communist hands and Communist plans." It also emphasized, via *Quadragesimo Anno*, the necessity of working-class activity.[5]

Two national social action conferences, held in 1938 and 1939, were among the SAD's first steps to involve the laity. The 1938 conference, organized around the theme of "what is necessary to establish a Christian social order," was a huge success: about 5,000 laypersons, 23 bishops, and more than 700 priests attended. A priests-only meeting was particularly important. Concerned with practice, these participants discussed the basics of getting involved in the labor movement and communicating the Church's social teaching to working people. While never mentioning communism, the agenda for action outlined ways to implement the Church's positive program against it.[6]

Jesuits created the first CIO-period Catholic labor schools in the United States. A directive from the Jesuit father general resulted in the November 1935 opening of the School of Social Sciences at St. Joseph's College in Philadelphia. This school, which averaged more than a thousand enrollments for the next three years and became a "clearing house for Catholic thought and action," put forth both sides of the Church's program. On the one hand, it taught "an integrated program of the Christian social order" that sought to undermine "materialistic capitalism." Yet its curriculum was derived quite specifically from the struggle with communism for working-class hearts and minds. Forced to establish a set of courses de novo, the school's director obtained a current course list from the Workers' School in New York City. "As far as possible," he noted, "we matched each course in their program with one of our own." The director made it his policy to "give responsible parties any information of Communistic activities which are brought up to our attention."[7]

Jesuits soon opened more labor schools throughout the country: Xavier Labor School in Manhattan, Crown Heights School of Catholic Workmen in Brooklyn, and the Kansas City School of Christian Workmen. What set these schools apart from others was that they took their character, at least in the beginning, more from the priest-director than from their particular social context. Each developed its own characteristics and constituencies, though over a longer period of time than those (for example, the ACTU's) that emerged more organically from Catholic working-class activity.

The term "labor priests" was a media creation that came to be an acceptable Catholic description for those priests who actively supported trade-union struggles—almost entirely CIO—through public speaking, picket-line involvement, and a multitude of other activities. These labor priests played a particularly significant role in legitimizing CIO organizing drives and refuting charges of communism. They also took the offensive, often privately, against conservatives within their own ranks and tried to mitigate the impact of reactionaries within the hierarchy.[8]

Finally, there is the ACTU. While the organization derived its mandate from *Quadragesimo Anno,* in at least two of the three most important chapters—New York and Detroit—the Catholic Worker played a significant role its founding. In Chicago, the third of the three most important chapters, and in New York, white-collar workers played a very important role in the early years of the organization. Industrial workers were involved in each of these three chapters, but only Detroit's was deeply rooted in the industrial working class. Even a decade after its founding, auto workers composed the critical sector of the chapter's activist core.[9]

What was the goal of ACTU? It was simply to be a "real power for the Cause of Christ in the labor movement." ACTU activists intended to do this in two ways: "carry the message of trade unionism into every working-class Catholic home" and "carry the gospel of Christianity into every labor union."[10]

The labor school was one of ACTU's major efforts to further its goals. These schools educated working-class Catholics in their Church's social teaching, trained activists to participate in their local unions, and recruited members into ACTU. Yet, most of them were only moderately successful because, while representing only one aspect of ACTU activity, they were immensely time consuming. The Jesuit and diocesan labor schools were more successful; and in Detroit, ACTU had the best of both worlds, as the archdiocese ran the labor schools and the ACTU focused its energies on other activities. Detroit's parish labor schools began in February 1939. Eight units met that first term, and 45 the following fall. The schools continued well into the war years.

Two things stand out about these early schools. First, if those returning a set of surveys distributed in the Detroit schools (the majority of whom were Catholic CIO members) were typical, the originating schools had an important impact upon the participants. They consistently noted that the classes gave them experience and knowledge that enabled them to participate actively in union meetings: "to speak and ask for things that I think we need"; "more confidence to speak"; "better able to express my opinions"; "[i]n being able to take the floor at a meeting any time." The schools, moreover, imparted a set of duties: "supplied me with knowledge of obligations that I did not have"; "opening my eyes to the truth." Second, very few women attended the classes. More than 1,000 men and about 60 women registered for classes in the fall of 1939; the average attendance was just over 500 men and nearly 30 women.

The Detroit parish schools were not exceptional. No other school went as far as Xavier's outright banning of women (a policy later changed), but few enrolled many women; ACTU, moreover, was heavily male in composition and leadership. Jesuits seem to have been particularly conscious about keeping out the "good pious ladies who might be called professional lecture attenders."[11]

This emphasis on working-class men was deeply embedded in Catholic laborism and Catholic anticommunism. Part of it, as we have seen, derived from the fear that Catholic working-class men could be lost to the Church. Part of it came from the perception, based upon the contemporary reality of women's subordinated role, that men could best defend "Mother Church." Yet another source was the Catholic Church's commitment, shared by many others, to industrial unionism in factories; in 1940, less than 22 percent of all working women were in manufacturing. Still another reason was the attitude of labor priests toward women and the sexual politics of Catholic piety.[12]

We briefly have surveyed, then, the origins of the Catholic Church's commitment to industrial unionism and the accompanying institutions. If anti-Communism was central to Catholic laborism, it was not the only focus of that activity. Catholic working-class groups aided the organizing drives of left-led unions and often aimed their demands for union reform at racketeer-dominated unions. Labor priests often participated in Popular Front groups that fought discrimination, and Catholic institutions recognized left-led unions as bargaining agents. Those in the clergy, laity, and hierarchy who viewed Communism in the CIO as the only significant labor issue, moreover, were an isolated minority.[13]

Still, in some areas, anti-Communist activity took on prime importance before 1945. A discussion of these cases illuminates both the strengths and weaknesses of Catholic working-class anticommunism as well as its methods and values.

Catholic anti-Communist activity before the war was generally unsuccessful. One outstanding example was the Xavier Labor School's effort to overthrow Michael Quill's leadership of the Transport Workers Union (TWU). Father Charles Owen Rice's efforts at the United Electrical, Radio & Machine Workers's (UE) No. 601 Westinghouse plant were equally unsuccessful. He picked off several Communist labor leaders and helped anticommunist candidates win elections in 1941 and 1944, but, as he later noted, "each time our results" were "[n]ullified and frittered away." The significance of the election of the veteran ACTU activist and toolmaker Paul Ste. Marie as president of UAW No. 600 also was ephemeral, as he failed in his reelection campaign.[14]

During the war, however, one ACTU chapter and one labor school scored substantial and lasting victories against the CIO left. In Michigan, the Detroit ACTU played a central role in an alliance that drove the Communist–left group out of the Michigan CIO. Before discussing this effort, however, it is necessary to examine the "conference" method that the Detroit ACTU and most other chapters used in their union work.

Paul Weber, the nation's most important and intellectually innovative ACTU activist, developed the conference method. Detroit Archbishop Edward Mooney had been hesitant to give ACTU official approval because he feared that separatism would galvanize anti-Catholicism. His opposition, coupled with the decision to refrain from discussing the internal aspects of specific unions at general membership meetings, led the Detroit ACTU originally to define itself as purely educational. Weber, however, persuaded Mooney to allow ACTU to become activist. There were groups within the labor movement, he argued, who would "sooner or later isolate and persecute" Catholics whether they organized separately or not. "[E]ducated" Catholics could not defeat Communists who were not only educated but *"organized."* Catholics needed to be able to "fight fire with fire." Weber's solution? The conference: organize Catholics independently, but then work closely with "trustworthy non-Catholics who follow our fundamental principles."[15]

Weber outlined the conference guidelines that governed Detroit ACTU work for the next decade. ACTU conferences were to act as a "caucus-within-a-caucus." If action was needed, Catholic members of a local were to meet at a closed conference meeting. Conference leaders were then to establish contact with non-Catholics; a second meeting then would be held with both Catholics and non-Catholics present, where the former were to function as individuals. "But since they are in accord on fundamentals," Weber argued, "and have previously threshed out their specific disagreements, they can be depended upon to act as the spearhead of the rank-and-file movement."

Basic assumptions about the class capacities of the rank and file accompanied Weber's thinking: "I think it is time we recognized that unions, however much we deplore the fact, are run by minorities." Given that reality, Weber argued, the "best hope of any existing union is to be run by an enlightened, honest, Christian minority." That minority must offer a positive program around which the rank and file could rally, just as "fellow travelers" rallied around the Communists. And this minority's commitment to the positive required the "qualities connoted by the words 'revolutionary' and 'utopian.' Nothing short of this will do."

Several things stand out about this decision to adopt the conference method. First, there are obviously parallels between the conference method and the Communist fraction. One need not have been a Communist, a "fellow traveler," or anti-Catholic to have perceived as sophistic the Detroit ACTU's argument that there was a significant difference: the purpose of a conference was "religious"; the purpose of a "caucus" was "political." Second, most Catholic labor activists, clerical and lay, assumed that a "minority" ran and would run unions; they, moreover, were extraordinarily pessimistic about the rank and file. They might not have put it as starkly as Father Philip Carey, S.J., director of the Xavier Labor School, who remarked that working people were contented "like Carnation Cows" when material conditions were good—but most would have agreed with him. Third, in the case of Weber and the best of the ACTU activists, a kernel of anticapitalist radicalism was present.[16]

The Detroit ACTU immediately established conferences in the UAW and soon had them meeting all over the city. It was in coalition with Michigan Socialists and with the help of President Philip Murray of the CIO, however, that conferences proved most effective. Just after Ste. Marie's smashing victory at UAW No. 600, the two groups united in efforts that culminated in driving Communists and those who worked with them out of the Michigan Industrial Union Council (IUC).

By mid-1942, Harry Read, editor of the *Michigan CIO News,* a founder of the Chicago ACTU and current member of the Detroit chapter, was working closely with the Socialist August Scholle, head of the Michigan CIO, against the Communists and those who worked with them. Murray, who had met with Read about the situation, was "fully cognizant of what we are doing and approves of it." The left's rise to power in the Wayne County CIO in late 1942 jolted Scholle into a recognition of the ACTU's strength and commitment. ACTU activists had "stood to their guns," while there was a "breakdown" in the "Socialist Front and the independent group." Scholle, according to Read, was now "different" than when he arrived in Michigan: he now saw "clearly that we have the right analysis and answer; and that we alone have it."[17]

The complete victory of the anticommunists at the June 1943 convention of the Michigan IUC came out of this Socialist/ACTU alliance.

ACTU activists were convinced that only they and the Socialists understood what was at stake, but unaffiliated anticommunists joined them to drive out the left from IUC offices and defeat them on virtually every policy issue. John Gibson, "socialist" leader of the Dairy Workers and "one of the brilliant youngsters developed by the Reuther caucus," easily defeated Patrick Quinn, an independent leftist who worked with the Communists, for the IUC presidency. Catholics and socialists, according to one observer, constituted "almost 65 percent" of the convention delegates.[18]

The ACTU alliance with the Socialist Party and those who "just *think socialistically*" (emphasis in the original) was an uneasy one. ACTU leaders had to educate the clergy, just as they had learned themselves, about the necessity of this alliance; they, for example, pointed out that Walter and Victor Reuther were "sound leaders, whose socialism, we think[,] will be mitigated by events." No matter how tenuous, however, this alliance was one of the central factors in the former's ascendancy to the UAW presidency.[19]

There had been skepticism among those fearful of an anti-Catholic backlash about ACTU conference methods. The Detroit ACTU's successes, however, suggested that these fears were unfounded. A 1943 meeting of labor priests approvingly discussed the Detroit experience. By 1945, Father Benjamin Masse, S.J., editor of *America* and an opponent of the developing myopic anticommunist focus, noted that there was no evidence that the Detroit ACTU was creating a "religious ghetto" in the labor movement. It had, he thought, been "able to count on considerable right wing support independently of religious affiliation."[20]

In Michigan, then, the Detroit ACTU defeated the Popular Front with an adroit alliance, national CIO approval, and better organization. We shall now turn to Connecticut, where Catholics were even more successful in the struggle against Communism, though for a set of different reasons.

Father Joseph F. Donnelly began Connecticut's labor schools and publicly attacked "outside" IUMMSW (International Union of Mine, Mill & Smelter Workers) organizers in October 1942. He made the statement only after consulting a national CIO officer to make "sure of the ground on which" he "was treading." As labor schools spread throughout Connecticut—Donnelly became their full-time director— many IUMMSW locals became a center of opposition to the Reid Robinson administration. Out of a disputed election, in which a Connecticut oppositionist ran against Robinson for president, came a national CIO-imposed administratorship that, from IUMMSW's perspective, isolated the Connecticut membership from the rest of the union.[21]

Donnelly's schools did not develop into a membership organization and therefore never adopted the conference method, but they gradually turned to educating the state's CIO leadership rather than the rank and file. They learned to direct "particular efforts to a small and special group and reach the less interested by other means" and set up in each industrial area "a center from which might flow into the local labor movement the sound principles and planning of the Church's social teachings." Donnelly's schools attracted relatively small numbers, but he argued that since the "leadership of the labor movement" was "carried in a very few hands," they were succeeding in educating those who mattered most.[22]

The Diocesan Labor Institute's statement of principles noted that "strictly union problems are ordinarily the affair of unions," but this was no ordinary time and anticommunism was central to its early history. In 1945, Donnelly reported that his institute had made a "noteworthy contribution" to the total elimination of "Communist representation" in the Connecticut IUC. In 1942, Communists had controlled it.[23]

The Catholic Church began shifting the emphasis of its laborist activities in 1944. In a change that was completed by 1946, its personnel and its public positions moved to an entirely anticommunist position. Anticommunism, as we have seen, was always central to its concern for the Catholic working class, but this now became its sole focus. Four reasons can be identified for this change:

First, there was considerable concern within Catholic circles about the Communist role in the CIO–Political Action Committee (CIO–PAC). This role galvanized a key labor priest who had never accepted the wartime alliance with the Soviet Union; it was he who first forced a debate within Jesuit labor circles. The discussion increased with the release of the Dies report and then spread to the pages of America.[24]

Second, many American Catholics, both lay and clerical, became increasingly horrified at Soviet activity in Eastern Europe. Accompanying this was a concern that some Eastern European Catholics, impressed with the Red Army's victories, were coming under the influence of left ethnic leaders.[25] In each of these cases, Poland played a central role. Committed to the idea that there could be "no good Europe without a free and independent Poland," clerical and lay Church leaders, after considerable efforts to pressure Washington, could only stand by as events unfolded in Poland and Eastern Europe. In November 1946, the American bishops issued a statement in which they argued that the conflict between Russia and the West "touche[d] on issues on which there [could] be no compromise." Russia was "no less aggressive against" human freedom in "the countries it has occupied" than the Nazis and Fascists. All other matters, the bishops argued, were secondary to "the need of unity in protecting man in the enjoyment of his God-given native rights."[26]

Third, Catholic men, both clerical and lay, became increasingly worried during the war that the American family, which they equated with patriarchy, was disintegrating. They shrilly responded to working mothers, day care, increasing juvenile delinquency, dissemination of birth control information, and the growing independence of women.[27] What was novel about this response, not entirely new nor limited to Catholics, was that increasing numbers of important Catholics apparently came to identify the underlying threat in these areas as communism.[28] The struggle against communism, then, also became a struggle to restore patriarchical power in the family.

Fourth, Philip Murray's condemnation of Franco's regime in November 1945 produced much criticism within Catholic labor circles. It also seems to have unleashed a more general frustration with his refusal to frontally attack Communists in the CIO. For at least some Catholic laborites, Murray's anti-Franco position was yet one more frightening example of Communist influence in the CIO.[29]

Several developments indicated the direction in which the Catholic Church was heading. In 1944, a labor priest whose stated goal was to defeat the TWU played an important role in a viciously racist strike in Philadelphia. Just as significantly, a fellow Jesuit labor priest tried to smother criticism of this activity through the most tendentious apologetics. In October 1945, the New York ACTU opposed a rank-and-file strike that developed into a revolt against the corrupt leadership of the International Longshoremen's Association (ILA). As an ACTU leader noted, "When it became clear that the choice was between Joe Ryan and the Communists, our members in the Longshoremen's Association went back to work." And, in November 1944, the bishop's administrative board appointed Father John Cronin to do an extensive study of Communism in America. Cronin, who had led an anticommunist struggle in the Baltimore shipyards, had done much to alert Church officials to the growing danger of Communism. The bishops' subsequent appointment of him as an assistant director of the SAD undercut those clerics who opposed the growing focus on anticommunism, legitimizing the most reactionary and providing Cronin an institutional base for future anticommunist activities.[30]

The Catholic Church, then, both clerics and laity, began in 1945 an unrelenting war on CIO Communists and those who worked with them. Virtually everything became subordinated to this struggle as the positive aspects of the Church's labor program faded in importance. Yet it was not just communism against which the Church battled; now the enemy also was secularism, destruction of the patriarchal family, and apparently, for many, modernity in general. It was, moreover, an international crusade in which American Catholics, united after more than a decade of divisions, could play an important role.

Before we examine this crusade, however, an assessment of Philip Murray's role is needed. Murray was a devout and profoundly antisecular Catholic who saw his CIO labor work as at one with his Catholicism; as he told a labor priest in 1946, "What the CIO is trying to do is basically in the social encyclicals of the Church."[31] Historians often have pondered why it took Murray so long to move openly against the CIO left. What they have ignored is evidence that Murray had undermined the left well before 1949.

First, as we have seen, Detroit ACTU activists had Murray's approval for their anti-Communist alliance with Michigan socialists in the CIO bureaucracy. Second, the CIO national office often intervened against the left unions; it is inconceivable that James B. Carey and Allen Haywood would have acted without Murray's approval.[32] Third, while Murray condemned raiding, not only did it continue unabated—and here Reuther's UAW was one of the most active CIO unions—but his own Steelworkers participated in it.[33] Fourth, Murray bankrolled Father Rice's anticommunist activities for more than two years.[34] While many Catholics were unhappy, as we have seen, with Murray's refusal to move aggressively against communism, it appears that even when the left–center alliance appeared secure, significant CIO forces were undermining it with Murray's approval and aid.

In 1950, Murray characterized efforts to destroy the UE as a "good fight, a noble fight, and holy fight." Echoing Murray's judgment—it was a "just and beautiful fight"—no one better typifies the crusade mentality of this anticommunist struggle than Rice.[35] With the absolute assurance of a deeply embedded Manichean view of the world and the requisite pugnacious temperament, Rice spent years fighting Communists and other leftists. Only Father John Cronin did more to defeat the labor left.

Rice was exceptional in many ways. Not only was he more talented than most other labor priests, he also was well connected to national CIO leaders—not just Murray, but also James B. Carey. He also had a sympathetic superior who worried little about his periodic appearances on the front page of newspapers. He, moreover, acted in a public and direct way that was not the preferred mode of Catholic labor priest intervention in the postwar period. Rice's relationship with Murray was a particularly important component of his activity. Whatever happened—no matter who attacked him or what trouble his interventions brought him—he knew he had the direct backing of the top CIO leader in the country.

In other ways, however, Rice was not so different from most postwar Catholics. In his religiosity and view of the world, he was in the mainstream.

Rice corresponded with Catholic members of every expelled union, but he focused most of his energy on the UE, as did the Catholic Church as a whole. Not only was it by far the largest of the left unions and heavily Catholic in composition, it also was solidly based in a important industry that acquired strategic value as the Cold War took center stage. Rice involved himself in the UE in a myriad of ways. First, he functioned as a one-man committee of correspondence for oppositionists throughout the union. Rice's *Our Sunday Visitor* (*OSV*) articles were particularly important, for this intensely antimodernist national Catholic newspaper gave him access to the kind of Catholic layperson throughout the country with whom he ordinarily had little contact. Acting as adviser, cheerleader, and confidant, Rice kept up a stream of correspondence that comprises a large part of his papers. Second, Rice became personally and deeply involved in the battles within UE District 6. His participation in the huge Westinghouse No. 601 local was particularly deep. Heavily involved in 1939 to 1941, and again from 1946 to 1950, Rice met with oppositionists to plan strategy, wrote leaflets, and interceded with fellow clergy for support.[36]

Rice's access to outside forces particularly benefited the No. 601 opposition. His arrangement of HUAC subpoenas just before an important election drew the desired front-page coverage in Pittsburgh. He, moreover, was closely connected with the local Democratic Party and may have been involved in its intervention at No. 601. There was also Rice's connection to the FBI, a relationship that is difficult to document precisely but probably served well both him and members of the future IUE (International Union of Electrical Workers).[37]

Rice's second most important involvement in an expelled union was in the United Office & Professional Workers of America (UOPWA). He directly intervened in this white-collar union to support the insurance agents' early secession movement and then became embroiled in a bitter public discussion with two of its Irish leaders. Receiving scores of

letters on the basis of his *OSV* articles, Rice became an organizing
center just as he had in the UE.[38]

One outstanding characteristic of Rice's anticommunist efforts was
its sheer opportunism—his acceptance of aid from virtually anyone.
He received a car from Chevrolet's central office for "important work
for the welfare of . . . [the] country and sane industrial relations." In
1948, moreover, he tried to make contact with General Electric management in Erie, Pennsylvania, to provide him with potential recruits
for his battle with UE. Rice's defense in the matter of the car, which he
noted would have "wiped" him "out" if it had become public, is that it
"was not sinful."[39]

How, then, do we assess Rice's role? First, he was not omnipotent,
as his opponents often implied. He failed at UE No. 506 in Erie, where
the left Catholic John Nelson made an irresistible target, as well as at
Farm Equipment Workers (FE) No. 236 at Louisville, Kentucky. Second, local conditions played an important role in his success as well as
his failures. Third, as Rice himself increasingly has noted in the past
25 years, the national anti-Communist climate established the necessary condition for his success. Yet we must assign him a central role in
the successful purge of the CIO left. Enormously talented and ener-
getic, virtually unscrupulous and unsupervised, Rice turned contacts,
advantages, and opportunities to his best purposes. His willingness
to write for the ultraconservative *OSV* was a decidedly bold move,
one Rice now characterizes as a "pact with the Devil."[40]

Rice's public interventions into the internal affairs of the UE and
UOPWA were not standard operating procedure for Catholic anticommunists. His UOPWA efforts, in fact, received the private condemnation of an ACTU veteran.[41] More typical were two other modes of
activity: the labor school as an organizing/informational center for
anti-Communists, and behind-the-scenes intervention.

We see both in the organization of the anticommunist UE Members
for Democratic Action (UEMDA) in 1946. A short-term failure but a
long-term success, UEMDA came primarily out of four areas of dissent within the UE; in three of them, Catholic laborites played a
significant role. Pittsburgh was one. Another was St. Louis, where
little evidence exists for the activity of Father Leo Brown, S.J. That was
the way Brown wanted it, yet through oral histories we know that
Brown gave critical advice to James Click and was involved in other
ways in UE. Considerably more is known about efforts in the Greater
New York area. The New Rochelle Labor School, which began in 1940,
played a central role in organizing antiadministration forces in UE's
District 4, where dissidents soon were meeting at the New York

ACTU offices. Several alumni of the Xavier Labor School brought along their UE local and the *Searchlight*, edited by an ACTU activist, attracted further support. Brown persuaded Click to visit New York for a meeting and Donnelly, in Connecticut, put them in touch with District 2 dissidents. They soon had Philadelphia contacts, probably through the Jesuit labor school.[42]

Pittsburgh hosted a UEMDA meeting at which it chose an opposition slate for the approaching 1946 UE convention. Although the administration handily defeated it, this first revolt within UE, in which Catholics played an important role, had long-range consequences. It involved many future IUE leaders, provided a network for future collaboration, and produced many of the early secessions that weakened the UE well before the all-out anticommunist onslaught developed.

The role of Catholic priests, with the exception of Rice and several others, in the UE battle seems to have shifted in 1949 and 1950. One reason was that a sizable anti-Communist group, in which Catholics were significantly represented both in the leadership and the rank and file, had developed and was functioning fairly independently. Second, since antiadministration forces had found it exceedingly difficult to exploit bread-and-butter grievances, they increasingly turned to ideological issues in their attacks on the UE. Here, the Church could play a role with which most of its personnel were more comfortable than with direct involvement: condemnations of the UE as Communist dominated in the pulpit and in official communications by bishops.

Father Eugene F. Marshall was a priest whose UE involvement indicated this always had been the best role for him. His parish included most of the Catholics who constituted a majority of the work force at the GE plant in Pittsfield, Massachusetts. In October 1946, Marshall, on consecutive Sundays, attacked two Catholics from the GE local who had given their convention votes to the incumbent UE president, who was "as red as the flag of Russia." In 1949, Marshall raised the ideological ante: the vote between the IUE and UE was a "choice between Washington and Moscow, and ultimately between Christ and Stalin." In 1950, as the GE representation elections neared, Marshall, bolstered by Rice's personal appearance, again framed the issue in purely ideological terms. The local bishop, moreover, urged Catholics to vote against the Communist conspiracy.[43]

In case after case, from 1949 on, we find bishops and priests framing a political issue in religious, and therefore moral, terms, while convinced they were doing just the opposite; as one priest put it, it was "not a matter of politics, but . . . a moral obligation." We also find James B. Carey, who acquired a new priest adviser when Rice became a liability, seeking clerical support from the pulpit whenever he thought it would be of use.[44]

The UE bore the brunt of the Catholic Church's efforts to destroy the left in the CIO, but other expelled unions experienced Church involvement or condemnation. The Jesuits seem to have been particularly interested in IUMMSW. In 1946 and 1947, they intervened, probably with Murray's tacit approval, to support the secession movement. Later, priests delivered sermons against that union, ACTU distributed leaflets, and an Arizona bishop officially condemned it in 1954. The Church also intervened against the FTA (Food, Tobacco, Agricultural, & Allied Workers) in California, and New York ACTU publicly attacked the UOPWA during a 1947 strike. The New York ACTU chapter ran conferences in the UPW (United Public Workers) and the ACA (American Communications Association), as did the Detroit ACTU chapter in the UOPWA. Local priests attacked the Fur & Leather Workers in the Triple Cities (Binghamton, Johnson City, and Endicott) in New York State, while west coast chapters of the ACTU fought the ILWU (International Longshoremen's & Warehousemen's Union).[45]

In the process of its successful drive against the expelled unions, as well as the Communists and those who worked with them in other CIO unions, the Catholic Church itself underwent several changes that had significance for its membership, the working class as a whole, and subsequent American history. Two will receive just brief mention here; the other, a more extended discussion.

First, by the mid-1950s, if not before, labor priests no longer worried about losing Catholic working-class men. Substantial evidence, moreover, indicated that Catholic men were attending church regularly as piety intensified during the Cold War. On the one hand, Catholic anti-Communist activism had been decidedly masculine as gendered appeals were made to working-class men. On the other, among men *and* women, there was the growth of primarily "feminine" devotions: from Our Lady of Fatima to Our Lady of Necedah to the Rosary Crusade for Peace.[46]

Second, an influential, well-organized, and well-financed conservative grouping emerged within the Catholic Church during its anticommunist crusade. Loosely organized at first, these conservatives became increasingly vociferous after 1946 as their criticisms of the SAD found hierarchical support. In 1953, Chicagoans founded the Council of Business & Professional Men of the Catholic Faith, which became the core of the Church's ideological right. These conservatives, who benefited from swimming with the currents of anticommunism and growing Catholic affluence, narrowed the ideological boundaries of Catholic social theory and practice in the 1950s.[47]

Third, the Church gradually abandoned its commitment to the Industry Council Plan (ICP). While there were as many variations on this plan as there were socialist visions of the future, the Detroit ACTU leader Paul Weber worked out what became the plan of choice for Catholic laborites. Weber's writings developed an anticapitalist and democratic program for ending class conflict and attaining "economic democracy." He asserted that only when capital and labor, organized in unions, equally shared key economic decisions—including prices, investments, and working conditions—would class struggle end. Weber's plan, ironically, given the Church's holistic vision, partook of functionalism and economism, but it was more than a mere groping toward what might have become an antistatist socialist-democratic program.[48]

Weber, at times, offered a solution to the chief problem for Catholics who supported industrial councils: how to get from capitalism to economic democracy. Many left that question for the future or discussed it in terms of a spiritual rebirth. In the home of the ACTU chapter that was most proletarian in composition, Weber several times transcended these platitudes to argue that the working class ought to force management to accept economic democracy. After noting that "union militance is intelligent or stupid according to whether it is directed at the right OBJECTIVE," Weber continued: "The sane objective of labor's struggle is to ENFORCE a condition of partnership. We battle capital because capital and the usurper, management, will not give us our rightful voice as partners to production." Or, after proposing that unions demand wage increases without price increases in postwar strikes, Weber urged that militance be "directed at the objective of winning an equal voice with management in industry councils."[49]

Weber, apparently exceptional in his willingness to assert the necessity of forcing capitalists to accept industry councils, often lapsed into the wishful thinking and irrelevance that characterized other proponents of the plan. Nevertheless, until the late 1940s, it was not considered unorthodox in Catholic circles to argue that the working class, through their unions, had a right equal to that of capital to govern the economy.

Church conservatives, never happy with the ICP, waylaid it the late 1940s. When other methods of attack failed, a procapitalist bishop went to the Vatican, itself in the process of making its own peace with capitalism. The assault had the desired effect. In 1950, the SAD's clerical chair leveled a semiofficial attack on the specifics of the plan—precisely where workers were to have equal power with capital. He suggested profit sharing as an example of the way in which the plan could be implemented. The NCWC administrative board, moreover, declined to publish a report on industry councils brought in by a committee it had appointed.[50]

The significance of this abandonment cannot be overemphasized. The ICP was not just the cornerstone of the Church's positive program of anticommunism; it was not just the outline of the new society the Church wanted. It was potentially the greatest Catholic contribution to its working-class membership and the American working class as a whole. To espouse the program in the abstract, argued Father William Smith, S.J., might remove the basis for controversy but would make it irrelevant: "The content of this organizing and ordering [the details of the ICP] is not some nebulous, negative, vague, or illusory plea for co-operation in general. The objectives are of the stuff that industrial relations are made of—wages, prices, profits, production—the vital elements around which the class struggle now revolves."[51]

Rather than forcing "an end to class war," then, Catholic laborites kept trying to convince themselves throughout the 1950s that industry councils were right around the corner. What they could point to were insignificant ventures in profit-sharing and labor–management cooperation plans, often in declining industries. None of these had anything in common with the version of the ICP that had been the norm among the laborites before the conservative counterattack, let alone with Weber's vision of the war years.[52]

The irrelevance of the Church's social program to its working-class members' concerns, as well as the impact its anticommunist crusade had on the ability of working people to defend themselves against capital, perhaps is best illustrated in Connecticut, where the Diocesan Labor Institute had been so successful. In the mid-1950s, institute officials, faced with diminishing attendance at school classes, met with Catholic "lower-level union officers and staff" in an effort to revitalize the school. The labor priests were shocked at what they learned: these men spoke of the Church's irrelevance to the factories and the need for married women to do waged work outside the home. They, moreover, had no vision for the future.

"Immobilized collectively, Connecticut working-class people," according to Ronald Schatz, "worked out individual and family responses to their common problems." Neither the Connecticut labor priests nor any other Catholic laborites appear to have understood that their role in the purge of the CIO partly accounts for the demobilization of the Catholic working class in particular and the American working class as a whole. Communists and other left-wing labor leaders had been banished, class confict had been muted, and Catholic working-class men went to church regularly. The facade of tranquility that had been erected, however, was cheap and flimsy, what Gustavo Gutiérrez calls "facile, low-cost conciliation."[53]

No matter how easy it is to comprehend the Catholic response to CIO Communists and those who worked with them; no matter how well one can understand the ways in which Catholics and the Catholic Church were under siege, literally and figuratively, in the postwar world; no matter how often Communists acted just as their worst enemies said they did and would act—the ultimate judgment about the Church's role in the CIO purges must be a harsh one. In 1944, the Jesuit John LaFarge, cutting against the grain of the developing Catholic anticommunist consensus, suggested that "[a]nti-Communism" could be as "dangerous as Communism itself."[54] In hindsight, he was wrong. Anticommunism was *more* dangerous—to the Catholic Church, its working-class membership, and the American working class as a whole. In this crusade, the Church betrayed the divine promise, made through Isaiah, to "create new heavens and a new earth," to "create Jerusalem to be a joy and its people to be a delight" (for Isaiah 65:17–22, see the dedication page). South and Central American peasants took up this struggle for the Kingdom of God and the Kingdom of Justice some 20 years later.

ACKNOWLEDGMENTS

A longer version of this essay was given to the Chicago Area Labor History Group and the Wayne State Labor History Conference. I thank the participants in those meetings as well as Susan Figliulo, Gary Gerstle, James Livingston, and Michael Meranze for their helpful criticisms. I am thankful for travel grants from the Harry S. Truman Library Institute and the Henry J. Kaiser Family Foundation and a Beeke-Levy Research Fellowship (Franklin and Eleanor Roosevelt Institute). Because of space limitations, documentation has been kept to a minimum. In most cases, the citations are merely representative.

McCARTHYISM
AND THE LABOR MOVEMENT:
The Role of the State

ELLEN W. SCHRECKER

McCarthyism, the anticommunist political repression of the late 1940s and 1950s, devastated the labor left. The onslaught against the unions whose members and leaders were in or close to the CP came from all sides. Corporations, other unions, even the Catholic Church—all joined forces to drive Communists out of the labor movement. But it was the federal government that guaranteed the success of the endeavor. It legitimated the efforts of other groups, bringing public support and the blessings of patriotism to hitherto private efforts. It also brought the power of the modern state to the task.

Labor historians who have traced the decline of the left-wing unions acknowledge the importance of the federal government's intervention, but largely as one among several elements. They do not place it at the center of their interpretations, perhaps because the diffuse nature of the official campaign against the labor left conceals its impact or because the left unions had so many other enemies that the state gets lost in the crowd. Moreover, since the destruction of the labor left so obviously benefited employers and rival unions, it is easy to assume that the beneficiaries of those developments were responsible for them as well. Yet, corporations and other unionists had been battling the labor reds for years. Victory came when their efforts were subsumed into the broader national campaign against American Communism. And here the state took the lead.

The federal government had long been involved with the labor movement, but its interest had been primarily economic. With the advent of the Cold War, the concern for national security came to dominate official policy. Because of the CP's ties to the new Soviet "enemy," domestic communism, which had previously been treated as a extremist political movement, was now seen as a threat to the nation's very existence, its adherents as potential spies and saboteurs. Not surprisingly, the process of eliminating the supposed danger of Communist subversion drew the federal government into those areas of American life in which the CP had been active. The government encountered little resistance; in fact, the private sector eagerly embraced the official campaign against communism. There may have been hypocrisy here; patriotism has often clothed less noble considerations. Still we cannot deny the sincerity of the general concern for national security. If they benefited in other ways from the anticommunist crusade, that does not necessarily mean that the opponents of the left-wing unions were not also dedicated to what they felt were the higher interests of their country. Such considerations had become so pervasive, in fact, that when the CIO expelled the Communist-influenced unions in what was presumably a matter internal to the labor movement, it invoked the language of national security and charged the left-wing unions with failing to support American foreign policy.[1]

Eliminating Communists from the labor movement was crucial to Washington's quest for what came to be termed "internal security." American Communists had been active and influential in key industrial unions and, according to most estimates, controlled approximately 20 percent of the CIO. Naturally, the government justified its attack on the labor left in terms of national security. The ideological scenario thus invoked had considerable power. Unions were central to the nation's economy; under Communist influence they could wreak immense harm, especially in vital defense industries. Communists were perceived as being incredibly powerful and invariably disloyal. "A single Communist," so former Congressman Fred Hartley explained, "in a position of power within the labor movement could act under the direction of Russian agents so as to seriously hinder this country's ability to defend its people and wage war against its enemies." This conviction was widely shared. President Truman and Secretary of Defense James V. Forrestal also feared that Communist unionists could undermine national defense. And within the labor movement, someone like James Carey, the labor left's most persistent opponent, invoked national security when he sought support against the reds.[2]

Though the "subversive" danger was, as we now have come to realize, largely hypothetical, the position of some of the left-wing unions in specific industries gave it plausibility. The United Electrical, Radio & Machine Workers of America (UE), with its base in the crucial electronics industry, was considered a particular threat. But any left union or activist could endanger the nation's security. The American Communications Association (ACA), for example, could strangle vital communications from its position in the telegraph industry. The International Union of Mine, Mill & Smelter Workers (IUMMSW) could sabotage copper production. Perhaps the greatest danger was the threat of political strikes by Communist-dominated unions in key industries. References to Communist-led work stoppages before and after World War II seemingly gave substance to these fears. Though economic rather than political factors caused these strikes, the fact of Communist involvement was to transform them into potent symbols of the threat to national security, cited repeatedly throughout the federal government's 15-year campaign against the labor left. Although there is no evidence that the CPUSA ever encouraged its labor members to sabotage America's defense, some of the Party's other activities—especially the practice of its most important labor members of concealing their political affiliation—did corroborate its image as an undemocratic conspiracy.[3]

The enormity of the supposed danger explains not only the intensity of the response to it but also the broad range of federal efforts to drive Communists out of the labor movement. From congressional committees and the FBI to the National Labor Relations Board (NLRB), Subversive Activities Control Board (SACB), and Immigration & Naturalization Service (INS)—almost every agency in the federal government became involved. If there was any central direction, it came from the FBI. The bureaucratic maneuvering of J. Edgar Hoover and his near-monopoly over official domestic intelligence gathering enabled his organization to structure the campaign, select its targets, and supply its ideological rationale. We can often trace the FBI's hand in many of the initiatives taken by other agencies or groups and individuals outside the government.[4] Even so, the collaboration was not always smooth; political infighting and bureaucratic rivalries created obstacles. The unions, moreover, fought back, taking advantage of whatever opportunities the legal system offered. As a result, the government did not achieve all of its aims. A few left-led unions survived, and many of their leaders stayed out of jail. But they had become marginalized; communism disappeared as a significant force within the American labor movement.

Though some elements of the drive against the labor left like the Taft–Hartley Act's non-Communist affidavits were more effective than others, it was the multifaceted nature of the onslaught that ensured its success. Each of the Communist-influenced unions had to face a variety of official actions directed both at individual officers and members and at the union as a whole. Besides the many legal and illegal FBI probes and harassments, there were congressional investigations, Smith Act indictments, contempt and perjury prosecutions, deportations, Internal Revenue Service (IRS) audits, denials of security clearances, grand jury sessions, SACB hearings, as well as all the various NLRB proceedings that directly affected the unions' core economic functions. The cumulative impact of all these actions simply overwhelmed the already embattled labor left.

Congressional committees played an important role. Because they received so much publicity at the time, the House Un-American Activities Committee (HUAC) and its senatorial siblings, the Senate Judiciary Committee's Internal Security Subcommittee and Joe McCarthy's Permanent Investigations Subcommittee of the Government Operations Committee, came to be identified in the public mind as the main agents of McCarthyist repression. Information obtained through the Freedom of Information Act, however, has forced us to revise that interpretation and give at least equal billing to J. Edgar Hoover and the FBI. Nonetheless, the committees did wield real power. Their most important function was to serve as agents of exposure and ensure that politically undesirable individuals would become publically labeled as Communists and thus vulnerable to sanctions from other governmental agencies or, more commonly, private employers.

Labor was a target of the committees from the start. Red-baiting was a classic antiunion tactic; and the CIO's early successes soon attracted charges of Communist influence. HUAC's first hearings in 1938/39 amplified those charges, and in the years that followed, it and other committees continued that promising line of investigation. Between 1946 and 1956, over a hundred hearings dealt with the problem of Communists in the labor movement. Though a few of the early sessions, especially those of the House and Senate Labor Committees in 1947, had some legislative purpose, most involved what would become the standard exposure routine and provoked the usual consequences—criminal prosecutions, broken strikes, internal union purges, and the dismissal of individual workers.[5]

Criminal indictments were perhaps the most dramatic outcome of a congressional hearing. They reinforced the ideological message of the hearings in the strongest possible way. Not only did they punish the individuals involved, but they also, and perhaps more importantly, publicized the issue by emphasizing the seriousness of the problem. The first prosecution of a union official arose out of the House Labor Committee's 1947 investigation into the allegedly Communist-led strike against the Allis-Chalmers Corporation. Although caused by economic factors, the strike was to figure in the standard mythology of the Cold War as an instance of attempted Communist sabotage within the defense industry. The committee bolstered its case by pressuring the Truman administration to indict Harold Christoffel, the former president of the Allis-Chalmers local, for perjury for having denied that he was a Communist.[6]

Contempt of Congress, rather than perjury, soon became the indictment of choice for uncooperative witnesses. By the 1950s, there were few left-wing unions which did not have at least some of their leaders or rank-and-file members facing contempt proceedings, either for taking the Fifth Amendment during the period when the protection afforded by the privilege against self-incrimination was still being litigated or, later on, for provoking test cases to limit congressional inquiries. Many of the key test cases, including those of the Hollywood Ten (most of whom were, after all, active in the Screen Writers Guild), were those of left-wing unionists. Julius Emspak, UE secretary-treasurer, was only the highest ranking of the dozens of UE people who faced contempt prosecutions. President Abram Flaxer of the United Public Workers (UPW) was indicted for refusing to turn over his union's membership lists to HUAC. Nor were such indictments the prerogative of union leaders; dozens of rank-and-file members of the left-led unions also faced contempt charges.[7]

Although few of these people actually went to jail, their contempt cases often dragged on for years, draining their unions of money, morale, and manpower. The impact of congressional investigations was more immediate when they took place, as they often did, during strikes or union election campaigns. Both HUAC and the House Labor Committee held hearings while the Allis-Chalmers strike was in progress. A few months later, HUAC investigated Local 22 of the Food & Tobacco Workers of America (FTA) in the middle of a strike against R. J. Reynolds. The pattern was to recur throughout the

McCarthy period, with congressional investigators "coincidentally" serving subpoenas during strikes involving the left-wing unions. The employers involved no doubt appreciated HUAC's assistance, and there is evidence that, at least in some cases, they probably instigated the hearings.[8]

Anticommunists within the labor movement also worked with the committees. The publicity generated by congressional hearings weakened the labor left by highlighting the Communist issue, which was usually the most effective element in the internal union campaigns against the left. In 1949 Father Charles Owen Rice, the most important Catholic anticommunist activist, arranged for a HUAC investigation of UE's East Pittsburgh Westinghouse Local 601 during an election for delegates to the national convention. HUAC hearings into the supposed Communist domination of the United Automobile Workers' obstreperous Ford Local 600 helped UAW leader Walter Reuther purge that local.[9]

The most common consequence of a congressional investigation was that the men and women who refused to cooperate with the committee lost their jobs. This procedure was perhaps the single most important component of the national anti-Communist campaign. Once the committees perfected their techniques and gained greater public acceptance, private employers routinely collaborated. Having unfriendly witnesses on their payrolls created bad publicity. The committees also hinted that government contracts might be withdrawn unless the offending workers were let go, and in at least one case the U.S. Air Force actually held up a contract for that reason.[10]

These dismissals put enormous pressure on the left-wing unions, especially since many of the unfriendly witnesses were important local leaders. Political solidarity required the reinstatement of these people. But even more important was the unions' need to retain their legitimacy and economic clout as unions. Thus, UE, ACA, and the International Longshoremen's & Warehousemen's Union (ILWU), as well as the United Steel Workers of America, the American Newspaper Guild, and even the anticommunist IUE, sought to handle these cases through ordinary grievance procedures. Though many of the fired workers remained unemployed and even blacklisted, some got their jobs back.[11]

Other elements of the government's campaign against the left-wing unions received less publicity but were just as effective. One important and early weapon belonged to the INS, which had been trying to denaturalize and deport left-wing labor leaders since the 1930s. The traditional distrust of foreigners as well as the lack of constitutional barriers to deportation made immigration proceedings a tempting tool for political repression. The case of ILWU leader Harry Bridges is well known, but the INS also had tried to deport other union leftists both before and after World War II.[12]

Again, as with the congressional hearings, deportation proceedings were often ancillary to strikes or union elections, though national security was, as usual, the stated justification. Superficially, the deportation campaign was unsuccessful. A few left-wing labor leaders had to leave the country in the late 1940s, but most, including Bridges and the UE's James Matles, were never expelled. Here, again, it was not the stated goal of the deportation proceedings that ultimately mattered, but their contribution to the overall pressure on the labor left.[13]

The government's employee security programs provided a particularly potent weapon against the left-led unions and their members. Actions against individuals often affected their unions as well. Thus, for example, when several of the militant leaders of a United Office & Professional Workers of America (UOPWA) local were dismissed as security risks from their jobs in an electronics firm in 1948, the local collapsed. Elsewhere, the refusal to grant security clearances often hampered local officials from processing grievances and carrying out other union business. Some unions were particularly vulnerable. The federal government's loyalty–security program tore such a hole through the activists in the UPW that it effectively destroyed the union. UE was also affected because so many of its members worked in defense plants where the even more stringent standards of the military's industrial security program applied.[14]

The biggest purge took place on the waterfront. A month after the Korean War broke out in the summer of 1950, the Truman administration called a meeting of shipowners and the anti-Communist maritime unions to protect the nation's shipping. The measure which emerged from that conclave and which Congress enacted three weeks later authorized the U.S. Coast Guard to set up a port security program. Using information supplied by naval intelligence and the CIO, the program targeted members of the ILWU, National Maritime Union (NMU), and the National Union of Marine Cooks & Stewards (NUMCS). By the time the federal judiciary ruled against it, the program had thrown more than 2,700 merchant seamen and longshoremen out of work.[15]

The federal government's various employment security programs were normally directed against individual workers, but Washington occasionally cracked down on the Communist-oriented unions themselves—often with the assistance and encouragement of rival unions. In September 1948, concerned about the possibility of "a political strike or other organized sabotage," the Atomic Energy Commission (AEC) ordered General Electric not to accept UE as a bargaining agent at its new Knolls Atomic Power Laboratory near Schenectady, New York, even if the union was to win the forthcoming representation election. The AEC also ordered the University of Chicago to break its contract with the UPW workers at the Argonne National Laboratories.[16]

Naturally, the unions fought back. In the beginning, they resorted to arbitration and tried, with mixed success, to put the dismissed workers back on the payroll. The overall political atmosphere determined the outcome, though occasionally, especially in the early years if it was clear that there was no sensitive work involved, the unions did obtain the redress they sought. Once the Korean War broke out, arbitrators became more reluctant to overturn security dismissals. Even more destructive than the individual dismissals, however, was the oft-repeated threat that the government might not award work to or even cancel contracts at plants where left-wing unions represented the workers. Such a threat was especially damaging to UE and severely handicapped the union in its attempts to parry raids from other unions.[17]

More public, though less extensive, were the Smith Act indictments of such union leaders of Jack Hall of the ILWU, Irving Potash of the International Fur & Leather Workers Union (IFLWU), William Sentner and David Davis of UE, Karly Larson of the Woodworkers Union, and Juan Emmanuelli of the Unidad General de Trabajadores de Puerto Rico. Although the federal judiciary ultimately threw out all these cases, the financial and personal strain of the prosecutions was considerable and certainly increased the burdens on the unions involved. There were other less formal types of harassment as well. IRS audits seemed to be common, as were visits from the FBI.[18]

We are only just beginning to grasp the dimensions of the Bureau's activities. The labor left was one of Hoover's main targets, and the FBI's enthusiastic though covert cooperation with journalists, labor leaders, business executives, clergy, and politicians undergirded many of the ostensibly private moves against the labor left. Cooperation with other government agencies was even more extensive. The Bureau routinely fed material to HUAC and the other congressional committees. NLRB records indicate that FBI agents dealt "almost daily" with the board, especially when they were searching for evidence to bolster criminal proceedings against left-wing labor leaders.[19]

Much of the material that the FBI was seeking from the NLRB concerned the non-Communist affidavits that Section 9(h) of the Taft-Hartley Act of 1947 required all union officials to sign. Of all the official measures that affected the left wing of the labor movement, the Section 9(h) affidavits were to have the most far-reaching impact. Initially, however, the affidavits were almost an afterthought, attached to a piece of legislation designed to weaken the entire labor movement, not just its Communist elements. Though both the House and Senate wanted an outright ban on Communist labor leaders, Senator Robert A. Taft convinced his colleagues to substitute the more easily enforceable affidavits.[20]

The law required every officer of a local and international union to file an annual affidavit with the NLRB affirming that

I am not a member of the Communist Party or affiliated with such party.

I do not believe in, and I am not a member of, nor do I support, any organization that believes in or teaches the overthrow of the United States Government by force or by any illegal or unconstitutional methods.

Unions whose officers did not file the affidavits could not use the services of the NLRB. They could not be officially certified as bargaining agents or obtain union shop agreements; nor could the NLRB process their unfair labor practices complaints or let them participate in representation elections. The only other sanctions embodied in Section 9(h) subjected officials who falsified their affidavits to the standard criminal penalties for perjury.[21]

At the time, it was by no means clear that the 9(h) affidavits were going to have much of an impact. Communist labor leaders could presumably retain power by simply ignoring the law and doing without the services of the NLRB. In addition, Section 9(h) had been so poorly written that its implementation threatened to become an administrative nightmare. There were constitutional problems as well. The affidavits, with their prohibition against "belief in" and "support" of communism, raised important First Amendment issues of free speech and association, issues which, it was clear, the U.S. Supreme Court would have to decide. Moreover, as a result of his veto and subsequent attack on the bill, President Truman had so thoroughly identified himself with the opposition to Taft–Hartley that his election victory in 1948 seemed to promise a rapid repeal.[22]

Above all, at least in the first few months after the Taft–Hartley Act went into effect, the hostility of organized labor itself threatened to nullify the law. Several hundred thousand workers walked off the job to rally against the act. Furthermore, many non-Communist labor leaders refused to sign the affidavit since it discriminated against labor and was, they argued, an unwarranted interference with the internal affairs of unions as well as a menace to civil liberties. The Communists and their allies, the primary targets of the affidavit, were even more ferocious in their denunciations of the "Fascist," "evil," "slave labor," "antiunion" Taft–Hartley Act and, in some cases, were sustained in their refusal to sign by membership referenda.[23]

Even before the law went into effect, several unions planned to test it in court. The case that the U.S. Supreme Court ultimately decided was that of the ACA, but many other unions, including the United Steel Workers of America, also mounted constitutional challenges. It took several years for these cases to reach the Supreme Court, a delay that was to prove crucial to the fate of the left-led unions. As the Cold War intensified and public anti-Communism deepened, opposition to Section 9(h) diminished. In July 1949, after the U.S. Court of Appeals upheld the law and it was clear that Congress was not going to repeal Taft–Hartley, the United Steel Workers abandoned the field and signed the affidavits. Fate was even crueler. Two of the Supreme Court's most liberal justices, Frank Murphy and Wiley Rutledge, died in the summer of 1949, and Justice William O. Douglas fell off a horse. As a result, of the six justices who actually participated in the decision, only Hugo Black believed that Section 9(h) was unconstitutional; though Felix Frankfurter and Robert H. Jackson disliked some of the language in the affidavit, they agreed with the majority that the danger of Communist subversion justified the imposition of political tests for union officials.[24]

In any event, by the time the Supreme Court's decision appeared, the issue was moot. The left-wing unions had already complied with Taft–Hartley. For many of these unions, their failure to sign the affidavits simply exacerbated the problems that they were already facing—from internal opponents, outside raiders, and the Catholic Church. Because most of the alleged Communists had been effective bread-and-butter unionists, their opponents had had only limited success in persuading rank-and-file members to oust the left-wing leaders or affiliate with a rival union. Taft–Hartley brought the federal government into the battle and, while not necessarily giving the anticommunists a decisive edge, certainly changed the nature of the struggle. Given the deepening Cold War and the changing political climate, it is possible that the labor anticommunists would have triumphed during the late 1940s even without Section 9(h). Nonetheless, the affidavits provided a convenient focus for the labor left's internal opponents. By initially refusing to sign, the left-wing leaders provided their antagonists with what seemed to be yet another indication of their political extremism and apparent lack of patriotism. More importantly, however, noncompliance was a concrete act with real consequences. The serious problems that accompanied noncompliance finally enabled the anticommunists to invoke economic as well as political arguments against their left-wing opponents.[25]

In some unions, like the UAW, the conflict over Section 9(h) gave the anticommunist forces a long-awaited opportunity to purge their rivals. In other unions, like the UE and IUMMSW, the warfare simply escalated. Thus, for example, in the IUMMSW, where the infighting had been particularly intense, the international leadership's failure to sign the 9(h) affidavits encouraged further outbreaks of secessionism. Dissident leaders claimed, with some justification, that the policy of noncompliance had weakened the union by exposing it to outside raiders. The internal feuding over the affidavits in IUMMSW and elsewhere also diverted attention from economic issues to what one union official called "the false issue of sign or resign."[26]

Like the internal schisms, the external raids that had long plagued the labor left intensified under Taft–Hartley. Other unions, traditional rivals and newcomers alike, leaped at the opportunity to force representation elections from which the noncomplying unions were barred. With the enormous handicap of having to ask their supporters to vote for a "no union" option, the noncomplying unions lost more elections than they won. As these losses accumulated, it became clear that noncompliance threatened the left-wing unions' very survival.[27]

Raiders received additional advantages from the NLRB's rigid policy of enforcement. That agency had been restructured by Taft–Hartley, with the creation of a strong general counsel to balance the supposedly prolabor board. In order to appease his conservative critics, President Truman appointed a Republican lawyer, Robert Denham, to the new post. To what extent Denham's reputedly promanagement proclivities influenced his treatment of the left unions is unclear; the records that I have seen certainly indicate considerable hostility, but, given the general antagonism to the left-led unions even within the liberal community, it is doubtful that a less conservative general counsel would have offered the left unions much more assistance. What is clear is that by refusing to process any of the noncomplying unions' unfair labor practice complaints against employers, the NLRB made it hard for those unions to service their members and thus further increased the economic appeal of their rivals.[28]

Nor did employers shrink from taking advantage of the noncompliance status of the left-wing unions. In many instances, antagonistic managements simply refused to bargain, citing the unions' failure to comply with Taft–Hartley as their excuse. They almost succeeded.

Deprived of the support of the federal government, the noncomplying unions had only their own economic power to rely on. The
weaker ones had no choice but to accept the poor contracts they were
offered. The stronger ones walked off the job. Either way it was a bad
situation. The strikes that followed were often long and sometimes
bloody. Outside raiders stepped up their attacks and employers, insu-
lated from NLRB sanctions, returned to the antiunion tactics of what,
one observer called, "the pre–Wagner Act jungle."[29]

Compliance was the only solution. Some unions had tried to establish "fronts" in which an international would handle matters for a
noncomplying local or the complying locals would be ostensibly severed from the errant international. But such tactics had their limitations; and by the summer of 1949 the left-wing unions were ready to
submit. Too many elections were being lost, and the unions' capacity
to deliver the economic goods to their members was seriously threatened. And so, one by one, the conventions and executive boards of
the left-wing unions voted to comply with Taft–Hartley and have
their officers sign the 9(h) affidavits. The decision provided some
relief; and in the immediate aftermath of compliance the left-wing
unions did win some elections. But the raiding continued and actually
intensified, especially after the CIO purge in November 1949.[30]

Compliance posed its own problems. After all, many officials of the
tainted unions *were* Communists. In order to comply with Taft–
Hartley they would either have to quit the Party or resign from their
union posts. Some gave up their jobs. Others left the Party. Secret
members resigned in secret, while more public ones adopted a policy
of what the NLRB's disgusted staff members called "Resign and Sign"
and left the CP with a flourish, often issuing statements to the effect
that they were acting under duress and that their political beliefs
remained unchanged.[31]

Other unions complied by reshuffling their leadership and/or revis-
ing their constitutions. In making these changes, the left-wing unions
were simply following the lead of the hardly radical AFL, which had
rewritten its constitution to eliminate all its vice presidents after John
L. Lewis refused to sign. Thus, for example, Donald Henderson resigned as president of the FTA and became its "national administrative director," a position that presumably did not require him to sign a
9(h) affidavit. Other unions simply eliminated officers' positions in
order to put themselves into compliance. One Furniture Workers local
got rid of 32 such positions.[32]

These subterfuges, obviously designed to circumvent the law,
rarely worked. The NLRB insisted that "compliance with Section 9(h)

would have to be achieved in substance as well as in form," and it soon challenged the status of some of the unions that had juggled their leaderships. For example, it disqualified the FTA from a representation election at an Alaskan salmon cannery and asked "National Administrative Director" Henderson to send in a sworn statement describing his new duties and "stating that these functions have not in the past been performed by him as president of the union or by any other officer." When the NLRB did not initiate action to decertify a union for such practices, hostile employers or rival unions often urged the board to do so.[33]

An even greater problem for the NLRB was not the officers who did not sign 9(h) affidavits but the ones who did. From the start, General Counsel Denham believed that many of the left-wing union officials were still "subscribers to the basic principles of the Communist Party." Nonetheless, Denham and his colleagues could not act on their suspicions, for the language of the Taft–Hartley Act required the NLRB to accept the affidavits once they were submitted, "unless, of course, there could be produced definite and positive proof of the falsity of the sworn statements." Obtaining that proof was the job of the Justice Department, not the NLRB, though Denham did try to initiate the process by forwarding the suspicious affidavits to the Justice Department and FBI.[34]

Then employers, who presumably had even stronger motives for seeking decertification of the left-wing unions, forced the NLRB's hand. Several companies simply refused to bargain, claiming that the fraudulence of the unions' 9(h) affidavits deprived them of NLRB protection. At first, the NLRB claimed that its hands were tied. It refused to decertify the unions and, albeit reluctantly, continued to process their unfair labor practices complaints. Once the Eisenhower administration took over and a Republican majority controlled the board, NLRB policy changed. The key case involved the IUMMSW. The board held up action on a union complaint against the Precision Scientific Company of Chicago and instead ordered an probe into the company's charge that the union's secretary-treasurer, Maurice Travis, had falsified his affidavits.[35]

The formal hearings, which took place in May and June 1954, resembled all the other anticommunist proceedings of the period. The government's witnesses were the same group of former IUMMSW officials and professional informers who had already testified about the union before Congress and the CIO and who were later to appear at the union's SACB hearings and perjury trials. The results were also the same. Since the board shared the widespread belief that Communists always lied, it had little trouble ruling the union out of compliance on the grounds that Travis had not really left the Party. The U.S. Supreme Court was to reverse that decision in December 1956, but Travis had resigned long before in order to protect the union's certification. Thus, even though the NLRB had officially lost its case against the IUMMSW, in reality it had won. It had successfully used the threat of decertification to force a left-wing union leader out of office.[36]

Decertification proceedings were, however, an awkward way to use the 9(h) affidavits to eliminate Communist labor leaders. The most promising approach, certainly the most straightforward, was to use the sanctions provided for in the law and prosecute individual union officials for falsifying their affidavits. From the first, the NLRB had been pressing for such prosecutions and it sent copies of hundreds of suspicious 9(h) affidavits to the Justice Department and FBI. Despite FBI investigations and rumors of imminent indictments, nothing much happened in 1949 and 1950. The wording of the affidavits stood in the way of a successful prosecution. As Attorney General J. Howard McGrath explained, "Difficulty is experienced in the maintenance of prosecutions under this section because of the necessity of proving that an affiant *at the time of the making of his affidavit* was a member of the Communist Party or affiliated with the Party" (emphasis in the original). In other words, the government had no way to prove that the officials had lied. The FBI, which could have provided such evidence, was reluctant to let its informants testify in public and, in most cases, had no evidence for Party membership after the affidavits were signed.[37]

Because of these obstacles, it was not until 1951 that the Department of Justice took action and indicted Anthony Valentino, the business agent for a Camden, New Jersey, Packinghouse Workers local that had once been affiliated with the FTA. Though the attorney general claimed that he had sent about 80 cases to grand juries in 1952, he got only three indictments, all of equally obscure people. It was clear that the Justice Department, at least under the Truman administration, was loathe to indict people it could not convict.[38]

In this area, too, the situation changed when the GOP took over. Less solicitous than the Democrats about both civil liberties and organized labor, the Eisenhower administration toughened up the enforcement of anticommunist measures across the board. Attorney General Herbert Brownell ordered a review of all the 9(h) cases that had been referred to the Justice Department and began to obtain indictments. I have not come across a complete list of all the 9(h) prosecutions that were undertaken. I have the names of some 30 people but am by no means sure that the list is complete. Nor, given the present unavailability of Justice Department files, is it clear why some of these prosecutions were undertaken. There is some evidence that various journalists, employers, and union rivals occasionally suggested specific prosecutions. The availability of witnesses seems to have been an important factor. Thus, for example, Chicago UE official John J. Killian was apparently indicted after having been identified as a Communist by an undercover agent in a Smith Act trial.[39]

Some of the people indicted were relatively obscure local UE officials in the Midwest, while others like IFLWU's leader Ben Gold, IUMMSW's Travis, and President Hugh Bryson of NUMCS were more prominent. In addition to the prosecution of individual union officials for falsifying their affidavits, the Justice Department experimented with the use of conspiracy indictments against groups of left-wing unionists. From the prosecution viewpoint, conspiracy was an easier charge to prove and, given the government's problems with obtaining evidence, conspiracy charges must have seemed particularly tempting. Thus, for example, after it lost its initial case against Valentino, the Justice Department reindicted him and a colleague for conspiracy. The government also prosecuted 16 IUMMSW leaders and opened a major case in Ohio against Fred Haug, a local leader of that union, his UE activist wife, Marie Reed, and an assortment of Ohio CP officials.[40]

The 9(h) trials conformed to the standard pattern of most McCarthy-era proceedings. The government relied on a combination of professional witnesses and textual analysis to tie the defendants to the CP and its advocacy of "force and violence." The willingness of such informants as Harvey Matusow to doctor their testimony enabled the prosecution to overcome the problem that had so plagued the Truman administration: finding evidence about the defendants' Communist beliefs and affiliations *after* they had signed the affidavits. Of course, the Eisenhower administration, with its strong probusiness orientation, was far more sympathetic to such prosecutions on ideological grounds as well.[41]

Again, as with so many of the other anticommunist prosecutions of the period, the federal judiciary ultimately overturned most of the 9(h) convictions, usually because of the dubious veracity of the government's witnesses. But the litigation was exhausting. Often it took years before the 9(h) defendants were acquitted. IUMMSW fought its conspiracy case from 1956 until the U.S. Supreme Court finally overturned the conviction almost ten years later.[42]

While most of these prosecutions ultimately foundered, they galvanized the NLRB to decertify the unions involved. The conviction of

Anthony Valentino in October 1952 began the process. Less than a month later, the NLRB moved to decertify his local. The action had the desired effect. Valentino, under pressure from within the labor movement as well as from the federal government, gave up his union post. Since Valentino's was only the first of what the NLRB expected would be many more 9(h) convictions, the board decided to hold up all NLRB action in cases in which there were outstanding 9(h) indictments. The unions involved fought back; again, as in all the board's other attempts to use 9(h) directly against the left-wing unions, the federal judiciary ruled against the government. The NLRB then tried to decertify those unions whose officers had been convicted of 9(h) violations. Again the unions appealed. The U.S. Supreme Court again agreed, ruling on December 10, 1956, that "The sole sanction of Section 9(h) is the criminal penalty imposed on the officer who files a false affidavit, not decompliance of the union nor the withholding of the benefits of the Act that are granted once the specified officers file their Section 9(h) affidavits."[43]

The Taft–Hartley affidavits, it seemed, had lost their bite. Actually, 9(h) had been problematic from the start and the officials, businessmen, union leaders, and politicians who wanted to eliminate Communist influence from the labor movement had long been critical of its inadequacies. As early as 1948, the final report of the special joint committee set up to oversee the Taft–Hartley Act recommended strengthening the affidavits and extending them to management. Those officials in the NLRB and Justice Department who had to enforce Section 9(h) also proposed changes. They wanted to revise the definition of "officer" to eliminate the practice of evading compliance by constitutional revisions; they also urged that the affidavit be made retroactive so that union officials could not quit the party one day and sign the 9(h) form the next.[44]

During the early 1950s, Congress toyed with several different measures that either revised the language of the affidavits or else eliminated them altogether in favor of some other, presumably more effective, mechanism. Early in 1953, Senator Hubert H. Humphrey explored the options in a series of subcommittee hearings. Humphrey was particularly attracted by a measure that had long been pushed by the International Union of Electrical Workers' James B. Carey of extending to all defense contractors the AEC's policy of refusing to deal with UE. There were other proposals as well, including measures that would make it illegal for unions to have Communist officers, put the left unions on the attorney general's list, establish a new federal agency to investigate Communist labor unions, and permit employers to discharge workers who belonged to subversive unions.[45]

In his State of the Union address in 1954, President Eisenhower explicitly endorsed a new law against Communist-led unions. Congress responded by passing the Communist Control Act of 1954. The measure amended not the Taft–Hartley Act but the Internal Security Act of 1950 (McCarran Act). It gave the task of eliminating left-wing unions to the Subversive Activities Control Board, which was authorized to register labor organizations as "communist infiltrated." Once the SACB listed a union, it would lose all its NLRB privileges until it cleaned up its act. Because these new procedures were directed against institutions instead of individuals, NLRB and other officials believed that they would finally be able to purge the left-wing unions. Opposition to the measure was minimal; there were no hearings, and the measure passed the Senate unanimously and the House with only two negative votes.[46]

The Communist Control Act, however, turned out to be no more efficacious than Taft–Hartley. Its passage did lead to the resignation of Ben Gold, who had been resisting NLRB attempts to use Section 9(h) to decertify his union, but SACB procedures proved to be just as vulnerable to litigation and delay as Taft–Hartley. The Justice Department filed its first petition—against IUMMSW—in July 1955. It filed its second, and last, petition against UE in December of that year. Hearings in both cases began in the spring of 1957. Essentially reruns of earlier proceedings, they used the same informers and relied upon the same evidence.[47]

Again, legal maneuvering prevented effective enforcement. After years of litigation, the Justice Department dropped the case against UE on April 10, 1959, probably because it realized that the evidence it had against that union was so tainted by FBI illegalities that it would not stand up in court. The case against IUMMSW lasted longer. The Justice Department did not drop it until 1966, by which point Supreme Court decisions in other cases had so gutted the SACB that any further action before it was fruitless.[48]

In 1959, Congress again tried to eliminate Communists from the labor movement. The antiracketeering Landrum–Griffith Act repealed the Section 9(h) affidavits and in Section 504 made it illegal for a Communist or ex-Communist who had been out of the Party for less than five years to become a union official. Though the FBI checked out more than 500 people for possible prosecution, the Justice Department made only one serious attempt to enforce this section of the act. In 1961 the government indicted Archie Brown, an open Communist who was a member of the executive board of ILWU's Local 10 in San Francisco. The Ninth Circuit Court of Appeals, however, overturned Brown's conviction in November 1964 on the grounds that Section 504 violated both the First and the Fifth Amendments. The Supreme Court upheld that decision the following year.[49]

By the mid-1960s the federal government's campaign against the labor left finally sputtered to an end. Nonetheless, despite the ostensible failure of so many of its individual elements, the overall drive against Communist influence in the labor movement succeeded. Many liberal scholars and observers have claimed that the judicial dismantling of the structure of political repression indicates the effectiveness of the American legal system in combatting McCarthyism.[50] But such an interpretation is superficial; it ignores such underlying realities as the enormous imbalance of power between the federal government and its left-wing adversaries. Nor does it account for the federal judiciary's reluctance to intervene until the worst of the repression was over and the Communist movement was essentially defunct. Finally, such a triumph-of-the-law interpretation overlooks the inescapable conclusion that however favorable to the left individual court decisions may have been, the government did achieve its goal of eliminating significant Communist influence from the labor movement. Thus, while the left-wing unions won legal victories and retained some of their members, the cumulative effect of the political repression they faced was fatal. The drain on their resources was simply too great. By the mid-1950s, most of the top leaders of the left-wing unions were, as Harvey Levenstein noted, "involved almost full time in staying out of prison." Though most of them won their appeals, the anticipated impact of their cases on their unions forced the more vulnerable individuals, like Travis and Gold, to resign. Even for those officers who retained their posts, the continued litigation was exhausting.[51]

It was also expensive. Although the unions often pooled their resources, their legal battles coming on top of the cost of fighting off constant raids were a serious financial strain. IUMMSW officials estimated that the union had spent close to $280,000 on its legal defense from 1953 to 1962. The smaller unions were particularly afflicted. Victor Rabinowitz, who represented the ACA's members and leaders in appearances before HUAC and the other congressional committees, recalls that by the late 1950s the union was in such desperate financial straits that "if I had enough money to pay my railroad fare [to Washington], I considered that it was not too bad."[52]

Ultimately, of course, the strain of self-defense ate into the unions' ability to function as labor organizations. Often they were unable to resist employers' demands and had to accept unfavorable contracts because they were simply too weak to risk a strike. Such a situation only debilitated them further and exposed them to additional attacks from outside raiders. Employers, of course, welcomed the prospect and often, according to the patriotic grumbling of rival unions, continued to deal with the left-wing unions precisely because they were so weak.[53]

It is important to realize that some of these organizations, especially IUMMSW, IFLWU, and some of the unions in the maritime field, were also dealing with declining industries. Thus, even if they had not had to face political repression, the 1950s and 1960s would still have brought hard times.[54]

The dénouement in most cases turned out to be the collapse of the left unions as independent entities. Even the ILWU, which observers believed was the strongest of the left-wing unions, had to give up all its locals outside of the west coast. Other unions merged with each other or tried to find friendly homes elsewhere. Only the ILWU and UE survived, albeit in a much reduced condition. The multiplicity of attacks, from employers and other unions as well as from official agencies, simply wore the weakened unions out.[55]

While it would be wrong to assign full credit to the federal government for what happened, Washington clearly was central to the process. The government was hardly monolithic. Its different branches and agencies operated independently and occasionally even came into conflict; still the overall impact of the state was definitive. Even when the government was not immediately responsible for some of the more devastating assaults on the left-wing unions, it often served as a catalyst, its actions providing opportunities for the unions' other enemies to exploit. Even more important was Washington's role in legitimizing anti-Communism and transforming the attack on the labor left into the defense of America's security.

Once we look at the demise of the left unions within the broader context of the overall political repression of the McCarthy period, the crucial role of the federal government becomes even more apparent. What happened to the labor movement during the 1940s and 1950s happened throughout American society. From Harvard to Hollywood, the same combination of direct governmental pressure and private-sector collaboration destroyed the influence of the American CP and all the ideas, individuals, and organizations associated with it. Once anticommunism became official policy, the left-wing unions, the most influential organizations within the Communist movement, were doomed. They were too important to ignore, and the state was too strong to resist.

FIGHTING LEFT-WING UNIONISM:
Voices from the Opposition to the IFLWU in Fulton County, New York

GERALD ZAHAVI

The house of the U.S. shoe and leather industry is infested with Communist ratholes. Not only has the industry made little effort to plug up these ratholes, but has fostered nourishment for the bustling family of rodents within. . . . And what of the tanners? To date—except for isolated individual cases—there has been only one group with the courage to stand up to Gold's Commie-directed union: the Gloversville tanners. They fought Gold a hard, long, costly battle—and won. It took moral guts to do it—a fight based strictly on refusal to do business with a Communist-led union. Today their house is pretty well purged of the Communist ratholes.[1]

Fulton County, located some 45 miles northwest of Albany, New York, in the southern Adirondack foothills, was a typically conservative upstate New York county in the 1940s and 1950s. Since the late eighteenth century, its small twin cities of Gloversville and Johnstown had been major centers of glove manufacturing; by the first decade of the twentieth century, they were producing more than 90 percent of all fine leather gloves manufactured in the United States. The county's thriving glove trade gave rise to and supported an extensive leather tanning industry that soon achieved international recognition. In the

1930s and 1940s, dozens of tanneries provided employment for close to two thousand workers.

During the Great Depression, Fulton County's leather industry attracted the attention of the Fur Department of the left-wing Needle Trades Workers Industrial Union (NTWIU). In the summer of 1933, NTWIU organizers arrived, helped workers organize, and in the wake of a six-week strike, won local employers' grudging acceptance of a tannery workers union. Although unsuccessful in coaxing the leather workers to affiliate with the national union, NTWIU organizers did leave behind a small cadre of Communist union activists and leaders. Thus, throughout the 1930s, the leather workers of Fulton County remained organized under the banner of the Independent Leather Workers Union of Fulton County, an autonomous local union headed by a generally respected and well-liked Communist Party (CPUSA) member named Clarence Carr.

With the coming of World War II and the growing assertiveness of local left-wing activists, especially Carr, the Independent—not without considerable internal struggle—finally affiliated with a national organization: the International Fur & Leather Workers Union (IFLWU). It transformed itself into Local 202 of the parent union in the summer of 1940. The IFLWU was one of the most openly left wing of the CIO unions. Led by immensely popular Ben Gold—a member of the CPUSA's national committee—it entered the postwar era with a heady sense of optimism that was soon shattered by the internecine battles of the Cold War years. Many of its leather locals, which affiliated with the International after the latter's 1939 merger with the National Leather Workers Association, were located in leather industry centers in conservative rural Pennsylvania, upstate New York, and New England—well outside the orbit of the New York and Chicago ethnic radical cultures that defined the ideological family of the International union. Thus, during the Cold War, they were potentially the most vulnerable of the International's locals to red-baiting and union raiding.

The association of the Fulton county tannery workers with the Communist-headed International always had been a source of contention both between employers and employees and within the union. Ideological controversy had been somewhat muted in the years of Soviet–U.S. cooperation during World War II, but with the domestic front of the Cold War reaching into Fulton County in the postwar years, factional fighting and external attacks once again arose. The local union's circumstances were not helped by the unwillingness of IFLWU leaders to abide by Section 9(h) of the newly passed Taft–Hartley Act; when IFLWU officers refused to sign "non-Communist" affidavits, Local 202, as a constituent union, was left without National Labor Relations Board (NLRB) protection. Thus, when negotiations over a new contract fell apart in late June of 1949, many of the county's tannery owners—organized under the Fulton County Tanners Association—took advantage of the vulnerability of the left-wing local and initiated a lockout.[2] The lockout soon turned into a nine-month strike, lasting into the spring of 1950.

In late 1949, local union leaders, to avoid NLRB decertification, decided to sever their ties with the IFLWU and return their union to its independent status. Their strategy proved ineffective; the NLRB refused to recognize the independence of the newly disaffiliated union and blocked its participation in a December 1949 union certification election. Yet, even in defeat, the left-wing union continued to command the loyalty of the workers; the majority voted "no union" in that election—an expression of solidarity with their beleaguered leaders. Their organization, however, was close to moribund. Months on the picket lines in the bitter cold of an upstate New York winter took their toll. Right-wing members of the general executive board and their supporters soon led an insurgent movement to create an alternative union acceptable to both the NLRB and the tannery owners. They succeeded in March 1950 and all but ended the strike. This apostasy by a small group of union members led to the formation of CIO industrial union Local 1712, the right-wing United Tannery Workers Union of Fulton County (later to affiliate with the Amalgamated Clothing Workers Union). Although a fragment of the original union survived and reestablished Local 202 of the IFLWU, the local never regained the prestige or influence of the pre-1949 period.

The complex course of events narrated above constitutes merely a bare outline of what transpired in the Fulton County leather industry in the 1940s and early 1950s. I have taken the time to trace it in order to aid the reader in following the first-hand accounts that follow. The oral histories presented here, edited from more than 250 pages of typed transcripts, examine the culminating months of almost two decades of struggle in Fulton County. Although they deal specifically with the strike of 1949/50, they do not present a *balanced* picture of all sides of that conflagration. This is intentional.[3] The selections are extracted from taped conversations held with four active leaders of the *anti*–Local 202 campaign. Together, they constitute a detailed portrait of the opposition to left-wing unionism in one upstate New York community.

The four men profiled below—Lydon Maider, a labor-relations lawyer deeply involved in local industrialists' attempts to replace radical left-wing labor leaders with more conservative alternatives; George H. Meyer, the head of the local leather manufacturers' association in 1950; and two union members, John Sutliff and Harold Taylor, active in the right-wing opposition faction within the union—offer us a unique perspective on the motives and tactics of those who sought to purge the labor left in the post–World War II era. Such a perspective, especially sensitive to the corporate, shop-floor, and local dimensions of this drama, is all too lacking in most scholarship on the left-right split in the CIO in 1949/50.

What emerges from their four accounts is a real sense of personal and collective drama. On the one hand, we witness a group of employers in conflict with a left-wing militant union, conscious of their common class interests, actively trying to forge a strong sense of unity through the mechanism of an employers' organization—the Fulton County Tanners Association. This was not always easy, as suggested by the Maider and Meyer interviews. Fulton County tannery owners were a diverse lot, not always given (or economically strong enough) to act in concert with fellow employers. The most astute among them were influenced by their New Deal and wartime experience of business discipline and government oversight. They took the advice of "corporate liberal" professionals—lawyers and labor-relations specialists—as well as national trade organizations quite seriously. In the postwar years, they tried to limit intraindustry competition and cultivated cooperation in order to overcome a perceived common threat. They sought to regain, to borrow Howell Harris's wonderful book title, their "right to manage," a right they believed had been deeply eroded in the previous two decades.[4] In fact, as the following interviews reveal, their right to manage was threatened not only by a militant Communist-led union but also by community and state agents—ministers and priests, civic organizations, peace-advocating fellow industrialists, and New York State mediators. All, according to the tanners, were meddling intruders in a private war.

By the 1940s, Fulton County tannery owners, unlike their predecessors, had come to recognize the self-disciplining value of unions; thus, they did not attack unionism per se. But they did attack radical unions. Local 202 represented all that they feared and loathed: an intransigent, militant, and powerful workers' organization with ultimate loyalty not to themselves but to "outsiders," and worse than that, *Communist* outsiders! Ironically, Local 202 was the catalyst of their unity. The testimonies of lawyer Lydon Maider and President George H. Meyer of the Tanners Association offer us a glimpse into the inner world of capitalist class formation and strategy on a local level; they identify the obstacles employers faced in fighting a well-established left-wing union, how they overcame them, and at what price.

On the other hand, the accounts that follow also yield some important insights into the workings and motives of right-wing union factions that struggled in Fulton County and elsewhere to seize the reins of power from Communist leaders and their supporters. Locally, right-wing union leaders like John Sutliff exploited the vulnerability of Local 202's left-wing officers and the frustrations of a group of young union members starting their adult lives in the postwar era. They formed a working coalition built on anticommunism and expediency that ultimately broke the power of the Local's Communist leadership. Although many of the younger members of this coalition had few complaints about Clarence Carr and his fellow left-wing leaders, their intolerance of material deprivation and their lack of long-term historical ties to the union's officers (forged in the struggle to build the union) partially explain why their loyalty could not survive months of material hardship. As Harold Taylor suggests in somewhat exaggerated terms in his interview, the "guys from under thirty-five . . . were the instigators of this whole 1712 thing."

However we may choose to judge these men, or whatever judgment they might make of each other and themselves, we should not lose sight of our need to learn from them. Their actions and motives, multiplied by the experiences of hundreds of similar communities throughout the nation, ultimately helped transform the U.S. labor movement—and U.S. capitalism—in the post–World War II era just as powerfully as the actions of Philip Murray and the 1950 CIO convention.

Lydon Maider   *Maider has an impressive mind, a fine memory for details, and a tendency toward precision. He is scrupulous about gauging the veracity of his own recollections. It is clear that law runs in his veins. We met in his spacious law office in Gloversville in February 1988. Back in 1949 and 1950, he was the local attorney of the Tanners Association of Fulton County. As such, he helped chart the tactics and strategies of the employers during the nine-month battle waged against Local 202.*

[After World War II] it was decided that this loose relationship that these tanners had should be formalized. And the Tanners Association of Fulton County, Incorporated, was formed. All of the tanneries in the two cities except G. Levor & Co. became members of it.[5] The association employed a man by the name of John Forster, who had been a very successful mediator employed by the New York State Mediation Service. John Forster had come up through the Carpenter's Union. I think he was a native of Troy or thereabouts. He had a very forcible personality. He gave the impression of being and was, in fact, a very honest man, and he had the confidence of everybody he came in contact with. He was a very successful mediator.

They opened an office on North Main Street in Gloversville. He, in effect, was the personnel officer for each one of these individual members. He not only handled the labor relations, but he handled many of their personnel problems. These individual tanners varied in the number of employees they might have. Most of them probably didn't have more than 50 employees. . . . None of them were really big enough to hire a full-time guy like Forster to do personnel work, see? That was a practical solution, and it was a good one. It worked. So, thereafter, all negotiations with the union were handled by him and I served as their legal counsel. I think I may have had something to do with [formalizing the organization]. I was quite friendly with a lot of these people. My experience during the war [as a Navy labor-relations lawyer] and handling problems over there got me to believe that what they needed was to have some kind of centralized control over their labor-relations problems. I came in contact with a lot of labor-relations people, particularly in larger industries than I was used to seeing around here, and I was convinced that they were going to have problems if they didn't do that.

It was a very successful thing, and I feel sure as I sit here that, had they not done it, they would've had all kinds of problems. This man, Forster, was a strong personality and he could see a problem coming, and he could go to one of the manufacturers, one of his employers, and advise them, you know, and try to influence them to do something that they might not be inclined to do. After all, you have to realize that these tanners basically were fellows with very limited backgrounds educationally and in other ways. Anybody running a tannery—let's say of 50 people—is probably somebody who came up through the tannery someplace. So this labor relations thing was a new problem that came up during his lifetime, and they weren't very well suited to deal with a lot of these things. But some labor relations situations that might turn up in tannery might have an effect some other place. So there was a great need for a leveling of policy. . . .

My recollection is that the union made financial demands that were considered excessive and couldn't be met. They wouldn't renegotiate. They were absolutely adamant about any reduction in those demands. Of course, what happened was—it was perfectly apparent to me, and I think everybody else at the time—that this was a union policy that had a definite Communist background to it. One of the points that I remember making in the argument of the National Labor Relations [Board] case that we later had was that there was to be later in the summer or early fall of that year a convention of the CIO, and I think it was to be in Cleveland, and the big question that was coming up was whether the International Fur & Leather Workers Union would be thrown out of the CIO. It's my belief that what they were trying to do here was to come up with a big wage settlement that might influence that whole thing out there. Now, I have no way of proving it. It is circumstantial evidence. . . .

I think they struck every association member. Sure, they claimed it was a lockout, and I think you can say in a way it was. I think—I don't think there's any question about it. The policy that was adopted was this: We can't operate this industry unless it's unionized. We are looking to have our people represented by a responsible union. This is a Communist union. After Taft–Hartley, you can't make us negotiate with you unless you file affidavits. Therefore this is the thing to do. If we can't negotiate with these people, we might just as well say, "All right. We'll have a lockout."

My own personal feeling was that it would bring about a settlement. Now, as you read these newspaper things, I think one of the things you'll see generally stated from the policy of the tanners—I wrote most of them—the continuous idea was: "We can't operate this industry without a union representing the people. We want a good responsible union that represents our people in a practical way and we can get along with anybody who can do it. We can't get along with this Communist bunch." It was as simple as that. . . .

There's no question that it generated into a lockout. But it didn't start as one. It simply drifted into one on the theory that this is the best way to force a settlement here. You could never have induced that group of businessmen generally to have a lockout and have everybody agree to it. It was, in effect, forced on them—the circumstances; they had no other alternative. It was my opinion that they were within their legal rights to do this and that, as a matter of strategy, it was a good policy to follow. It was my belief that it would get over soon. And I think it would've except for this Communist angle probably. I think it became a policy issue with that union. They had to have . . . a big wage settlement. I'm convinced that that was part of this whole thing. . . .

There are two things that I remember that I think are worthy of note, and that is this. A labor dispute of the magnitude of this one in this small community has a tendency to attract people to try and do something. One of the things that happened was that Carr or some of his people got in touch with one of the ministers of one of the leading churches, the Presbyterian Church over here, and he was going to do something. He was gonna try to intervene in some fashion or other. Whether he was going to preach on the subject—I think that's what he was planning to do. And he was going to try to influence the tanners to do business with this Communist union. And I remember a definite effort on the part of some of the tanners—some of the people, and myself included—to try and get to him, to try to influence him not to do that, because we didn't think he understood what this thing [was] all about. The thing is that every time something like that happened, it tended to delay the ultimate of it because this looked like some new and important event and it tended to influence these men to stick to Carr. . . .

That's one of the events that I remember which caused us a great deal of trouble. And we felt, and I feel now in retrospect, that it set back the ultimate settlement of this thing and getting these people back to work. . . .

The other—another incident that happened: there was a man here in town, older than I, who ran a textile mill here, and he was one of these opinionated people who felt that he carried a great deal of weight in the community and he had seen this thing going on and he wanted to stop it. And he thought he could influence it. And he got his nose into it. He set up a meeting that I attended at Amsterdam, at the hotel there. John Forster and I went to it. It was highly secret. I can't think who it was that we conferred with. This man set it up, and our—John Forster's and my—objective was to put out this bonfire, because every time some movement like this got started it was feed for Carr and his people. You could bet that anything like that would throw the thing back for a couple of weeks; it would take that length of time for it to burn out, see. And it was the same sort of thing as this minister's thing. He was gonna start something of the same kind. . . . The idea was to set up an effort on the part of the New York State mediation people to come in here and do something about it. We tried to keep people out of here, you see. We didn't need any mediation; nobody needed to talk with us about talking with the union people; we'd talk with anybody, except we wouldn't talk with this Carr bunch, you see.

I think . . . I don't know what your impression of this whole thing is, but you should not have the impression that this was ever an antiunion activity on the part of the Tanners Association. Because the view of the Tanners Association (and I think it was probably influenced by me a good deal, but it was the official view and it was thoroughly honest) [was] that you could not operate this industry without a union situation. . . . I know as a practical person that there are many people, and they may be right to some extent, that think they would be better off if they didn't have a union representing their people. I don't think there were many of those tanner employers who thought that. There may have been one or two. . . .

One of the problems here with this whole thing was to keep these people [association members] from defecting. Actually, some of these people were financially very weak. And the Tanners Association created a fund to keep some of these people alive. . . . Marshall McKay—now, he was financially weak and he defected. He's the only one, I think, that did. He defected and made some kind of contract with Carr—a sweetheart contract maybe, or some kind of an arrangement. . . . That would be an important incident in a way. Anytime anything like that happened, you could immediately feel it in all the developments. It was difficult for these people. [But] none of the other tanners, I think, had a great deal of respect for McKay. I don't think they trusted him, to tell you the truth . . . because they knew he was weak and they knew he might do exactly this. He didn't have any background really with the tanners much. He was new in the management situation. He was looked upon as a bookkeeper-type fellow who had gotten into the management. . . . This incident was really bad, because if he needed money they were doing things to help these people that were weak.

G. Levor & Company [a large local tanning firm] were never involved in this tanner's group either. But they sat on the sidelines and watched this whole thing happen. My recollection is that . . . that whole experience was a hard time for them because they had a not insignificant capacity for producing glove leather. And what were they to do in the time of this strike when their competitors who were in the Tanners Association [were] out of business? Were they going to try and capitalize on it? These people . . . were extremely high-type people and extremely loyal to people of their class. My recollection is . . . that they did not lift a hand to try to make it hard for the tanners. They were sympathetic with them because they had opposed Local 202 and they had fought Carr . . . in the 1930s. I do not believe that they ever did a thing to make it more difficult for their friends in the industry. . . .

I think what happened was that after the strike was really over and the people were back to work, the CIO came in here; and John

Maurillo was the guy who did it, who came. My recollection is that he was not a union representative of any particular union, but he represented the CIO. . . .[6] The CIO was recognized by the rest of the tanners. There was no election held. I think they just recognized them. They negotiated an agreement with them. I participated in it, I'm sure. . . . After that, the CIO turned the thing over to the Amalgamated [Clothing Workers of America]. . . . They had professional leadership. They'd send somebody in here that had had experience in some other place than just Fulton County. Whereas instead of negotiating with Clarence Carr and the local people who were just ordinary guys, now we had some professional-type people coming in here. Maurillo was one of them, and the people who came up here from the Amalgamated were good, sound, professional people that you could talk business with, you know. I've always looked upon the coming of the Amalgamated as a very definite and positive improvement in the whole situation. They took a very proper view of things and were a good influence here.

George H. Meyer   *"We were the only people who ever beat . . . the Fur Workers . . . through a strike," Meyer proudly boasts. A "technical tanner," his good friend Lydon Maider calls him. Meyer was a graduate of Pratt Institute, which offered a special course in tanning. He began his career as an employee of Du Pont but came to Gloversville to join the Liberty Dressing Company back in 1927. He ultimately became head of the firm. During the turbulent strike of 1949–1950, he was the president of the Fulton County Tanners Association and thus one of the more important strategists in the campaign to destroy Local 202. He is retired now, residing in Florida in the winter and on the shores of Sacandaga Lake, north of Gloversville, in the summer. We met on a warm and sunny day in mid-July 1988 at his house on Sacandaga Lake.*

Carr came down and threatened me one day. He came down there one day, one afternoon. I guess I wasn't feeling very good, very happy, that day. He came to me about 4:00 o'clock in the afternoon and said, "We got to get something settled about this beamhouse," and he mentioned whatever the problem was. "Well," I says, "That's no problem. What're you botherin' with that for? That's petty." "Matter of fact," he says, "if you don't settle this, I'll take 'em out tomorrow at 8:00 o'clock." "Can I depend on that?" "Well," he says, "let's talk about it." If they had, I would have taken his contract and I would have tore it right up and I would have said, "Now you'll never get another one." In this particular instance, I think it was after the war. It was after 1945. They were starting again to get raunchy. They were starting to get very, very—they were changing policy. They were goin' back to the old ways again. . . .

They became very "Russianized" during that time. We would go to negotiate a contract, and they were starting to send in their lieutenants, fellahs like George Pershing, Meyer Klig. . . .[7] They ran the show; they were professionals. They were gangsters. They'd stall until you couldn't accomplish anything. They put the demand out. The demand would be there. They'd keep talking about the demand, but they'd then start on other things. You know—get the Marines out of China—we had to discuss that in the meeting. I said, "What the hell does this have to do with . . ."

I was president of the Tanner's Association—1949. I don't think I came on until '49, '50. Well, leading up to this thing here, we started to have our negotiations for a new contract. Prior to that, every year, they appeared to be just as anxious as we were to operate for a period by extending the contract by mutual agreement for either 30 days or 60 days because we hadn't concluded negotiations. The reason we hadn't concluded negotiations—sometimes negotiations for a new contract would take nine months—it was all their fault. They couldn't ever decide to settle. They never would believe us. We would tell them something, and we insisted this is a fact and this is as far as we're gonna go, this is it. They wouldn't accept it; they wouldn't believe it. They always thought there was another drop in the lemon, that they could squeeze a little bit more out of the lemon. . . . They just killed time. They figured that they could wear down the tanners by just going on and on and get what they want. What they found out, I guess, I don't know, it didn't work with me. It didn't work. I'd just keep them there: "go ahead, talk."

I hated the Communists! I hated the Communists! Hell, I would have shot them on sight. Oh sure—and they [the other tannery owners] knew that. "Want a dirty job done? Get George. He's a bulldozer." They were stalling. Now, the thing was that we were trying to get this settled and we asked for an extension. For some reason or other, we would never get it, but we were always negotiating with someone from New York. Carr might be there, but it was the guy from New York who was carrying the ball. Just the same when [Harold] Pozefsky was there, he carried the ball.[8] We were really arguing with Pozefsky—or discussing with him, negotiating with Pozefsky. All the other fellahs were there as backdrop. They would sit there on the bench; there'd be 12 or 15 of them; they'd be falling asleep because they didn't know what the hell was going on, you know. The firing line would be the table, would be Pozefsky and Carr, or Pozefsky and somebody from New York. When the guy was from New York, then he'd be taking over, see? I'd be sitting on this side, and Maider would be over here—we changed off different places—this was the firing line, right here.

We said, "Every other year, we have an extension. Why don't you want to extend the contract beyond June 30th? We're going on vacation for the first two weeks, then we'll come back." We'd blame each other: "You didn't accept our terms." So we'd get right back to square one, that sort of thing. . . . We had the suspicion, Maider and I, that they [didn't] want to close. There's something in the air; there's something comin'. The union didn't want to settle. They didn't want to renew the contract. They wouldn't give an extension. This is the first time that they refused to extend the contract. We kept saying to each other, "Why don't they want to extend it?" . . .

We didn't have any ultimatum. We hadn't been given any ultimatum. All at once, we got a telephone call. "Do you know that the Independent Leather Company is on strike?" The moment the contract was over; what was it, the 30th of June? Well, anyway, whatever day it was, "What d'you mean the company is struck? Let's have a meeting right away." So we had a meeting. They discussed it. I said, "Look, men, this is just one thing. This is war! This is war! . . . You know what I want to do. You fellahs have to decide whether this is it or it isn't. This could be a long one. It could be tough because they're well organized, they're in there. They'll have every plant. They're gonna shut us up one by one; they're gonna beat us. There's only one thing to do: a strike against one of us is a strike against all of us. And that means a close up. We have no contract with them. The contract is over. We start all over new. We fight. It's win or lose. . . . It's gonna cost us a barrel of money, a barrel of money. We got to support each other; we got to do everything possible to beat this thing." Then Maider came in and said, "It's evident: they want to get rid of John Forster; that's one reason why they didn't renew the contract. They wanted to be out; they wanted to strike. They wanted to destroy us one by one, and they have to get him outa' the picture. And they want to bust the association. If they put a break in the line and half the people quit and the other half don't want to quit, one by one, the association will crumble." So we decided the next morning; we would close the plants—every one. A strike against one is a strike against all.

I thought it would be [a] long [fight] because they had a very tight-knit organization; they were fully organized. They had everybody in the plants that was a union member; they had complete control of the membership. And when they had a meeting, they knew just how to run it. They'd meet in the Eagle's Hall, and the lieutenants were scattered in the hall and if anybody came up with any opposition— Ho ho, they'd go right after that guy. "Hey! You want to get thrown out?" They shut him up. In other words, they always had this station. I got the picture from my lieutenants, and they could absolutely control the men. They got what they wanted; they always had a show of hands. No matter what they wanted, the hands always showed yes. They never had any organized opposition.

I had very many problems. I had a lot of problems keeping them [association members] together. We had to change diapers several times. Some of them wanted to give in, not right at the beginning, but after four or five months. I used to tell the other standbys, "Well, I had to change another diaper today." . . . There was one outfit that we supported in order not to have them thrown out. You see, we had to support—we paid their payroll, we paid their rent. . . .

[Marshall McKay, of Teetz-McKay Leather]—we could tell by his attitude—he wouldn't play along if we did support him. I even had the head of the Tanners Council go there and have a long talk with him, and he came out and he said, "George, I don't think we can hold him."[9] We promised him support. We offered him support. We even pleaded with him. We said, "Don't do it because it's breaking the chain; the chain is no stronger than the weakest link, and don't be the weak link in the chain." But it didn't work and we lost him. But he didn't hurt anybody else particularly. We had a couple of, two or three, places where the diapers had to be changed. . . . They got their check. They got their check every week.

They [the union] tried all kinds of tricks. They tried to get the ministers to negotiate. . . . The superintendent of schools had a meeting with me one night, a long meeting, begging me to stop the strike. They thought he could have an influence, I guess, and he was a friend of mine. They just tried everything. And the Chamber of Commerce, and they were headed by the president of the silk mills, all the big wheels in the city, and they called me in on the carpet and they wanted me to stop the strike. . . .

The way they [the union leaders] got them [the workers] to vote "no union," Bernie Woolis, he brought—just like platoons—he brought them in to the labor rooms.[10] Each had a shot of whiskey, then they went down and voted, see? "Vote no union! We're gonna beat them! Vote no union!" Oh, sure, they didn't give up any affiliation. They were just told to vote that way and like a bunch of sheep, they did. And they had a shot of liquor to help 'em. . . . Well, yes. He [Clarence Carr] had a following, and he held them together because they were his boys. He was one of the boys. He went hunting with them and fishing with them, and he staked skins with them and he would go down in the beamhouse and talk for them, and that. They looked to him as a big brother. I give him that, I give him that. But when it came to a lot of other things, he was just a . . . he was radical. He was wild.

There was no union; they put themselves right out of business. Then we went and we talked with the CIO and we talked with the [AFL]. We said, "Look, we're not antiunion. We just want some people that we can talk with." We gave the [AFL] guy the real third degree. We met him down in Albany, Jack Forster and myself, and we told him Jack Forster was an ex-[AFL] man in the Carpenter's Union. And this fellah, I guess, was in the butcher's union, see? We talked with him like a dutch uncle, and we said, "Look, we'll cooperate with this business. We aren't anti-union; we want a union. The reason that we want a union is our own self-protection. We don't want people undercutting us and getting this and taking advantage of labor," and that sort of thing. "Listen, we're grown up. We've had a union—a lousy one. Now, for once, we want a good union and see if we can't get along with them. We'll work with the union." So they came in, they voted for that, they voted against them, 540: no unions.[11]

[The CIO] . . . well, they finally took it over, they finally took it over. . . . We had our own union. We wound up with our own union. Sure. They called it a company union, but—it was a company union—I negotiated with them just like negotiating with the other fellahs. But we were fair. We never had a walkout. We never had a strike; we never had a fight with them. We worked with them; we cooperated.

Maybe Lydon Maider said this to you—we discussed this several times—"George," he said, "they'll never be as strong again. . . . In the memory of all these workers, this industry, and this city and the town and everything else, they'll never forget this because it was a very, very bitter experience." It was a very costly experience. It hurt a lot of people. No question about it. If I had all the money that we spent, I would be very nice. But, look, somebody had to win and somebody had to lose. It was a fight to the finish. It was such a determination on the part of the manufacturers, they put up such an example of staying power, of unity, that he said, "I don't think they'll ever try to break in again and try and do that. Another thing is, they would never hold 'em because they would always look back and say, 'Look, they beat us, they beat us, they can hold out, they can hold out forever.' Therefore," he said, "I think its gonna bring labor peace; it's gonna clean up the whole area." And it did. The whole thing changed. The whole picture changed.

[The people that replaced Carr], well, they were better men, they were fairer, and I would say they were better educated in the sense of their relationship; they were more realistic. They weren't schooled in this background of firebrand Communism. They didn't sit in the rooms with these racketeers. It was a different generation. It was a different bunch of men. Those people—those fellahs there—they were good workers; they were respected by the manufacturers. But these other people didn't have their respect. They were just a bunch of crud.

John Sutliff   *Respected for his "reasonable" and "business-like" approach to labor–management relations by local employers yet strongly disliked by many workers, Sutliff remains, even today, a controversial labor leader in the community. From the late 1930s and through the early 1950s, he was a major antagonist of Local 202's left-wing leaders. During the early months of the 1949/50 strike, as a member of the union's general executive board, he was "running, probably controlling, about a third of their strike." In the last few months of the strike, however, he abandoned Local 202 and the Independent and charted his own course, helping to create the right-wing CIO United Tannery Workers Union of Fulton County. When I spoke to him in January 1987, he was living in retirement in Gloversville.*

Jesus Christ, they sat right down and bragged about it! Clarence Carr would get right up and tell you—his expression was . . . "I don't try to tell you what to be, but I *am* a Communist." He said it. Many times right in the meetings. . . . And I have to say this literally and honestly, of all the years I worked with Clarence—and I done a lot of things for him, and many things, eventually, against him—at no goddamn time did that man ever approach me to join the Communist Party! But he told me and told people right in the room, "Yes, I am a Communist." In fact, he run on the Communist ticket one time.[12]

Clarence Carr said it, and he said it from right up. Stayed one all the way up through. He was born in Johnstown as far as I know. I mean, he lived in Johnstown. His first wife and him lived in Johnstown. He worked in various tanneries. I never personally dug into his background as far as to find out, well, how the hell, where he got involved in the Communist Party or anything. When we formed our first union and he became the president—we went from 1933 until 1949—Clarence Carr was right in there. He had maybe one or two occasions where somebody ran against him for the presidency. He had it pretty much wrapped up, and the membership ran from—like I said—three thousand and it dwindled down to about, oh, a couple of thousand. But no opposition.

But Clarence Carr, back in the late thirties, started to manipulate his friends, including me and people in the organization. He started to manipulate all of us to join International Fur & Leather [Workers Union]. But they were Commies. . . . Then in the forties, I don't know, '41, '42, or '43—something like that—they jumped into Local 202.[13] Well, there was about a five-year period there that frankly he was hitting us on the head to join Local 202. . . . About a half dozen of us guys . . . fought them not to affiliate. We didn't want International Fur & Leather because of its communistic background and its way of going. . . . See, what they were doing at that time, we'd have a membership meeting, and at that time we'd have maybe a hundred people to a meeting. They'd take over the goddamned meeting. And if we got up and said 20 words, we were out of order. They got up and said 2,500 words, they were alright. Jesus Christ, they were peddling the bullshit everywhere it went, and if one of our guys got up and tried any of this shit—bang, down he'd go!

We set up a goddamned group within the group to fight them in meetings so that we'd get the floor and be able to say what we wanted to say. So we fought them during the late thirties, early forties, before the affiliation of 202, we fought them not to affiliate. We even brought the priest in here, Father English, and had him speak in the Eagles Club down here. We beat 'em three, four times. But like they said, the Commies'll get you sooner or later. And I guess they even proved it to me eventually. . . .

It wasn't only a short time thereafter when we ran into that '49 strike. Anyway, what they were out to do, and they helped them to do it—this International group—they picked two plants here. That strike didn't need to happen. But that was preplanned by the International, and this was one of the reasons why I was against affiliating in the first place. Well, they just successfully swung it by manipulation. They rigged the goddamned thing up so that there was a strike, and they sucked the employers and give them the business. So the employers took a position: they told the negotiators, "If ya' strike one, you strike us all." The union told our people, "This is not true. We'll get the support. . . ." Blah, blah, blah. And we had about, I don't know, eight [to] ten thousand dollars left; they had drained the goddamned treasury something terrible, the local people here—Carr and the group. We were with International Fur & Leather. But you see, what they did, and this went over the heads of, well, I'd say probably even me at the time: the first thing you know, he's [Carr] telling the people that if we had a strike, International Fur & Leather is gonna support us. Follow me? And therefore we can't lose. But we're only gonna strike one plant. They told us who. We'll support them; we'll all keep on working, and we'll lick this goddamned [Tanners] Association. Well, that was the biggest goddamned bunch of trumped up lies that I ever heard in my life. They pulled that strike on Independent Leather like this. And it wasn't within 24 hours and I knew the whole goddamned industry was going down. I could see it. . . .

The tanners . . . hired a lawyer in Amsterdam. They were desperately trying to set up the Textile Workers [Union of America] to come in and raid. They did, well, everything in the goddamned book, really. They weren't no angels. But this fight went on and on and on, and the only ones that was really getting screwed was the workers; I mean, hey, you couldn't sell it! They wouldn't vote Textile, which I wouldn't myself. I helped them beat the Textile.

They got an election order here with the [International] Fur & Leather off the ballot. Local 202 was off.[14] So frankly what happened at that point, the minute they did that, if you didn't vote Textile, you didn't have any other place to go. . . . So, what I wanted the workers to understand, but they didn't understand, the ones I could get ahold of and the fellahs that I knew. I said, "Tell them that it's fine to vote 'no union' and I don't want the goddamned Textile either. But if we vote 'no union,' I wanted them to understand that they just don't have any union and the only thing we have if we vote 'no union' is that after the vote is counted, and everything else, then we'll get a group together and we don't have Clarence Carr in there . . . and we don't have this one and we don't have that one trying to negotiate with these employers." . . .

So when we started talking this way, this is when—as I said, I couldn't convince them, nobody could convince them—so this is when there was a small group of about ten guys and myself. We got together, talked it over, and we said, "How in hell? We gotta get an escape route." So, in the meantime, I had had a call from a lawyer in Amsterdam. I knew damned well he worked for the Tanners [Association]. He was employed by them; they were puttin' money down there. The minute I heard the setup, I says, "No way. I don't want no part of it." They had a meeting right here in Gloversville; some of the guys got some dough, you know. I said, "Bullshit to you guys. I don't want no part of him." I said, "There's a guy working with him that works for the CIO as a national organizer." I said, "Him, I want to talk to."

So we got this guy [Peter Aversa]. . . .[15] I talked to him a couple of times and I said, "Can you do this and this and this and this?" He said, "I don't know. I can try." That was when [James B.] Carey and [Philip] Murray headed up CIO. I said, "Pete, I think we can handle them locally here with a committee providing [that] we can get a little leverage here somehow." And he said, "What kind of leverage do you need?" I said, "There's an unorganized plant in town. Now I've heard all this bullshit about scabs, charters, what have you. . . . Now if they grant a charter to this plant that we organize, then what stops that plant, after it gets its charter, what stops that from actually signing up the rest of the guys? And plant by plant, we get recognition from the employer on a recognized basis. What stops them from actually granting us an escape on their charter?" "Well," he says, "let me get back to you in a couple of days."

So he left and came back. He said, "If you can get me this and this and this, we'll see what we can do." So what we set was a couple guys on a committee. They flew into Philadelphia. They wanted me to go. I said no. But they flew into Philadelphia. They got a hold of Murray and Allan Haywood, and they agreed to give us the charter providing we had the unorganized plant.[16]

We organized the plant overnight. We got a charter. We released it publicly: "We took the plant away from the Fur & Leather today." We did all this, and the goddamned workers in that plant vote tomorrow to go back into the Fur & Leather! So we had an organization one day; it was in the newspaper release. The next day, Jesus Christ, they disaffiliated with us, went back with them. And the third day, we had 'em back in and had them sign the charter and elect officers. We had a local. And from that time on after we once got that damned local (it was the Bradt Tannery down here), after we once got the local and got it set up, [of] course International Fur & Leather, Woolis, well, everybody in the goldbrickin' country said we were strikebreakers and we were scabs and we were this and we were that. This is the way we busted it up.

Harold R. Taylor   *"To me, this is ancient history. Well, I haven't thought about it in so many years. I haven't given it much thought." Taylor is a man who lives in the present and clearly enjoys his retirement immensely, although he still visits "the boys" at the mill once in a while. Back in 1949/50, he helped Sutliff build the foundations of the United Tannery Workers Union* *but was shoved aside in the internal politics of the new union. I interviewed him at his home in Gloversville in June 1987. His story is one of compromise and expediency, but also of regret. Ironically, Taylor looks back with nostalgia at the older local he helped bury, and for its Communist head, Clarence Carr, he has only praise.*

Well, I joined [Local] 202 about 1946. I was about 21. I just got out of the service. . . . I was a member of 202, Clarence Carr's union, but I had no involvement in their politics whatsoever. In the meetings I went to—it was about our own little problems right here, labor problems, working problems. As far as national politics, no, no.

I think there was a law against having too much of a closed shop, but there was an unwritten law that you better, you know. That's the way it was. It didn't make no difference to me. In those days, union dues were a couple of bucks a month. It didn't amount to that much money. . . . [My father] he was under the same devil-may-care type of thing that I was. He joined the unions just to get the work, that's all.

[Carr] was a good man, he was an honest sincere man, and he was very dedicated to the men under him, his workers. And right off the bat, I mean, if you was in this little place and you had problems in the shop, that was always arisin' every day in some shop along the line where the boss tried to put somethin' over on the worker or the worker thought the boss was tryin' to put somethin' over him. Everything would stop. Oh my god! Every time you got mad [you'd have a wildcat strike]. Most anything would lead [to a strike]. If the boss looked at you wrong, or if he cussed at you. I remember one time we had a wildcat strike against Ernie Stern [general manager of the Bradt Tannery] because he talked so dirty and nasty in front of the girls in the office. We just got together as a group and went up and said, "That's it, we're all gone." He'd swear a little bit, and cuss a little bit more, but then he'd give in. . . . If they come down and they said "do this" or "hurry up" more or less of a push-push-push, see, and they wanted you to hurry up—this is what most of it happened over. They wanted to speed you up, speed you up. And you would say, "Wait a minute, you're going full blast now; if you want to speed up, more money." If you mention more money, no, no, no. Well, then, you'd say, "Alright, if that's the way it is, we'll have a strike." So you go on strike.

I mean we'd have these little wildcat strikes, and it wasn't over a half an hour [before] Clarence Carr would be there to fight for you, to straighten it out. . . . You might lose two or three hours, and that would be it. You'd go back to work. That's the kind of guy he was. He was always right there, behind his men.

Well, I had just gotten married in February of '49. Come June they called a strike, and I was working at the time for . . . Martin-Deischel. That was a long, long strike. And what few dollars that I had, my wife and I went through that. Of course, what kept us going was that she was working a little bit, and not making too much money. But we couldn't get no unemployment insurance; we couldn't get anything in those days to help. And the union went busted; they couldn't help you either, 'cause it was a local—202 was a local union. They didn't have a great deal of backing [from the International]. Being [that you were] young and single, or just married, they figured well you could go out and get yourself a job and do anything you want to do. After a while, after a period of six months, then I did go get a job. I think that was Bradt Tanning Company.

You know, you have this type of thing. After everything goes on for a period of time, it hurts everybody, not just the workers. . . . There was a lot of support for the workers. Of course, too, you want to remember back in those days they had little stores on the corners where you could go into the store and you could charge your groceries. It's not like it is today if you don't go in with the green stuff you don't get nothin'. In those days, I mean, a lot of people just ran up bills and bills and bills. And so the small man carried 'em for as long as he could. And this is what helped the striker. Today, nowhere in God's world this would happen. If you didn't get your unemployment insurance today, you'd be licked. You couldn't go nine months. . . .

So at that particular time, all the rest of the men from 202, a lot of the staunch workers, and the old-timers, they were going broke and losing their homes and mortgaging them. They were blowing what money, what few dollars, they had. It got to the point where it wasn't good for the community, really, 'cause you had all these workers just walking the streets. So they came—a group of them—came down to Bradt's [Tannery]. They wanted to know if we would try to start a little union there because then we wouldn't be breaking anything; then they would more or less join in on us. This is where [Local] 1712 came in. So, there was three or four other guys and myself. They were older men than I was. [John Sutliff] was one of the instigators coming to us. He did not work there. He was one of the group that was dissatisfied. He came to us to see if we would get together to form a union, which we did—because we could see the handwriting on the wall. In fact, most of us were all ex-members of 202, but we were just lucky enough to go get jobs. This is how it was, because everybody that worked in the mill in those days was a member of 202. But we seen the handwriting on the wall, so then we joined our own union and affiliated with 1712 somehow.

It became apparent to us that these people just were not gonna deal with Clarence Carr. Of course, that was going back to the time when everybody was a Communist that disagreed . . . which is not necessarily so. I'll say one thing personally for the man: he was a good man. And he was out for the workin' man. I didn't have nothin' against Clarence Carr. Years afterwards I got out of the leather business—oh, in the fifties I got out of it—and I went to work in the hardware business, and then I owned my own hardware store. And through the years he done business with me, when he was living. And we got along very well. No, there were no bitter feelings whatsoever. And Clarence Carr's right-hand man, Charlie Hildreth, him and I are very friendly right today. Well, he was secretary, second in command in 202. . . .

I thought it was a good idea [to start another union] because I had suffered too. I had gone—as a young fellow—I had gone many weekends without being able to go out and buy a beer and be one of the gang, and I lost my car. We did have a home—we moved in with my in-laws. So how would you actually feel? You'd want to have it settled and get it over with, and get out on your own. I just felt, I had just come through a war and we were young veterans and we weren't Communist, by no means. We were just out there trying to make a decent wage, to get a decent dollar. For God's sake, I made more money in the Army than I made in comin' home. . . .

Older men were dyed-in-the-wool 202. The 202 members were men of my father's age. The younger men, like myself, we were more or less the guys—the fellows who just got out of the war—[who] took the bull by the horns and changed things around a little bit. The older men didn't do this so much; I'm talking about the fellows that were 40, 45, 50 years old at that time. They were more or less hanging in there with Clarence Carr. . . . I would dare say that the guys . . . under 35 . . . were the instigators of this whole 1712 thing. Anybody any older, well, some of these old guys had been there for years and they had saved a few bucks; it didn't bother them a bit, you know.

The [Tanners] Association was very strong at that time against them [202]. They wanted to get rid of the unions. They didn't give a damn whether Carr was a Communist or a Socialist, or whatever he was. Besides that, at that particular time, you'd ask them the difference what was a Communist, what was a Socialist, and nobody would know the difference. . . . They were hurting, too. They had made their brags what they would do—this and do that—but not for Carr. So if you got somebody else in here, well, where's their argument? They gotta start negotiatin'. They lost their argument. They couldn't come out and start hollerin' Communism all the time. Then, who knows—maybe 1712 had more Communists in there than anything else had, who knows. . . .

Well, after it got off the ground, we had an election. And, of course, we had to have an election of officers. They elected a president, vice president, secretary, treasurer, and so on and so forth. That was a temporary type thing in order to get a charter, to get it going. . . . Of course, the fellows that were elected first, they got washed out because they had the big Karg mill. This is where the other union developed, in there. But we were just a little go-between in there. That's all we were. They had hundreds and hundreds of people working there, and John Sutliff was in that one. So they washed out all the little guys that helped them in the first place. . . . Now, what was happening, 202—and some of the hardheads of 202 weren't standing still, you know—they'd just as soon go bang heads as not. But what the three or four of us went and done, we went out and put our name[s] out there so to give them some heads to bang. But after we went and did this, and after it was all settled—of course, fortunately enough, none of us got banged around, but we were there—we were exposed to 'em. Then, all these people from Karg's [Tannery]—John Sutliff was one, and I don't care too much for that man, either, to be honest with you—went and pushed us right out. We had nothin' to say, nothin' to do, anymore. And that's the way that he operated all those years that he was there. . . . Why did he do it? Who knows why. He just wanted power, I guess. He brought in the people from Karg's. Then you see all your presidents and your vice presidents and your officers right down the list are all Karg men, after that. Because they were hiring three or four hundred people where everybody else had maybe forty [or] fifty men in their shops. So they were big.

[Under 1712] Sutliff went to the boss. He got the boss's side, and that's as far as he would go. That's the kind of guy he was. Some of the [gripes] never got resolved. He never come to the men. . . . He was on the boss's side. I think he was paid off by 'em. Anyway, that's the kind of guy he was. I just couldn't see it that way, and neither could anybody else, because they figured they had no protection from him. They were sold out. I never heard any regrets about [abandoning 202]. They had to go somewhere. But there was an awful lot of regrets about puttin' John Sutliff in there for so many years, I know.

It was the younger men from the war changed this thing around a little bit. I don't know. Easy going and . . . they all wanted something. After the strike, they all wanted something; years after that, they didn't have the guts to say, "Well, this is it, and we're gonna fight for it—again." And it just never happened. They never got any big lump sum. They got piecemeal—crumbs. Over the years, that's what they've had, crumbs.

THE SHOP-FLOOR DIMENSION
OF UNION RIVALRY:
The Case of Westinghouse in the 1950s

MARK MCCOLLOCH

In the past 25 years, a good deal of outstanding labor history has been written about workers in the United States, from the American Revolution through World War II. Yet, most post-1945 labor history is an afterthought, consisting of sweeping generalizations, spiced with a bit of anecdotal evidence. Nowhere is this more true than for shop-floor issues. There, writers have fallen into one of two extreme schools: for the first, the shop floor in the union–personnel department era has become a harmonious, cooperative place; the other view is that, in return for higher wages and better fringe benefits, workers have relinquished control of the shop floor to a resurgent management.[1]

Yet, the shop floor has remained an arena of intense struggle. Workers spend almost half their waking lives there. What occurs there, moreover, affects most other aspects of their lives, including their health, standard of living, and financial security. This essay examines shop-floor issues at Westinghouse Electric Corporation in the 1950s, when it was the number two producer in the rapidly expanding electrical manufacturing industry.

Shop-floor issues intersect here with union ideology, as Westinghouse was the scene of intense interunion rivalry in the 1950s. The

United Electrical, Radio & Machine Workers of America (UE), founded in 1936, had succeeded in organizing a large majority of Westinghouse's production workers by the 1940s. It signed its first national contract with the firm in 1941 and substantially improved its contracts through 1948, a process that included a five-month strike in 1946. In late 1949, a long-smoldering left–right division within the UE resulted in a split and the formation of a right-wing dual union, the International Union of Electrical Workers (IUE).[2]

National Labor Relations Board (NLRB) representation elections were held at most Westinghouse plants in May 1950, amid an all-out anti-UE campaign involving the CIO leadership, governmental bodies such as the FBI and HUAC, sections of the Catholic Church, the electrical corporations, and the media. Very close vote totals resulted. Since the winner took all in each plant, the UE lost representation rights for 73 percent of the workers to the IUE. A significant minority of workers became nonunion or joined the International Brotherhood of Electrical Workers (IBEW). For the remainder of the decade the battle would continue, and the UE would be gradually reduced to representing less than 20 percent of the firm's production workers.

Most previous writers who have dealt with the fight between the UE and the IUE and its allies in the 1950s have ignored its shop-floor dimensions. The majority of those who have discussed the issue, regardless of their diverse political perspectives, essentially have agreed: there was very little difference between the functioning of the two unions on the shop floor or in collective bargaining.[3]

This essay will address just two of the many shop-floor issues at dispute in Westinghouse in the 1950s: seniority and incentive provisions and practices. It will examine how these changed over the decade and what role the major unions played in those changes. These two examples will illustrate the changing nature of shop-floor life and the variety of approaches to these questions taken by two very different unions.

The UE and the IUE approached these two issues from divergent conceptions of the role of unions in the United States. While the UE's enemies, such as IUE President James B. Carey, described it as "a Communist organization masquerading as a labor organization,"[4] there are very few people alive who are able to definitively depict the relationship of the leadership of the UE to the Communist Party in the 1936–1950 period. Clearly, however, some of the key leaders of the UE had close links to the CPUSA. By 1951, almost none of the UE heads had formal or close informal ties to the CP. What the UE always did have, however, was an implicit, sometimes made explicit, anticapitalist thrust. Its leadership believed that there *was* a working class and a "corporate class, striving relentlessly for increased productivity and higher profits." As a result, "intolerable burdens are placed upon workers in the shops. Severe economic strain is inflicted upon working class families."[5] The government was firmly on the side of the corporations in this class struggle. "The Truman administration and both parties, while putting on a big show of supposed differences, are thoroughly united in doing the job of big business against the American people."[6]

Beyond ardent anticommunism, it is difficult to pin down the ideology of the IUE in the 1950s. In addition to the naked personal ambition that would plague the IUE in this period, Carey and other IUE leaders seem to have seen themselves as representatives of an interest group, organized labor, in a pluralist, capitalistic society. While they hoped for a liberal brand of capitalism, wanted a "bigger share" for workers, and frequently tried to convince corporate officials that unions and companies shared common goals, capitalism was not only challenged but was often explicitly defended. The class struggle was rejected: "We are the best friends of industry, commerce and businessmen," argued the IUE, "for they cannot prosper if workers are unable to buy the goods on the shelf."[7] This required some concessions from management: "We do not want security without freedom, but we cannot have freedom without security."[8] Security also required expenditures by workers. The Republican Party was criticized in 1953 for "slashing defense appropriations to fulfill reckless campaign promises."[9]

Most of the UE staff members of the 1950s were men and women who came into political activity in the radical mass movements of the 1930s. Their political personalities had been shaped by these struggles. The IUE staff tended to be younger and less influenced by the "movement" atmosphere of the 1930s and 1940s. Finally, IUE staffers were substantially higher paid than those of the UE, often a factor in easing one's adjustment to the existing order.

Workers at Westinghouse toiled, as was the case at many manufacturing firms, under two different payment systems, daywork or incentive/piecework. Under daywork, employees received a set rate for each hour they labored; under incentive systems workers were, in part, paid by the amount or "pieces" that they produced. Usually, this meant a low "base rate," received regardless of output, and a bonus or incentive payment for each additional piece produced above a certain target, or "100 percent." Sometimes, the output of a number of workers was pooled and a "group incentive" rate was used.

Westinghouse, using efficiency experts, conducted "time studies" of incentive jobs to see how long it "should" take a worker to perform a certain job. It then set the "rate" with the "100 percent" and the amount paid per additional piece becoming a "recorded value." From the point of view of workers, a rate might be too "tight," that is, require too much speed and effort to achieve; or, from management's point of view, it might be too "loose," allowing workers to make a high wage without greatly increasing work pace.

A majority of the production workers at Westinghouse were paid on a piecework basis as early as the 1920s. During the 1930s the fledgling UE was critical of incentive systems but unable to mount the all-out fight necessary to abolish it. Instead, the union struggled to stop wage cuts and minimize abuse of the system.[10] During World War II, faced with government resistance to wage gains made by any other method than incentive plans and placing a high political priority on boosting production for the antifascist effort, the UE temporarily moved toward the qualified endorsement of piecework and concentrated on establishing systematic protections for workers.[11] Because of the tight labor market and juicy cost-plus government contracts, according to a recent historian, "piece-work prices were never higher nor management supervision more lax than during World War Two."[12]

Following the war, Westinghouse, like many other corporations, began to launch major attacks on incentive rates. The union defended the protections and the "loose" rates it had won. The period from 1946 to 1949 might be called a standoff on this issue, as workers relied on their contractual protections and their individual ingenuity to resist attempts to slash rates and speed them up.[13] The UE took an explicit stance against productivity drives by government and management, arguing that "corporations have hogged all the benefits of such increased production . . . making all technical improvements a curse rather than a blessing to the vast majority."[14]

By 1948, the UE had codified a formidable set of protections into its Westinghouse contract. Temporary or estimated rates, usually very loose, had to be established promptly on any new job. The 1948 contract stipulated, "they will become recorded values not later than 12 months from the date item repeats on a new manufacturing order."[15] The values could only be changed when a clerical error had been made or there was a change in method. Even then "only that portion of the value affected by the change will be adjusted."[16] If the workers felt a value was too tight it could be "handled in accordance with established local grievance procedure."[17] This usually meant that workers could at least obtain a new time study.

If Westinghouse wished to switch the payment method of any group of workers—daywork, incentive, or group incentive—the matter had to be negotiated locally first. While working on a new job, an incentive worker would receive either the new temporary rate or his/her old rate, whichever was higher. Finally, while the corporation wished to eliminate the widespread practice whereby workers created large "banks" of completed but unsubmitted incentive work or chits, it obtained only an acknowledgment that the issue would be "given serious consideration by Locals and local management."[18]

The 1949 split and the resulting six-month period of uncertainty over representation rights gave Westinghouse an excellent opportunity to attack these contractual protections. The IUE, Westinghouse, and the NLRB all supported a delay in the representation elections until the expiration of the UE contract. Once it had expired, the corporation stepped up its pressure on local wage rates. Although often weakened by the internal divisions Westinghouse workers resisted these efforts. At its huge turbine plant in Lester, Pennsylvania, Westinghouse began cutting rates and speeding up workers and proposed to unilaterally put its 1950 bargaining proposal into effect until a new contract was reached. UE Local 107 called for no interim changes, and its 6,500 members struck over the issue.[19] Rates were cut at the IUE's stronghold in Mansfield, Ohio, where workers did not "want to stick their necks out" in the existing climate of red-baiting and interunion rivalry.[20] In Springfield, Massachusetts, the company sent workers a letter denouncing their "exorbitantly high wage incentives."[21] In its Cleveland lamp plants, the company cut rates in the foundry and in the florescent assembly and ballast lines. Workers on group incentive tasks who previously earned 135–160 percent of their base rate had no incentive takeout.[22] At Newark, New Jersey, coil winders were producing 50 percent more than they had a year before but earning only slightly more, owing to wage cuts. A walkout of 100 UE workers there brought drastic change and a takeout of 180 percent the following week.[23]

Once the representation elections were over, in June 1950, the workers, now divided into two main unions, faced a harsh set of company take-away demands. Not all would be immediately achieved, but they foreshadowed Westinghouse's goals later in the decade. Refusing the UE demand to reinstate the old contract now that representation rights were settled,[24] Westinghouse called for a free hand to conduct time studies of any job (incentive or daywork) at any time. Time-study methods could include the use of photographs and movie cameras.

Workers were to give a newly studied job rate a "fair trial" before any grievances were filed.[25] Finally, the corporation demanded a contractual clause stating that increased "productivity" was a joint goal.[26]

On July 19, 1950, the IUE announced a 90-day partial contract with Westinghouse that was primarily designed to provide it with a dues check-off for the plants it had won. In April, the IUE's Westinghouse conference board had formulated a 19-point contractual program including strong incentive protections, but the July agreement did not mention these.[27] The UE continued to oppose the take-away demands, even when the company retreated a bit, stipulating that "cameras will not be used to determine established time values."[28] It warned that "a motion picture camera in the hands of Westinghouse is the same as a labor spy"[29] and noted that it had "refused to have anything to do with" Westinghouse's proposal for a productivity clause.[30]

In early October 1950, the IUE signed its first full contract with Westinghouse. The result was a step backward for workers, even if not a total surrender. The contract added a clause giving management the right of "establishing time values for wage payment purposes by the following methods: by time study, from formula or data, by comparison or by estimate." Another contract addition opened a door to Westinghouse when it allowed a time study on an entire job when one element was changed, even though such a study was not supposed to change the time value on the unchanged aspects of the job. The IUE contract also gave up the protective clause explicitly allowing grievances over these measures. On the other hand, many of the old UE contract protections, such as the ban on cameras, were retained.[31]

On November 1, 1950, the UE signed its contract with Westinghouse.[32] In some areas where the IUE contract had retreated, the UE also lost some ground. Yet, instead of simply dropping the explicit grievance statement, the UE contract changed it to "questions that arise concerning the values, including low values[,] will be handled in accordance with the established grievance procedure."[33] The right to check an overall value when one component was changed was conceded, but advance notification was required and only a general check, not a detailed study, could be made. Moreover, it could not be used to set a new time value.[34]

Westinghouse and its workers continued to skirmish over incentive rates, pace, and protections for the next four years. Resistance varied not only by union but by individual plant. Within the IUE, conditions were probably best at the huge East Pittsburgh plant, with its militant traditions and a large, well-organized group looking for an opportunity to return to the UE. There were scores of strikes over incentive issues at the plant, with results as varied as the circumstances involved. Average incentive takeout, which remained a fairly high 153 percent, may have actually risen until the end of the Korean War boom.[35] Westinghouse, however, resisted adding any additional sums to the incentive component of wage increases until 1954. As base rates rose, this had the impact of lessening the differential enjoyed by incentive workers. Thus, by mid-1952, a Class 4 incentive worker at the plant, with a minimum guarantee of 1.39\frac{1}{2}$, would gross only 1.92\frac{1}{2}$ for a takeout of 150 percent. This situation was still better than that at many other IUE plants. At Lima, Ohio, for example, an incentive worker with 150 percent production boosted his/her wages by only 25 percent.[36]

At most other IUE locations the situation was much worse. At the huge plant in Cheektowaga, New York, the IUE supplement, signed in October 1950, allowed Westinghouse to make time studies of all workers in the plant and agreed that "the union will cooperate to this end."[37] Those who could not keep up with the quotas would be assigned to lower grade jobs.[38]

At the plant in Sharon, Pennsylvania, values were cut on hundreds of jobs in 1951, resulting in the reduction of incentive earnings by 12–30 percent. When the workers resisted these cuts, Westinghouse ordered disciplinary furloughs for 4,500 workers and threatened to close the plant.[39] After a three-week lockout, IUE President James B. Carey arranged a settlement that marked a significant setback for the workers.[40]

At the Lima plant, Westinghouse instituted a new time-study procedure in October 1952. Under the old system, if the time-study man thought a worker was slacking off, the study would be halted and redone. Now, the efficiency expert could factor in a calculation to achieve an "ideal" pace. Westinghouse also claimed that any time an incentive group fell substantially below its peak output, the group was on a slowdown and could be disciplined. The local union argued that any effort over "100 percent" was voluntary and not subject to discipline.[41]

The unorganized newly opened plants and, in some cases, the 16,000 workers represented by the IBEW and other unions further undermined conditions. At the still-unorganized factory in Columbus, Ohio, Westinghouse used film cameras to set time values, which averaged 63 cents behind comparable jobs at the parent Mansfield plant. In Little Rock, Arkansas, IBEW Local 1136 had a contract calling for measured daywork with stiff quotas. This system of payment established a fixed daily output quota but provided no incentive bonuses. Discipline followed if a worker did not reach the quota. Workers there started at 64 cents an hour as late as 1952.[42]

Attacks continued on incentive protections at UE plants. At the union's stronghold in Lester, Pennsylvania, the combination of local militancy and strong support from the UE national office brought very high rates. For each incentive classification, the guaranteed rates at Lester ranged from 8 to 33 percent higher than at East Pittsburgh, which in turn averaged about 5 percent above the average for the other IUE locations.[43] At the Nuttall plant in Pittsburgh, a strike of 145 days was waged in 1952, in part over Westinghouse's attempt to cut time values on operations with temporary values. The settlement continued the ban on new time studies in most cases but allowed the timing of a handful of highly disputed operations.[44]

At its lamp plant in Trenton, New Jersey, where 90 percent of the workers were women and the IUE had a substantial base of support, Westinghouse instituted new quotas in 1952 that were 75 percent higher than in the past. It fired Carmela La Porte, a hand winder with six years of experience, for failing to meet the quota and threatened to move the plant to Little Rock if the UE resisted. Westinghouse then locked the workers out when the UE failed to accept this. A settlement was reached in April, reinstating the fired worker and agreeing to submit the new rates to arbitration.[45]

The national contracts signed by the UE and IUE in this period largely reflected a continuation of the positions won or lost in the 1950 agreements. The main improvement won by the UE in its 1953 contract was that its wage gains were folded into the incentive base rates, so that incentive bonus percentages were now calculated from a higher point, for the first time since 1948.[46] This was repeated in the 1954 contract, when, in addition, the UE turned back renewed corporate demands for a speed-up authorization clause and for the use of cameras in time studies.[47] The UE continued to attack productivity clauses and propagandized against incentive systems per se, for the first time since the 1930s.[48]

The 1954 IUE contract, which followed the UE's by two weeks, also folded increases into the incentive base rates and rejected the demand for cameras in time study and for the proposed speedup clause.[49] In order to get the same retroactive date as the UE, the IUE agreed to an earlier reopening of its time value and seniority clauses, which had been scheduled to run until November 1956.[50]

In 1955, the biggest and longest strike in the history of Westinghouse erupted. At the center of this dispute was the drive by the corporation to weaken incentive protections and to speed up output.

The Westinghouse offensive centered on three familiar demands: the right to restudy and reset incentive rates at any time; the right to time study dayworkers and impose production quotas on them; and the acceptance by the UE of a productivity/speedup clause. Mixed in with these issues were wage increases and fringe benefit offers based on the recently negotiated General Electric–IUE contract.[51]

The dispute began in August 1955, when the dayworkers at East Pittsburgh walked off the job to protest their timing with a stopwatch. The company then furloughed the plant's incentive workers. After a month, IUE President Carey intervened and reached a tentative agreement with Westinghouse. Time study of dayworkers would begin, experimentally, in one section of the East Pittsburgh plant, and its implementation elsewhere would be part of the national negotiations. The crucial last sentence of the Carey deal read: "the parties agree that the Union and the Locals will not interfere with studies of dayworker operations."[52] The IUE's Westinghouse conference board, however, with the East Pittsburgh delegates leading the way, repudiated this deal. The company's agreement to temporarily limit the settlement to the East Pittsburgh plant allowed the package to pass the conference board, but the dayworkers at East Pittsburgh still voted to oppose it. Carey pressured the local's executive board to ratify it, and they did so, with a few dissenting votes.[53]

On October 16, 1955, a national strike of the IUE plants began, and the UE plants joined the picket lines on October 21. The UE called on the two unions "to work out to the fullest extent possible common strike objectives, to carry out a joint fight against the company on the national level and to achieve the fullest cooperation in the strike struggle."[54] The IUE, however, rejected this approach and separate, although somewhat parallel, negotiations became the pattern. Despite the divisions between the unions and significant back-to-work movements at Mansfield, Columbus, and some other locations, most production workers held with the strike.[55]

Throughout the conflict, the UE continued to oppose the implementation of a productivity clause that they saw as "designed to weaken the ability of the union in its continuing day-to-day struggle to protect existing work standards"[56] and urged the IUE to stop negotiating over the "ground rules for the study of dayworkers and to reject it totally."[57] The two unions reached settlements in March 1956 that represented a mixed picture: both unions had to agree that Westinghouse could conduct time studies of dayworkers under certain conditions, but the UE contract limited this to "measuring or improving production, method analysis or for budget purposes," in other words, no measured daywork.[58] The IUE clause allowed Westinghouse to apply individual production standards to "direct dayworkers," those who did easily measured production tasks, as opposed to "indirect," such as janitors, crane operators, tool room workers, who made up about one-third of the nonincentive work force, and agreed to a very explicit productivity clause for them.[59]

For UE Local 107 the strike was not yet over, as it continued to try to protect its local supplement. Despite jailings and substantial fines, the strike there continued for another five months. When a settlement was finally reached, measured daywork had been defeated. The incentive system was, for the most part, scrapped. Workers were shifted to daywork, with very high rates.[60]

Westinghouse would continue to attack incentive rates. Unlike the situation at General Electric, where the major focus was on the cutting of rates, Westinghouse was primarily interested in ending incentive entirely, if it could substitute measured daywork.[61] New factors present in the late 1950s would give the corporation additional sources of strength in this fight. These included substantially higher unemployment, the continued geographic dispersion of new plants, which made threats to run away more convincing, and a certain "war weariness" evident among the workers after the long 1955/56 test of strength.

The pattern of the late 1950s can best be seen at the East Pittsburgh plant. In 1957, Westinghouse announced that it was planning to move 3,500 jobs from the East Pittsburgh plant to a new location at Trafford, Pennsylvania, about six miles away. The company plan called for hundreds of incentive workers to switch to measured daywork, with wages pegged at their old average earned rate, with a cap of 130 percent of the daywork rate for a job in the same labor grade. If the local rejected the deal, the company threatened to move the jobs out of the area entirely.[62] As President Paul Carmichael of IUE Local 601 told the workers, in an attempt to persuade them to accept the plan, "Westinghouse told us frankly it would consider Trafford only if it could get the same consideration from us that it could get at Athens [Georgia] or Kansas."[63] Still, many of the incentive workers rejected this plan, and Westinghouse agreed to sweeten the cap maximum to 140 percent for those who transferred. Even so, the average worker lost about 25 cents per hour in the transition.[64]

The corporation continued to press the issue of incentive rates at East Pittsburgh. Because of an accumulating pattern of rate cuts, by 1959 it took an incentive takeout of 120 to 130 percent to equal the daywork keysheet. Some workers over 40 years of age now preferred even a measured daywork job over the daily struggle needed to sustain higher incentive earnings.[65] Even so, several thousand workers at the plant who remained on incentive at the end of the decade sometimes continued a stubborn, defensive resistance. A representative dispute arose in April 1960, when 300 workers in E aisle walked out in support of a group of women coil tapers, demanding a new time study because of a new method that would have cut their earnings by 30–40 percent. After a protracted struggle, several new time studies were made and the rate was cut only modestly.[66]

Elsewhere in the IUE plants the picture was darker. At the huge new Columbus plant, opened in 1953, the company was producing as many refrigerators in 1959 with 3,200 workers as with its prestrike work force of 4,200; moreover, there had been steady rate cuts.[67] At the new location, in Metuchen, New Jersey, where almost all workers had been switched to measured daywork, workers struck in 1959 to protest the continued raising of daywork quotas and the attendant speedup. In Cheektowaga, New York, the company retimed the measured daywork jobs, with no boosts in pay. At Bloomfield, New Jersey, the IUE local president reported that there were now twenty-eight time-study men in his plant, as opposed to four in the UE period.[68]

The picture was more mixed in the few remaining UE plants. Workers at the Chicago maintenance and repair shop had an average takeout of only 117 percent in 1959, but high base rates. They fought attempted rate cuts and defeated efforts to move them to measured daywork.[69] Similar efforts were pushed back at the Nuttall gear plant.[70] At Lester, where huge military contracts were received in the late 1950s, wage rates remained high for the new dayworkers and they successfully resisted efforts to impose work quotas.[71]

To summarize: over the course of the 1950s, most workers at Westinghouse lost ground on incentive issues. The key factors in this retreat were the splitting of the UE in 1950, the lack of a coherent strategy and will to resist on the part of the top IUE leadership, and the structural and cyclical economic changes of the late decade. By 1960, a significant move toward daywork had been made. Except at the UE locations, this was usually measured daywork. For those workers who remained on incentive, some fall in takeout occurred, especially in 1950 and in the 1957–1960 period. This falloff, which was not universal, came from the steady pressure of the company, combined with the significant concessions on the use of cameras and retiming protections on the part of the IUE.

One of the major changes wrought by the UE at Westinghouse from

1936 to 1949 was the institutionalization and improvement of seniority. This occurred both by the codification of existing practices and by a substantial strengthening of these rules. By 1949, the UE's contractual seniority provisions were qualitatively different from the vague consideration that the company had given length of service in the preunion days in at least three ways:

First, seniority was *the* paramount consideration at time of layoff or rehiring and of great importance for job bidding. The 1948 contract's rehiring provision read: "accumulated service will govern if the employee can do the job with only such training as an employee with previous experience on the job would require."[72] Promotions followed the same principle if the person could perform satisfactorily after a brief period of adjustment.[73]

Second, the UE had succeeded in winning fairly broad seniority units. In most cases this meant departmental seniority, with units of a thousand workers or larger. In the case of smaller factories, plantwide seniority had frequently been won. Seniority units were not usually determined by the national contract but by a hodgepodge of local supplements. Nonetheless, the UE had consistently fought for broad seniority units, because they were more equitable and would generate the greatest internal solidarity.[74]

Finally, the UE had made considerable headway in achieving seniority lists that were undivided by race, ethnicity, and—more significantly—by gender. The latter was the most salient because of the firm's past negative practices. Westinghouse, supported by the opinions of a substantial fraction of the work force, had maintained separate seniority practices for men and women, including pre–World War II provisions calling for the nonhiring of married women; single women were let go when they married. Following World War II, when these provisions were relaxed owing to the labor shortage, Westinghouse attempted to return to these policies. They were resisted by most UE locals, which received strong leadership from the UE national office. By 1949, most locals had unified seniority lists. When right-wing local leaders attempted to resurrect or defend the discrimination against married women, the UE opposed them, usually successfully.[75]

Westinghouse took advantage of the 1949 union split to limit seniority protections. The company's goals on the seniority front were partially revealed in the 1950 contract negotiations. Westinghouse proposed the elimination of a companywide seniority credit for pensions and other fringe benefits, and its replacement by plant seniority. No seniority rights would exist at all until a worker had accumulated one year on the job. After a layoff of one year, those with seniority of less than five years would be eliminated from the call-back list. Five percent of each bargaining unit was to be designated by management as exempt from seniority provisions in cases of layoff.[76] The company proposed that the upgrading procedure be "based on seniority if the employee can do the job. Management reserves the right to determine if the employee can do the job."[77] Furthermore, Westinghouse called for the fragmentation of seniority units in most cases. When some plantwide seniority was to be retained, a seniority differential of 30 days would be required to bump within a section, 6 months to bump within a department, and 18 months to bump in the plant.[78]

From March 1950 to the signing of national contracts in the fall of 1950, many of the hard-pressed locals either struck to protect their local seniority supplements or made concessions of various dimensions. IUE Local 601's supplement, reached in September, was perhaps the most important. It replaced the old plantwide formulation of work sharing with a clause that made each section negotiate the extent to which work sharing would take place. Because it hopelessly fragmented any struggle over this issue, this came close to allowing the company to unilaterally determine such policy. Bumping would be confined to division. If a worker with more than seven years of seniority were bumped and not placed in another job, he/she could go on furlough for 30 days. If the company still did not place him/her, their status would be "negotiated."[79]

With their bargaining position partially undermined by a patchwork of these concessions at the local level, the 1950 IUE contract codified a significant retreat on seniority. It explicitly favored layoffs over work sharing in times of economic downturn. New negotiations were authorized at the local level over the configuration of seniority units. If any local had conceded a special seniority differential before allowing bumping, the principle was locked in, with locals allowed only to negotiate on the amount of the differential.[80] The upgrading clause was tightened subtly by allowing seniority to govern only "if the employee's experience, although not necessarily on the same type of work," indicated that he/she could do the job.[81] Finally, perhaps most ominously, Westinghouse got the right to grant from 1 to 2 percent of the workers in any unit exemption from seniority, as it saw fit. None of these provisions were present in the 1950 UE contract.[82]

While the national IUE contract did not discriminate against women in seniority provisions, many of the supplements reached by its locals did. The new contract at Local 202 in Springfield, Massachusetts, was representative of about a dozen such cases. It specified that "married women will not be considered for employment if their husbands are able to work."[83] If a female employee did marry, she might temporarily remain on the job but would be the first to go in case of a layoff.[84] At Mansfield, the IUE Local 711 seniority supplement read, "male and female employees shall be considered as separate groups except in such cases when female employees are engaged in male jobs."[85]

A mixture of retreats, stubborn defense, and occasional recapture of pre-1950 seniority rights characterized the inconclusive period that followed until the 1955/56 strike. In October 1951, a strike of the 6,100 members of IUE Local 1581 at Cheektowaga broke out over seniority issues. The old seniority supplement at the plant had been based on plantwide seniority. When it expired, Westinghouse proposed to substitute 65 seniority "families."[86] The local had been a thorn in Carey's side, and he intervened in the strike in a flamboyant but ineffective manner.[87] After 12 weeks of strike, a settlement was reached. Carey hailed it as "a victory for the union's demand for a combination of plant wide and occupational seniority,"[88] but a company official was "gratified that they've accepted the principle of occupational seniority."[89] In fact, the settlement retained plantwide seniority for layoffs but instituted occupational for upgrading bids.[90]

By the mid-1950s a trend toward growing resistance to further retreats became evident among the IUE locals. In the Local 601 elections in 1954 the Committee for a United Union slate (composed of former activists from *both* rival unions) denounced the incumbent's support for occupational seniority. The committee maintained that the "present local seniority supplement is almost word for word [identical] with the one the company posted on the bulletin boards in 1950, in violation of the contract."[91] The committee's candidates won most local offices, including the presidency.[92]

In the same year, IUE Local 617 at Sharon, Pennsylvania, with some new leaders in office, reversed its old position on separate seniority lists for married women. They filed a grievance over Westinghouse's refusal to recall married women in strict seniority order, took the grievance to arbitration, and won it.[93] At Cheektowaga the local executive board intervened to defeat a membership meeting motion to first lay off married women with employed husbands.[94]

Tension over seniority grew in 1954. IUE members at the new Columbus plant struck in September, with the local leadership calling for plantwide seniority and the company demanding occupational seniority with longer probationary periods.[95] At the East Pittsburgh plant, where more than 1,200 workers had been laid off in the past year, almost all workers with under ten years of service were off the job, but the picture was a chaotic one. Because of the occupational seniority clause it was possible to find men with 25 years of service bumped down to common labor, while junior workers retained higher grade jobs that required little specialized training.[96] Because of occupational seniority and other patterns of discrimination, all married women were gone from production jobs in the plant and only one-third of 1950's 1,500 women workers were left on the job.[97]

The new Local 601 leadership called on workers in East Pittsburgh to draw the line on layoffs at the ten-year mark, arguing that "you must share the work with your fellow employees."[98] While the IUE national contract brought no relief to East Pittsburgh, the local did win back some ground in its local supplement. Workers could now bump back into a job in another section of their department, if the job were the same labor grade and occupational number, and could cross divisions to bump into any job they had held during the previous year. Finally, they could bump in the same labor grade in their own section, whereas previously workers had been forced to drop a labor grade to bump.[99]

The 1955/56 strike was not a major battleground for disputes involving seniority, and the new national contracts simply repeated earlier clauses. One reason for this was that the mid-1950s was a period of expansion for the firm. This changed, however, in the late 1950s when massive layoffs took place at Westinghouse. By 1960, almost 20,000 fewer production workers were on the job than at middecade.[100] At the East Pittsburgh plant 3,600 were on layoff by early 1959.[101] At Sharon, almost half the 1955 work force of 6,400 were idle by mid-1958.[102] For most workers, the saliency of their seniority provisions increased sharply in the late 1950s.

Throughout the IUE, a mood more conservative than in the mid-1950s prevailed. Nowhere was this more evident than at East Pittsburgh. Most of the local's relatively militant 1954–1956 leadership was defeated for reelection in May 1956.[103] The local's new president, Paul Carmichael, moved rapidly toward a rapprochement with Westinghouse. By October 1957 he told Pittsburgh's major daily paper that "now there is complete understanding. The company provides the jobs and it is our job to eliminate trouble and yet assure the best working conditions for the men we represent."[104] He was reelected by a landslide in 1957 and by a substantial margin in 1959.[105]

The local leadership responded to the huge layoffs of 1958/59 in several ways. An agreement was reached with the company, allowing the layoff, without restrictions, of all persons of less than ten years of service. In the case of job reductions beyond the ten-year line there could be job sharing, to be determined by each section. Once again, this usually meant that the company actually selected the cutback method it preferred in each section.[106] In some sections, all high-seniority workers had three- or four-day weeks; others had alternative weeks off; and some sections worked overtime. Partially because of this, de facto section seniority was in effect. The company could breech the ten-year line simply by agreeing to discuss it with the union. In mid-1958 it did so; by the fall layoffs had reached the 17-year mark.[107]

East Pittsburgh took another important step backward during this period. In 1957, it changed its seniority supplement to remove the clause guaranteeing equal protection for married women, which had been reinserted in 1952.[108] Once again, a married woman had no seniority rights and could be fired if she failed to notify her foreman of her marriage.[109] Even in locations where special discrimination against married women did not exist, there were separate seniority lists for men and women at almost every major IUE location in the late 1950s.[110]

The situation was, as usual, even worse at the unorganized plants and at some IBEW locations. At the nonunion factory in Raleigh, North Carolina, Westinghouse gave vague consideration to seniority but admitted its system was "difficult to explain."[111] At the plant in Irwin, Pennsylvania, organized by the IBEW, women were still fired upon marriage.[112] Prior experience on a job was required in order to bump down at the Baltimore Air Arm IBEW location.[113]

I found no example, in this period, of the UE narrowing seniority units or establishing separate seniority units for women. The union fought for an explicit no discrimination by race or gender statement by Westinghouse, but the company replied, in 1958, that seniority for married women should be "a matter for local determination."[114] The UE's approach to the huge layoffs was to agitate for reduced hours at no loss in pay, a theme which it hammered at throughout the late 1950s.[115]

In the 1950s, most Westinghouse workers lost ground on incentive and seniority issues, but there were limits to the retreat and clear differences between unions. The varied approaches of the UE and IUE to these questions helped create different shop-floor working conditions for their members. On both incentive and seniority, the UE had firm, well-thought-out positions, consistently resisted take-aways, and usually succeeded in protecting shop-floor conditions for its dwindling thousands of Westinghouse members.

Unionized workers at Westinghouse who remained on incentive

still had protections and rates that were significantly better than in the nonunion era. Most of these who moved to daywork had, as a result of the struggles they had waged, won day rates well above the normal keysheet. Measured daywork and camera time studies were just two of the Westinghouse-sought innovations that the UE was able to block while they were being imposed on thousands of IUE members. The UE criticized incentive on moral grounds and urged that it be eliminated wherever possible, with the proper compensation.

Seniority provisions also remained significant, even at the end of the decade. At its unionized plants, the firm could not simply choose its favorites for retention or promotion. In some plants, the situation was better for married women than it had been in 1949, but the wholesale retreats by the IUE locals on this issue in 1950 and 1957/58 meant that, overall, women had gone backward on the seniority issue. While the UE did lose some ground on seniority units in the chaos of 1950, it was able to preserve most of its units. Finally, it successfully resisted separate seniority for married women.

While a certain convergence can sometimes be seen (both as a result of struggles by some IUE members and because any gain or loss in the chain helped or hindered the struggles of others), there was a clear difference in the practice of the the two unions. The behavior that flowed from two different conceptions of the relationship between unions and corporations did make a difference on the shop floor. In this area, as in almost any other, ideology and worldview—and the personalities and actions that they helped produce—counted for much.

"AN OLD SOLDIER"

TOM JURAVICH

Like an old soldier who stands at attention
He can't hear too well but he still heeds the call
His legs don't move quite as fast as they used to
  But that never stopped him from fighting at all

    He said, "Come on now, sit down for a minute
    I've got a story to tell you my son
    'cause you can't ever know where you're a-going
    Unless you know where you come from"

He talked about Flint back in the thirties
  Of organizing, how hard it was then
But mostly he talked of the good times he'd known
Of the spirit and courage of comrades and friends

With a gleam in his eye he talked of the future
  Like tomorrow was yesterday already gone
    Only this time a bit more impatient
For this time he knew that his time wasn't long

So thanks old friend for the songs and the stories
  Of all that we've been and all that we might be
    And the next time the going gets tough
    I'll remember you stood here long before me

NOTES

Abbreviations

Manuscript Depositories

AIS	Archives of Industrial Society, University of Pittsburgh
ALHUA	Archives of Labor History and Urban Affairs, Walter P. Reuther Library, Wayne State University
CHS	Chicago Historical Society
CUAA	Catholic University of America Archives
FDRL	Franklin D. Roosevelt Library
HCLA	Historical Collections and Labor Archives, Pattee Library, Pennsylvania State University
HSTL	Harry S. Truman Library
ILWUA	International Longshoremen's & Warehousemen's Union Archives, San Francisco
LC	Library of Congress
LMDC	Labor–Management Documentation Center, Martin P. Catherwood Library, Cornell University
NA	National Archives
SHSW	State Historical Society of Wisconsin
TI	Tamiment Institute, Elmer Holmes Bobst Library, New York University
UEA	United Electrical, Radio & Machine Workers of America Archives, University of Pittsburgh

Manuscript Collections

CIOSTO	CIO Secretary-Treasurer Office, ALHUA
CORP	Charles Owen Rice Papers, AIS

DBP   Daniel Bell Papers, TI
EDP   Ernest DeMaio Papers, CHS
GJP   Gardner Jackson Papers, FDRL
IUEP   International Union of Electrical, Radio & Machine Workers Papers, Special Collections and Archives, Rutgers University
RG 25   National Labor Relations Board Papers, NA

Preface

1. Mary Jo Buhle et al., eds., *Encyclopedia of the American Left* (New York, 1990), 788. This reference work contains adequate, in some cases excellent, sketches of most of the expelled unions.
2. Howard Kimeldorf, *Reds or Rackets? The Making of Radical and Conservative Unions on the Waterfront* (Berkeley, Calif., 1988).
3. George Rawick, "Working Class Self-Activity," *Radical America* 3, no. 2 (1969), 23–31.
4. Edward D. Beechert, "Racial Divisions and Agricultural Labor Organizing in Hawaii," in James C. Foster, ed., *American Labor in the Southwest: The First One Hundred Years* (Tucson, Ariz., 1982), 121–141; Beechert, *Working in Hawaii: A Labor History* (Honolulu, 1985); Leon Fink and Brian Greenberg, *Upheaval in the Quiet Zone: A History of Hospital Workers' Union, Local 1199* (Urbana, Ill., 1989), 21 (quote); Barbara Griffith, *The Crisis of American Labor: Operation Dixie and the Defeat of the CIO* (Philadelphia, 1988), 83.

Introduction

1. *1955 CIO Convention Proceedings*, 240–252 (quote, 252).
2. Determining trade-union membership figures always is tricky, but especially in the case of the expelled unions. My figures are drawn from Leo Troy, *Trade Union Membership, 1897–1962* (New York, 1965). In most cases, Troy's figures probably underestimate, drastically for several unions, the level of membership. I have, however, used his figures to simplify matters since this issue requires extended comment.
3. Daniel Bell and William Goldsmith interview with Pressman, March 20, 1956, DBP, Addendum, Box 2, folder 64.
4. Edward Beechert, *Working in Hawaii: A Labor History* (Honolulu, 1985), 292, 296, 299; Sanford Zalburg, *A Spark is Struck! Jack Hall & the ILWU in Hawaii* (Honolulu, 1979), 135, 124, 611; *The Dispatcher (TD)* July 30, 1943; Michael Torigian, "National Unity on the Waterfront: Communist Politics and the ILWU during the Second World War," *Labor History (LH)* 30 (1989), 422; Jane C. Record, "The Rise and Fall of a Maritime Union," *Industrial and Labor Relations Review* 10 (1956), 81–92; *March of Labor (MOL)*, April, 1951, 18, August, 1951, 26; *The Reporter*, July 5, 1949, 12–14; Ann Fagan Ginger and David Christiano, eds., *The Cold War Against Labor* (Berkeley, Calif., 1987), 592–601, 613; Mario T. Garcia, "Border Proletarians: Mexican-Americans and the International Union of Mine, Mill, and Smelter Workers, 1939–1946," Robert Asher and Charles Stephenson, eds., *Labor Divided: Race and Ethnicity in United States Labor Struggles, 1836–1960* (Albany, N.Y., 1990), 83–104; TD February 24, 1949, 1; July 7,

1950, 9; *Negro Handbook, 1949* (New York, 1949), 162; Robert Ozanne, *A Century of Labor–Management Relations at McCormick and International Harvester* (Madison, Wisc., 1967), 192; Ruth Milkman, *Gender at Work: The Dynamics of Job Segregation by Sex During World War II* (Urbana, Ill., 1987); Philip Foner, *Women and the American Labor Movement: From World War I to the Present* (New York, 1980), 367.

5. *1948 CIO Convention Proceedings*, 17–19, 160, 169–170, 175–177, 207–212, 218–219, 336ff.

6. *1948 CIO Convention Proceedings*, 164, 172; *1949 CIO Convention Proceedings*, 291–292; *Official Reports on the Expulsion of Communist Dominated Organizations from the CIO* (Washington, D.C., 1954), 30–31. The FBI reports, which are the source for the large number of CP members in the union's leadership as well Henderson's personal life, are in CIOSTO, Box 109, folder FTA Correspondence, 1946–1949. A "symbol number source index card," obtained through the Freedom of Information Act, verifies the FBI's microphone surveillance of the meeting on January 9, 1947, at which these issues were discussed.

7. These generalizations are based upon a vast array of sources; see, for example, *Proceedings of the Founding Convention: Distributive, Processing, and Office Workers of America* (New York, [1950]); Vicki L. Ruiz, *Cannery Women—Cannery Lives: Mexican Women, Unionization, and the California Food Processing Industry, 1930–1950* (Albuquerque, N.M., 1987); Michael K. Honey, "Labor and Civil Rights in the South: The Industrial Labor Movement and Black Workers in Memphis, 1929–1945" (Ph.D. dissertation, Northern Illinois University, 1988); Robert Korstad and Nelson Lichtenstein, "Opportunities Found and Lost: Labor, Radicals, and the Early Civil Rights Movement," *Journal of American History*, 75 (1988), 788–793, 801–806.

8. *Labor Fact Book 10* (New York, 1951), 108; *1949 CIO Convention Proceedings*, 289; Cochran, *Labor and Communism: The Conflict That Shaped American Unions* (Princeton, N.J., 1977), 314.

9. Sharon Hartman Strom, "We're No Kitty Foyles': Organizing Office Workers for the Congress of Industrial Organizations, 1937–1950," in Ruth Milkman, ed., *Women, Work & Protest: A Century of Women's Labor History* (Boston, 1985), 206–243; Harvey J. Clermont, *Organizing the Insurance Worker: A History of Labor Unions of Insurance Employees* (Washington, D.C., 1966); Mark McColloch, *White Collar Workers in Transition: The Boom Years, 1940–1970* (Westport, Conn., 1983), 43–50, 46, 51, 67–74; Counterattack, "Objective Study of United Office and Professional Workers of America, CIO," Special Report no. 1, enclosure with FBIHQ 100-350512-24; National Industrial Conference Board, Studies in Personnel Policy, no. 101: *White Collar Unionization* (New York, 1949); American Management Association, Office Management Series, no. 105: *Office Morale—White-Collar Unions* (New York, 1944); no. 111: *Operating the Unionized Office* (New York, 1945); no. 116: *Administering the Office Union Contract* (New York, 1946); American Management Association, Research Report no. 12: *Collective Bargaining in the Office* (New York, 1948).

10. Strom, " 'We're No Kitty Foyles' "; *DPOWA Founding Convention*, 11, 30; Counterattack, "Objective Study"; National Industrial Conference Board, *White Collar Unionization*, 8, 16; Strom, "Florence Luscomb," in Ellen Cantarow, *Moving the Mountain: Women Working for Social Change* (Old Westbury, N.Y., 1980), 32, 40–42; Louis Stark, "Trends in Office Unionization," *Office Morale—White-Collar Unions*, 14–15.

11. Joshua B. Freeman, *In Transit: The Transport Workers Union in New York City, 1933–1966* (New York, 1989); Bruce Nelson, *Workers on the Waterfront: Seamen, Longshoremen, and Unionism in the 1930s* (Urbana, Ill., 1988); Howard Kimeldorf, *Reds or Rackets? The Making of Radical and Conservative Unions on the Waterfront* (Berkeley,

Calif., 1988); William Z. Foster, *History of the Communist Party of the United States* (New York, 1952), 349.

12. J. Edgar Hoover to Rear Admiral Sidney Souers, February 15, 1949, PSF SF–FBI, Communist Party, HSTL; Troy, *Trade Union Membership.*

13. "Interview with Lewis Merrill," August 19, 1953, Theodore Draper Research Files (TDRF), Woodruff Library, Emory University, Box 14, folder 28; Bell and Goldsmith interview with Browder, June 22, 1955, Earl Browder Papers (EBP) (microfilm edition), Syracuse University, reel no. 8, series 3-153; Glazer, *The Social Basis of American Communism* (New York, 1961), 145 n25.

14. "Notes on an Interview with Lewis Merrill," DBP, Box 2, folder 55; "200 UE Communists Named!" *IUE News* clipping, May 22, 1950, GJP, Box 37, folder IUE–CIO; CIOSTO, Box 109, folder FTA Correspondence, 1946–1949; Millie Hedrick to General Officers, July 3, 1957, EDP, Box 16, folder 5.

15. For clear thinking on this issue, see Elizabeth Hawes, *Hurry Up Please Its Time* (New York, 1946), 42–43; David Roediger, "Foreword," in Jessie Lloyd O'Connor et al., *Harvey and Jessie: A Couple of Radicals* (Philadelphia, 1988); Mark Naison, "Communism from the Top Down," *Radical History Review*, no. 32 (1985), 100.

16. House Committee on Un-American Activities, *Investigation of Communist Activities in the Chicago Area, Part III*, 83rd Congress, April 29, 1954, 4268–4269.

17. "Reid Robinson," March 28, 1955, TDRF, Box 15, folder 33; Ronald Schatz, *The Electrical Workers: A History of Labor at General Electric and Westinghouse, 1923–1960* (Urbana, Ill., 1983), 196, 207–208; *Subversive Control of the United Public Workers of America: Hearings . . . Committee on the Judiciary*, 82nd Congress, 66; House Committee on Un-American Activities, *Hearings on Communism in the Detroit Area*, 82nd Congress, March 11, 1952, 3044, 3049, 3063ff; Strom, "Florence Luscomb."

18. Michael F. Urmann, "Rank and File Communists and the CIO (Committee for Industrial Organization) Unions" (Ph.D. dissertation, University of Utah, 1981), 142–146; Bell and Goldsmith interview with Browder, June 22, 1955; Harvey Klehr, *The Heyday of American Communism: The Depression Decade* (New York, 1984), 243–244; Glazer, *Social Basis of American Communism*, 124 n74, 125–126; "Notes on Interview with Merrill"; "Interview with Merrill"; "Communist Party: Sidney Mason, 1949 Affidavits and Explanation," IUEP, A2.05; Maurice Isserman, *Which Side Were You On? The American Communist Party During the Second World War* (Middletown, Conn., 1982), 20 n9; Robinson interview.

19. *Subversive Control of the United Public Workers of America*, 57–66; Blackie Myers, Max Perlow, Bob S, Ruth Young, and Roy Hudson speeches at June 18–20, 1945 Meeting of the National Committee of the Communist Political Association, Philip Jaffe Papers, reel 3, Woodruff Library, Emory University; Memorandum on Lee Pressman, December 5, 1945, attached to Hoover to Harry Vaughan, December 5, 1945, PSF Subject File—FBI P, HSTL; "General Intelligence Survey," August 8, 1944, 127, OF 10b, FBI, no. 2580, FDRL; FBIHQ 100-7319-235; blind memorandum attached to Hoover to Harry Hopkins, October 25, 1942, Hopkins Papers, Box 151, folder Communist Party, FDRL; FBIHQ 100-4931-1808; "Communist Party: Sidney Mason"; *Subversive Control of the United Public Workers of America*, 63.

20. Louis Goldblatt, *Working Class Leader in the ILWU, 1935–1977* (Berkeley, Calif., 1980), 243–246, 327, 419–426; *Daily Worker (DW)* November 17, 1943, 4; December 1, 1943, 3; Young speech—as well as others, especially John Williamson's report—at the National Committee Meeting, June 18–20, 1945.

21. "Memorandum on Some Organizational Problems," EBP, reel 1, series 1–17; House Committee on Un-American Activities, *Hearings on Communist Activities in*

the Chicago Area, 82nd Congress, September 1952, 3728, 3829; *Wage Earner* November 23, 1945, 2; FBI reports on FTA meeting of January 9, 1947; "Declaration of Policy," Merrill, "Personal Statement," EBP, reel 2, series 1-44; *Political Affairs (PA)* June, 1953, 34–35.

22. Joseph R. Starobin, *American Communism in Crisis, 1943–1957* (Cambridge, Mass., 1972); *Draft Resolution for the 16th National Convention of the Communist Party, USA* (New York, 1956), 46–49 (quote 46); Starobin, *American Communism in Crisis,* 155–180, esp. 173–176; Freeman, *In Transit,* 292–293, 292 n4; Arthur M. Schlesinger, Jr., ed. *History of American Presidential Elections* (New York, 1971), vol. 4, 3177–3181; CIOSTO, Box 47, folder H. Wallace.

23. Henry Foner, "Saul Mills and the Greater New York Industrial Union Council," *LH* 31 (1990), 347–360 (Foner generously provided me with a prepublication transcription of this important Mills letter); *PA,* January, 1949, 35–36; *Draft Resolution,* 48; David Shannon, *The Decline of American Communism: A History of the Communist Party Since 1945* (New York, 1959), 245–246; *Highlights of a Fighting History: 60 Years of the Communist Party USA* (New York, 1979), 309–313; *PA,* June 1953, 26–37; February 1957, 49–57; *Draft Resolution.*

24. Nelson, *Workers on the Waterfront,* 76.

25. Art Preis, *Labor's Giant Step: Twenty Years of the CIO* (New York, 1978); Chester Himes, *Lonely Crusade* (New York, 1947); Nelson, *Workers on the Waterfront,* 264–265.

26. *DW,* for example: August 16, 1943, 5; September 3, 9, 1943, 5, 5; October 4, 5, 6, 1943, 1, 5, 5; David Rothstein Papers, Box 10, folder 101, General 1943–1947, CHS; Francis Heisler to Murray, October 24, 1944, CIOSTO, Box 52, folder FE, 1941–1945; C. L. R. James et al., *Fighting Racism in World War II* (New York, 1980); Tom Kerry, *Workers, Bosses, and Bureaucrats* (New York, 1980), 112–130; National Committee Meeting, June 18–20, 1945.

27. "Yuri Afanasyev on the 19th Conference of the CPUSA," *New Left Review* 171 (September–October 1988), 86.

28. Aileen S. Kraditor, *"Jimmy Higgins": The Mental World of the American Rank-and-File Communist, 1930–1958* (Westport, Conn., 1988), chap. 8.

29. Ginger and Christiano, eds., *The Cold War Against Labor;* Elaine Tyler May, *Homeward Bound: American Families in the Cold War Era* (New York, 1988); John D'Emilio and Estelle B. Freedman, *Intimate Matters: A History of Sexuality in America* (New York, 1988), 282–284, 292–295; D'Emilio, "The Homosexual Menace: The Politics of Sexuality in Cold War America," in Kathy Peiss and Christina Simmons, eds., *Passion and Power: Sexuality in History* (Philadelphia, 1989), 226–240; Rosswurm, "A Betrayal of Isaiah's Promise: Labor Priests, Labor Schools, the ACTU and the Expelled Unions" (presented to the Chicago Area Labor History Group, September 15, 1989).

30. James Weinstein, "The Grand Illusion: A Review of 'Them and Us,' " *Socialist Revolution (SR)* 24 (June 1975), 87–103; Weinstein, *Ambiguous Legacy: The Left in American Politics* (New York, 1975); Weinstein, "Response," *SR* 27 (January–March 1976), 48–59; Members of DeKalb NAM, " 'Revolution and Democracy': A Critique," *SR* no. 19 (January–March 1974), 99–112.

31. Speeches by Louis Merrill, "Joseph S," and Ruth Young at National Committee Meeting, June 18–20, 1945; "Memorandum on Some Organizational Problems"; Williamson's speech to National Committee Plenum, July 1946, attached to Hoover to George E. Allen, July 19, 1946, PSF, Subject File—FBI Communist Data, HSTL; Klehr, *Heyday,* 239, 243; FBI reports on FTA meeting of January 9, 1947;

Mark Reutter, *Sparrows Point: Making Steel—The Rise and Ruin of American Industrial Might* (New York, 1988), 356; *PA*, January 1949, 34; February 1951, 71–72; Starobin, *American Communism in Crisis*, 96–98; Frank Emspak, "The Break Up of the Congress of Industrial Organizations, 1945–1950" (Ph.D. dissertation, University of Wisconsin, 1972), 40, 49, 50, 89–90, 383–384.

32. Stepan-Norris and Zeitlin, " 'Red' Unions and 'Bourgeois' Contracts? The Effects of Political Leadership on the 'Political Regime of Production' " (Working Paper Series 176, November 1989; Institute of Industrial Relations, UCLA) (I am thankful to Zeitlin for sending me a copy of this paper, which has now appeared in the *American Journal of Sociology* 96, no. 5 (March 1991), 1151–1200); Bell and Goldsmith interview with Browder, June 22, 1955; Browder, "United Electrical, Radio & Machine Workers Union (UE)," TDRF, Box 5, folder 15; Irvin Marnin, "The UE Faces the Split," *Fourth International*, November 1949, 298–303.

33. Barbara S. Griffith, *The Crisis of American Labor: Operation Dixie and the Defeat of the CIO* (Philadelphia, 1988), 83; Milkman, *Gender at Work; 1946 CIO Convention Proceedings*, 207–209; *1948 Convention Proceedings*, 214–216; *TD* October 10, 1949, 4, 6.

34. Toni Gilpin, "Left By Themselves: A History of the United Farm Equipment and Metal Workers of America, 1938–1955" (Senior thesis, Lake Forest College, 1981); Gilpin, "Labor's Last Stand," *Chicago History*, 18, no. 1 (Spring 1989), 42–59; William Regensburger, "Worker Insurgency and Southern Working-Class Combativeness," in Maurice Zeitlin, ed., *Insurgent Workers* (Los Angeles, 1987), 111–114, 119, 121–123, 130–131.

35. Charles S. Maier, "The Politics of Productivity: Foundations of American International Economic Policy After World War II," *In Search of Stability: Explorations in Historical Political Economy* (Cambridge, England, 1987), 121–152; Gilpin, "Labor Statesmanship v. Rank and File Unionism: Competing Models of Trade Unionism in Cold War America (presented to the Chicago Area Labor History Group, February 1987); *1961 UE Convention Proceedings*, 14–29, 131–142, 146–159; *1954 UE Convention Proceedings*, 97–105; *1960 UE Convention Proceedings*, 39, 119–123, 144–150; David Noble, *Forces of Production: A Social History of Industrial Automation* (New York, 1986), 154–158; *TD* March 5, 1948, 5, 8; March 19, 1948, 5; *1947 CIO Convention Proceedings*, 281–284; *1948 CIO Convention Proceedings*, 157–158, 242–244; Peter Weiler, *British Labour and the Cold War* (Stanford, Calif., 1988), 5, 89–90, 98–107; Ronald L. Filippelli, *American Labor and Postwar Italy, 1943–1953* (Stanford, Calif., 1989), 121–127, 198–204; Maier, "The Politics of Productivity."

36. Michael Ross, "American Unions and Western European Recovery," *Proceedings of Fourth Annual Meeting of the Industrial Relations Association, 1951* (Madison, Wisc., 1952), 94–99; Weiler, *British Labour and the Cold War*, 60, 69–71, 77–80, 105, 107, 110–113, 117; Filippelli, *American Labor and Postwar Italy*, xiii, 4, 11, 34–35, 45–50, 106–111, 127–129, 133, 177, 198–204; Lawrence S. Wittner, *American Intervention in Greece, 1943–1949* (New York, 1982), chap. 7; John Ranelagh, *The Agency: The Rise and Decline of the CIA* (New York, 1986), 216, 247; *New York Times*, May 8, 1967, 1, 36, 1, 37; Victor G. Reuther, *The Brothers Reuther and the Story of the UAW: A Memoir by Victor G. Reuther* (Boston, 1979), 424–427; Filippelli, *American Labor*, 106; Victor Marchetti and John D. Marks, *The CIA and the Cult of Intelligence* (New York, 1975), 70.

37. Korstad and Lichtenstein, "Opportunities Found and Lost"; Anne and Carl Braden Papers, Mss 6, Box 53, folder 17, SHSW.

38. David Brody, *Workers in Industrial America: Essays on the Twentieth Century Struggle* (New York, 1980), chap. 5; "In-Plant Strategies," *Labor Research Review* 7 (Fall 1985), 4–43.

39. Orlie Pell, *The Office-Worker: Labor's Side of the Ledger* (New York, 1938); Elinor Waters, "Unionization of Office Employees," *Journal of Business,* October 1954, 285–292; Albert Blum, *Management and the White-Collar Union* (New York, 1964) (American Management Association Research Study 63). Also see Vera Shlakman's four-part series in *Science and Society,* 1950 and 1951.

40. *Fortune* (F) November 1950, 54; June 1952, 74; November 1952, 78, 80; *1951 CIO Convention Proceedings,* 342, 344; *1952 CIO Convention Proceedings; 1954 CIO Convention Proceedings,* 365, 368, 417; Michael Goldfield, *The Decline of Organized Labor in the United States* (Chicago, 1987); Gary Burtless, "Earnings Inequality over the Business and Demographic Cycles," in Burtless, ed., *A Future of Lousy Jobs? The Changing Structure of U.S. Wages* (Washington, D.C., 1990), 88–89, 116; Lichtenstein, "From Corporations to Collective Bargaining: Organized Labor and the Eclipse of Social Democracy in the Postwar Era," in Steve Fraser and Gary Gerstle, eds., *The Rise and Fall of the New Deal Order, 1930–1980* (Princeton, N.J., 1989), 144–145; David M. Gordon, Richard Edwards, and Michael Reich, *Segmented Work, Divided Workers* (New York, 1982), 185ff.

41. Les Finnegan to Oscar Smith, n.d., Finnegan to Ben Mandel, August 16, 1949, Frank S. Tavener to Finnegan, September 2, 1949, IUEP, A2.05; "Mr. Carey," n.d., Joseph Hawkins to Murray, October 5, 1950, George L.-P. Weaver letters to various congressmen, March 10, 1950, CIOSTO, Box 51, folder IUE 1950; Box 64, folder UE May–December 1950; Box 175, folder IUE 1949/50; Carey to John Steelman, November 29, 1950 attached to Harry S. Truman to Carey, December 1, 1950, PPF no. 5140, HSTL; Sigmund Diamond, "Labor History vs. Labor Historiography: The FBI, James B. Carey, and the Association of Catholic Trade Unionists," in *Religion, Ideology and Nationalism in Europe and America* (Jerusalem, 1986).

42. Ralph S. Brown, Jr., and John Fassett, "Security Tests for Maritime Workers: Due Process Under the Port Security Program," *Yale Law Journal,* 62 (1953), 1165–1206; *1950 CIO Convention Proceedings,* 235–236; *1952 CIO Convention Proceedings,* 220–221.

43. Harvey, *The Limits of Capital* (Chicago, 1982), 415; Harvey, *The Condition of Postmodernity: An Enquiry into the Origins of Cultural Change* (London, 1989), chap. 14.

44. *The New England Economy: A Report to the President* (Washington, D.C., 1951); *1953 CIO Convention Proceedings,* 536–537, 540–541; *1954 CIO Convention Proceedings,* 360–362; F April 1950, 52, 54; *Subsidized Industrial Migration . . . : An American Federation of Labor Report* (Washington, D.C., 1955), 12–13, 49–50; Griffith, *Crisis of American Labor;* Irvin Sobel, "Collective Bargaining and Decentralization in the Rubber-Tire Industry," *Journal of Political Economy* 62 (1954), 12–25; Daniel Nelson, *American Rubber Workers and Organized Labor, 1900–1941* (Princeton, N.J., 1988).

45. Victor R. Fuchs, *Changes in the Location of Manufacturing in the United States Since 1929* (New Haven, Conn., 1962); Schatz, *Electrical Workers,* 233–235; Maurice Fulton, "Plant Location—1965," *Harvard Business Review* 33 (1955), 40–50; Leo Reeder, "The Central Area of Chicago: A Re-examination of the Process of Decentralization," *Land Economics* 28 (1952), 369–373; Paul M. Reid, *Industrial Decentralization: Detroit Region, 1940–1950* (Detroit, 1951); S. A. Kahn, "Stop Giving America Away!" *American City* May 1951, 106–107; *Monthly Labor Review* (MLR) March 1956, 332; "The Fight for Industries Is Rough in Some Places!" *Saturday Evening Post* (SEP) April 9, 1960, 10; *Subsidized Industrial Migration,* 18–26, 28–33; *Berkshire Evening Eagle,* October 22, 1953, clipping, Richard A. Lynch to Senator Smith, February 17, 1953, to Editor, June 1, 1953, IUEP, A2.07; Carey mimeographed letter, February 12, 1952, GJP, Box 13, folder Carey; "Industry Shifts Its Plants," *Business*

Week (*BW*) September 8, 1951, 22–24; *Subsidized Industrial Migration*, 36–40; Richard T. Selden, "Accelerated Amortization and Industrial Concentration," *Review of Economics and Statistics* 37 (1959), 282–291; Leonard C. Yaseen, *Plant Location* (Roslyn, N.Y., 1952); Stanley Frank, "The Great Factory Sweepstakes," *SEP* October 22, 1960, 34, 142, 144, 147, 148; "Should You Move Your Plant?" *BW* September 17, 1949; *1960 UE convention proceedings*, 146; *MLR* June 1956, 698.

46. Jackson to Carey, February 19, 1953, to Carey, September 4, 1953, GJP, Box 13, folder Carey; *Officers Report to IUE 1953 Convention*, 72; Herb Mills, "The San Francisco Waterfront: The Local Consequence of Industrial Modernization," in Andrew Zimbalist, ed., *Case Studies on the Labor Process* (New York, 1979), 127–155; *1954 UE Convention Proceedings*, 8–10, 119–120; *1960 UE Convention Proceedings*, 39, 233–251; *MOL* September 1952, 12–14; William D. Andrew, "Factionalism and Anti-Communism," *LH* 20 (1979), 240, 245–246; *F* October 1950, 48, 50; *1954 CIO Convention Proceedings*, 561–564, 616.

47. Jack Metzgar, "Plant Shutdowns and Worker Response: The Case of Johnstown, Pa.," *SR* 53 (September–October, 1980), 38; Samuel Bowles, David M. Gordon, and Thomas E. Weisskopf, *Beyond the Wasteland* (New York, 1984), chap. 4; Michele I. Naples, "The Unraveling of the Union–Capital Truce and the U.S. Industrial Productivity Crisis," and Bowles, Gordon, and Weisskopf, "Powers and Profits: The Social Structure of Accumulation and the Profitability of the Postwar U.S. Economy," *Review of Radical Political Economics* 18 (1986), 110–131, 132–167; Weisskopf, Bowles, and Gordon, "Hearts and Minds: A Social Model of U.S. Productivity Growth," *Brookings Papers on Economic Activity* 2 (1983), 381–450; Lichtenstein, "From Corporatism to Collective Bargaining," in Fraser and Gerstle, eds., *Rise and Fall of the New Deal Order*, 122–152; Lichtenstein, "Labor in the Truman Era: Origins of the 'Private Welfare State,' " in Michael J. Lacey, ed., *The Truman Presidency* (New York, 1989), 128–155.

Class and Race in the Crescent City

1. Irving Bernstein, *Turbulent Years: A History of the American Worker, 1933–1941* (Boston, 1970), 217–317; Edward Levinson, *Labor on the March* (New York, 1938); *Voice of the Federation*, June 3, 1937, 1, 4.

2. H. R. Bridges to M. R. Rathborne, November 17, 1937, ILWU Organizing Files, Box 12, folder on ILWU Organizing—Gulf—Correspondence and Reports with CIO Maritime Committee, 1937–1939, 1944 (hereafter, ILWU OF, Box 12, folder Gulf Correspondence with CIO Maritime Committee), ILWUA; "Minutes of the Full District Executive Board Meeting, International Longshoremen's and Warehousemen's Union, . . . San Francisco, California, Sunday, October 23, 1938," ILWU OF, Box 12, folder South Correspondence and Reports, 1937–1948.

3. Ben Jones to Mervyn Rathborne et al., December 12, 1937, ILWU OF, Box 12, folder Gulf Correspondence with CIO Maritime Committee; Paul Heide to Matt Meehan, October 22, 1938, ILWU OF, Box 12, folder Gulf Correspondence and Reports, 1937/38. The statement about "the white man . . . lead[ing] the negro out of the pit" was made by Caleb Green, a white southerner who became the ILWU's principal organizer and spokesman in the Gulf in 1939. *Proceedings of the Third Annual Convention of the International Longshoremen's and Warehousemen's Union*, North Bend, Oreg., April, 1–11, 1940, 140.

4. On the Big Strike, see Bernstein, *Turbulent Years*, 252–298; Howard Kimeldorf, *Reds or Rackets? The Making of Radical and Conservative Unions on the Waterfront* (Berkeley, Calif., 1988), 99–110; Charles P. Larrowe, *Harry Bridges: The Rise and Fall of Radical Labor in the United States* (New York, 1972), 32–93; Bruce Nelson, *Workers on the Waterfront: Seamen, Longshoremen, and Unionism in the 1930s* (Urbana, Ill., 1988), 127–155; Mike Quin, *The Big Strike* (Olema, Calif., 1949).

5. Gregory Harrison, *Maritime Strikes on the Pacific Coast: A Factual Account of Events Leading to the 1936 Strike of Marine and Longshore Unions* (San Francisco, 1936), 21; Nelson, *Workers on the Waterfront*, 156–188.

6. *Voice of the Federation*, June 3, 1937, 4; Mervyn Rathborne to John L. Lewis, July 14, 1937, CIO Records, Box A7-28, folder Maritime Union of America, National, CUAA.

7. Mervyn Rathborne to John L. Lewis, Aug. 27, 1937, ibid.

8. International Longshoremen's Association (ILA), *Proceedings of the Thirty-Second Convention*, New York, July 10–14, 1939, 34; Harry Lundeberg to William Green, July 7, 1939, quoted in Nelson, *Workers on the Waterfront*, 243.

9. Nelson, *Workers on the Waterfront*, 189–249.

10. CIO Maritime Committee, "For Immediate Release," n.d. [October 1937], in *The CIO Files of John L. Lewis* (microfilm ed.), part I, reel 7; Paul Heide to Harry Bridges, August 12, 1938, ILWU OF, Box 12, folder Gulf Correspondence and Reports, 1937/38.

11. John Robert Moore, "The New Deal in Louisiana," in John Braeman, Robert H. Bremner, and David Brody, eds., *The New Deal: The State and Local Levels* (Columbus, Ohio, 1975), 137; B. Halling to John Brophy, June 1, 1938, ILWU OF, Box 12, folder South Correspondence and Reports, 1937–1948; H. R. Bridges to B. B. Jones and B. Halling, May 13, 1938, ILWU OF, Box 12, folder Gulf Correspondence with CIO Maritime Committee; H. R. Bridges to Paul Heide, August 16, 1938, ILWU OF, Box 12, folder Gulf Correspondence and Reports, 1937/38.

12. Nelson, *Workers on the Waterfront*, 133–134, 259–260; Kimeldorf, *Reds or Rackets?*, 146.

13. Sterling D. Spero and Abram L. Harris, *The Black Worker: The Negro and the Labor Movement* (New York, 1968 [1931]), 182–205, quoted on 183, 199.

14. R. R. Tisdale to J. S. Potofsky, September 27, 1937, Amalgamated Clothing Workers of America (ACW) Papers, Box 221, folder 5, LMDC.

15. Eric Arnesen, "Learning the Lessons of Solidarity: Work Rules and Race Relations on the New Orleans Waterfront, 1880–1901," *Labor's Heritage* 1 (1989), 26–45; Arnesen, *Waterfront Workers of New Orleans: Race, Class, and Politics, 1863–1923* (New York, 1991), 245; Daniel Rosenberg, *New Orleans Dockworkers: Race, Labor, and Unionism, 1892–1923* (Albany, N.Y., 1988), quoted on 155.

16. Rosenberg, *New Orleans Dockworkers*, 142–174; Herbert R. Northrup, "The New Orleans Longshoremen," *Political Science Quarterly* 47 (1942), 530–533; Carroll George Miller, "A Study of the New Orleans Longshoremen's Unions from 1850 to 1962" (M.A. thesis, Louisiana State University, 1962), 23–26; Arnesen, *Waterfront Workers of New Orleans*, 204–252, quoted on 247.

17. Northrup, "The New Orleans Longshoremen," 533–534; Robert C. Francis, "Longshoremen in New Orleans: The Fight Against Nigger Ships," *Opportunity* 14 (1936), reprinted in Philip S. Foner and Ronald Lewis, eds., *The Black Worker: A Documentary History from Colonial Times to the Present* (Philadelphia, 1983), vol. 7, 401–406; *Statement by the New Orleans Steamship Association on the New Orleans Longshore Labor Situation, December 9, 1935* (New Orleans, 1935), 28, RG 25, Box 1320.

18. "Longshore Labor Conditions in the United States—Part II," *Monthly Labor Review* 31 (1930), 1055–1057; Douglas L. Smith, *The New Deal in the Urban South* (Baton Rouge, La., 1988), 3, 21–22, 232.

19. United States of America, Before the National Labor Relations Board (NLRB), "In the Matter of Aluminum Line [et al.] and the International Longshoremen['s] and Warehousemen's Union," September 29, 1938, ILWU, Disbanded Locals Files (DLF), Box 3, folder Local 202 Correspondence and General—NLRB Case; Northrup, "The New Orleans Longshoremen," 534–535. For contrasting assessments of the "independents," cf. Charles H. Logan to William [M.] Leiserson, September 4, 1934, William Morris Leiserson Papers, 1901–1959, Box 23, Charles H. Logan file, SHSW (unless otherwise noted, all Logan correspondence is from this box and file), and Robert C. Francis, "Dock Trouble in New Orleans," *Crisis* 42 (1935), 373.

20. Northrup, "The New Orleans Longshoremen," 535–537; "Strike of Longshoremen on the Gulf Coast," *Monthly Labor Review* 42 (1936), 392–395; Francis, "Dock Trouble in New Orleans," 373; Francis, "Longshoremen in New Orleans," 405–406; Gilbert Mers, *Working the Waterfront: The Ups and Downs of a Rebel Longshoreman* (Austin, Tex., 1988), 137–138, 157.

21. Ben Jones to Harry Bridges, n.d. [October 1937], ILWU OF, Box 12, folder Gulf Correspondence with CIO Maritime Committee.

22. Jones to Bridges, n.d.; Mervyn Rathborne, "Data Regarding Longshore Conditions in Mobile, Alabama," November 13, 1937, ILWU OF, Box 12, folder Gulf Correspondence with CIO Maritime Committee; Lester Rubin, *The Negro in the Longshore Industry* (Philadelphia, 1974), 114; "History of Unionization on Mobile Riverfront (1923–1938)," ILWU OF, Box 14, folder "History of Unionization on Mobile Riverfront"; John Carmody to Nathan Witt, February 13, [1938]; John J. Carmody to NLRB, February 23, 1938; George Googe to Warren Madden, January 5, 1938, RG 25, Box 900; NLRB, "In the Matter of Mobile Steamship Association . . . and the International Longshoremen['s] and Warehousemen's Union," September 29, 1938, RG 25, Box 901; F. Ray Marshall, *Labor in the South* (Cambridge, Mass., 1967), 207; statement of Joe Williams, n.d., ILWU OF, Box 14, folder South—Statements of Dockers, Mobile.

23. Mervyn Rathborne to Lee Pressman, November 13, 1937; Ben Jones to Mervyn Rathborne, November 28, 1937, ILWU OF, Box 12, folder Gulf Correspondence with CIO Maritime Committee.

24. [Bjorne Halling], "Report to the First Convention of the International Longshoremen['s] and Warehousemen's Union," April 6, 1938, ILWU OF, Box 12, folder South Correspondence and Reports, 1937–1948.

25. On Hortman, see esp. "Official Report of Proceedings Before the National Labor Relations Board, Case No. XV-R-168, In the Matter of Aluminum Line et al. and International Longshoremen['s] and Warehousemen's Union," New Orleans, June 27, 1938, 504–536, RG 25, Box 1319; *Louisiana Weekly* July 2, 1938, 1; Jones to Rathborne et al., December 12, 1937; [Halling], "Report to the First Convention of the International Longshoremen['s] and Warehousemen's Union"; Charles H. Logan, "Memorandum In Re New Orleans Steamship Association . . . and International Longshoremen['s] and Warehousemen's Union and International Longshoremen's Association," April 6, 1938 (hereafter, Logan, "Memorandum"), RG 25, Box 378.

26. Mildred Jeffrey to J. S. Potofsky, Dec. 13, 1937, ACW Papers, Box 221, folder 5; Ben Jones to H. R. Bridges, Dec. 2, 1937, ILWU OF, Box 14, folder Ben Jones Reports, 1937–38; Jones to Rathborne et al., December 12, 1937.

27. Alvin Schneider et al. to Harry Bridges and District Executive Board, January 3, 1938, ILWU OF, Box 12, folder Gulf Correspondence and Reports, 1938/39; testimony of J. Harvey Netter, in *Waterfront Investigation: Hearings Before a Subcommittee of the Committee on Interstate and Foreign Commerce*, U.S. Senate, 83rd Congress, 1st Session, Pursuant to S. Res. 41 on Waterfront Racketeering and Port Security, Part 2, New Orleans Waterfront, June 24–26, 1953 (Washington, D.C.: U.S. Government Printing Office, 1953), 785; David Lee Wells, "The ILWU in New Orleans: CIO Radicalism in the Crescent City, 1937–1957" (M.A. thesis, University of New Orleans, 1979), 5–6, 12; Paul Heide to H. R. Bridges, June 9, 1938, ILWU OF, Box 12, folder South Correspondence and Reports, 1937–1948; [Adrian] Duffy to [Bjorne] Halling, April 12, 1938, and April 14, 1938, ILWU OF, Box 12, folder Gulf Correspondence with CIO Maritime Committee.

28. Schneider et al. to Bridges and District Executive Board, January 3, 1938; *New Orleans Times-Picayune* July 6, 1938, 3; DWS [Donald Wakefield Smith], "New Orleans Waterfront Situation," March 28, 1938; B. Halling to Anthony Smith, n.d. [May 1938], RG 25, Box 378; Logan, "Memorandum," April 6, 1938.

29. Jones to Rathborne et al. Dec. 12, 1937; Smith Z. Erris, "To the National Labor Relations Board, Regarding the Situation at the Todd-Johnson Shipyard in New Orleans, La.," Apr. 24, 1938, attached to B. Halling to Ben Jones, April 23, 1938, ILWU OF, Box 12, folder South Correspondence and Reports, 1937–1948.

30. International Longshoremen's Association, *Proceedings of the Twenty-Eighth Annual Convention of the South Atlantic and Gulf Coast District*, Savannah, Ga., May 9–13, 1938, RG 25, Box 1321; Bjorne Halling to Joe Wright, June 1, 1938, ILWU OF, Box 12, folder South Correspondence and Reports, 1937–1948; Erris, "To the National Labor Relations Board," April 24, 1938; Paul Heide to Lee Pressman, August 29, 1938, ILWU OF, Box 12, folder Gulf Correspondence and Reports, 1937/38.

31. Edward F. Haas, "New Orleans on the Half Shell: The Maestri Era, 1936–1946," *Louisiana History* 13 (1972), 284, 305; Smith, *The New Deal in the Urban South*, 4–5, 198; Herman L. Midlo to George A. Dreyfous, April 28, 1938, American Civil Liberties Union (ACLU) Archives, Box 2034, folder New Orleans Shipyard Strike, Seeley G. Mudd Manuscript Library, Princeton University.

32. *Proceedings of the Second Annual Convention of the International Longshoremen's and Warehousemen's Union*, San Francisco, Calif., April 3–14, 1939, 134, 141; J. R. (Bob) Robertson to Lou Goldblatt, June 21, 1938; J. R. Robertson letter, June 26, 1938; Bob [Robertson] to Matt [Meehan], July 17, 1938, ILWU OF, Box 12, folder Gulf—New Orleans, 1938.

33. *New Orleans Times-Picayune* June 23, 1938, 1, 3; June 24, 1938, 1, 3; June 25, 1938, 1, 3; June 28, 1938, 1; *Louisiana Weekly* July 2, 1938, 1; Lucille Pettyjohn, notarized statement, June 25, 1938, ACLU Archives, Box 2034, folder CIO Strike Situation in New Orleans.

34. *New Orleans Times-Picayune* June 23, 1938, 3; June 24, 1938, 1; Robertson letter, June 26, 1938; Smith Z. Erris to Philip H. Van Gelder, June 28, 1938, Industrial Union of Marine & Shipbuilding Workers of America (IUMSWA) Archives, Series V, Box 69, folder Local 29 Correspondence, May–June 1938, University of Maryland (College Park) Library; Felix Siren to John L. Lewis, June 28, 1938; Matt Meehan to J. R. Robertson, April 29, 1939, ILWU OF, Box 12, folder Gulf—New Orleans, 1938; Harvey Schwartz, interview with J. R. (Bob) Robertson, San Rafael, Calif., December 29, 1972; Philip Lelli, interview with Burt Nelson, Seattle, March 28, 1987.

35. *New Orleans Times-Picayune* July 2, 1938, 1, 3.

36. Actually, during the summer of 1938, Robertson and Halling spent no more than

several weeks in the hospital. Two years later doctors performed a spinal fusion on Robertson, and on this occasion he spent some ten to twelve weeks in the hospital. *New Orleans Times-Picayune* July 8, 1938, 1; July 9, 1938, 1; *Socialist Call* July 16, 1938, clipping in ACLU Archives, Box 2034, folder CIO Strike Situation in New Orleans; Paul Heide to H. R. Bridges, July 8, 1938; Heide to Matt Meehan, July 9, 1938, ILWU OF, Box 12, folder South Correspondence and Reports, 1937–1948; Bob [Robertson] to Matt [Meehan], July 17, 1938; Burt [Nelson] to Matt [Meehan], July 30, 1938, ILWU OF, Box 12, folder Gulf Correspondence and Reports, 1938/39; Schwartz, interview with Robertson.

37. Paul Heide to H. R. Bridges, August 8, 1938, ILWU OF, Box 12, folder Gulf Correspondence and Reports, 1937/38; [Paul Heide] to Lee Pressman, August 19, 1938, ILWU OF, Box 14, folder Gulf Correspondence with National CIO, 1938/39; Heide to Pressman, August 29, 1938.

38. Ben Harper to P. H. Van Gelder, May 12, 1938, IUMSWA Archives, Series V, Box 69, folder Local 29 Correspondence, May–June 1938; B. Halling to Anthony Wayne Smith, May 18, 1938, ILWU OF, Box 12, folder South Correspondence and Reports, 1937–1948.

39. James A. Gross, *The Reshaping of the National Labor Relations Board: National Labor Policy in Transition, 1937–1947* (Albany, N.Y., 1981), 57–58; Mers, *Working the Waterfront,* 137, 143; Noel R. Beddow to David J. McDonald, March 6, 1940, United Steelworkers of America Archives, District 36 Records, 1936–1946, Box 11, folder 7, HCLA; see note appended to Charles H. Logan to George Googe, December 28, 1934; Logan to the National Labor Relations Board, October 19, 1935; Logan to William M. Leiserson, July 13, 1936; Logan to Leiserson, Mar. 23, 1937.

40. Logan, "Memorandum," April 6, 1938; Logan to [William M. Leiserson], August 15, [1939]; Logan to Leiserson, n.d.; Charles H. Logan to Richard W. Leche, September 7, 1937; [Donald Wakefield Smith], "New Orleans Waterfront Situation," March 28, 1938.

41. Logan, "Memorandum," April 6, 1938; B. Halling to Harry Bridges, May 26, 1938, ILWU OF, Box 12, folder South Correspondence and Reports, 1937–1948; Nathan Witt to Charles H. Logan, May 13, 1938, RG 25, Box 378.

42. Carmody to NLRB, February 23, 1938; Duffy to H[a]lling, April 12, 1938; *Riverfront News* July 15, 1938, ILWU OF, Box 12, folder Gulf Correspondence and Reports, 1937/38; "Official Report of Proceedings Before the National Labor Relations Board . . . ," 513.

43. *Proceedings of the Second Annual Convention of the International Longshoremen's and Warehousemen's Union,* 142; United States of America, Before the National Labor Relations Board, Fifteenth Region, "In the Matter of Aluminum Line [et al.] and International Longshoremen['s] and Warehousemen's Union," October 19, 1938, RG 25, Box 378; "Minutes of the Full District Executive Board Meeting, International Longshoremen's and Warehousemen's Union, . . . San Francisco, California, Sunday, October 23, 1938"; United States of America, Before the National Labor Relations Board, "In the Matter of Mobile Steamship Association [et al.] and International Longshoremen['s] and Warehousemen's Union," November 9, 1938, RG 25, Box 901.

44. Felix Siren to Anthony Wayne Smith, October 22, 1938, ILWU DLF, Box 3, folder Representation Election, NLRB; Heide to Meehan, October 22, 1938.

45. Richard A. Dowling to Lee Pressman, October 19, 1938, ILWU OF, Box 12, folder Gulf—New Orleans, 1938.

46. Marshall, *Labor in the South*, 207–208; Miller, "A Study of the New Orleans Long-shoremen's Unions," 36–37.
47. Charles Logan to William M. Leiserson, April 6, 1939; J. R. Robertson, "To the Officers and Members of all ILWU Locals," April 28, 1939, ILWU OF, Box 14, folder Gulf—New Orleans, 1939.
48. *New Orleans Times-Picayune* July 2, 1938, 1, 3; Siren to Lewis, June 28, 1938; Lawrence Hunt to Malcolm F. Halliday, July 8, 1938, RG 25, Box 378; Robertson letter, June 26, 1938; J. R. [Bob] Robertson to Harry Bridges, August 9, 1938, ILWU OF, Box 12, folder Gulf—New Orleans, 1938; Marshall, *Labor in the South*, 207.
49. Jane Speed to Walter N. Polakov, September 15, 1938; William Mitch to A. D. Lewis, September 29, 1938; Mitch to Gardner Jackson, October 25, 1938, *The CIO Files of John L. Lewis*, part I, reel 13; report, "Prepared by: J. Harvey Kerns, Field Secretary[,] National Urban League," n.d., National Urban League Records, Southern Regional Office, General Office File, New Orleans Urban League—Undated, Manuscript Division, LC.
50. Heide to Meehan, Oct. 22, 1938; Jones to Rathborne et al., December 12, 1937.
51. George B. Tindall, *The Emergence of the New South, 1913–1945* (Baton Rouge, La., 1967), 162–164; William Regensburger, "The Emergence of Industrial Unionism in the South, 1930–1945: The Case of Coal and Metal Miners," in Maurice Zeitlin, ed., *How Mighty a Force? Studies of Workers' Consciousness and Organization in the United States* (Los Angeles, 1983), 95–96; *Louisiana Weekly* September 10, 1938, 1.
52. Ralph Helstein, of the United Packinghouse Workers of America, quoted in Barbara S. Griffith, *The Crisis of American Labor: Operation Dixie and the Defeat of the CIO* (Philadelphia, 1988), 86.
53. Robert J. Norrell, "Labor at the Ballot Box: Alabama Politics from the New Deal to the Dixiecrat Movement," *Journal of Southern History* (forthcoming); Regensburger, "The Emergence of Industrial Unionism in the South," 89–96; *Alabama News Digest*, December 15, 1939, 5.
54. Bernard Mergen, "A History of the Marine and Shipbuilding Workers of America, 1933–1951" (Ph.D. dissertation, University of Pennsylvania, 1968), 139; IUMSWA Local 29, *Drydock News*, n.d. [June 1938], IUMSWA Archives, Series V, Box 69, folder Local 29 Correspondence, May–June, 1938; [Fred] Pieper to John L. Lewis, January 23, 1940, *The CIO Files of John L. Lewis*, part II, reel 11.
55. Johnson and Neil R. McMillen ("a matter of pride and preference"), quoted in McMillen, *Dark Journey: Black Mississippians in the Age of Jim Crow* (Urbana, Ill., 1989), 290.
56. Robertson to Bridges, August 9, 1938; Marshall, *Labor in the South*, 207; New Orleans Colored Citizens Committee to "My dear Longshoremen," October 12, 1938, ILWU OF, Box 12, folder Gulf Correspondence and Reports, 1938/39; "Stink-Mouth Bridges Can't Get Away with This Scheme!" ILWU OF, Box 12, folder ILWU–CIO Longshore Organizing—New Orleans, 1938, Leaflets, Bulletins, "Riverfront News"; see also "The Wolf in Sheep's Clothing—Beware," ibid.
57. Mers, *Working the Waterfront*, 147–148.
58. Francis, "Dock Troubles in New Orleans," 373; Dowling to Pressman, October 19, 1938; Siren to Anthony Wayne Smith, October 22, 1938 (emphasis in original).
59. Cf. Christopher L. Tomlins, "AFL Unions in the 1930s: Their Performance in Historical Perspective," *Journal of American History* 65 (1979), 1021–1042.
60. Sidney Fine, *Sit-Down: The General Motors Strike of 1936–1937* (Ann Arbor, Mich., 1969); Bruce Nelson, " 'A Class Line Across the Face of American Politics': Work-

ers, Organized Labor, and the Presidential Election of 1940" (unpublished manuscript, in author's possession); J. Wayne Flynt, "The New Deal and Southern Labor," in James C. Cobb and Michael V. Namorato, eds., *The New Deal and the South* (Jackson, Miss., 1984), 87.

61. "Minutes of the Full District Executive Board Meeting, International Longshoremen's and Warehousemen's Union, . . . San Francisco, California, Sunday, October 23, 1938"; Siren to Anthony Wayne Smith, October 22, 1938; Dowling to Pressman, October 19, 1938.

62. Charles H. Martin, "Southern Labor Relations in Transition: Gadsden, Alabama, 1930–1943," *Journal of Southern History* 47 (1981), 545–568; Daniel Nelson, *American Rubber Workers & Organized Labor, 1900–1941* (Princeton, N.J., 1988), 234–245, 257–262, 315–317; Roger Biles, "Ed Crump Versus the Unions: The Labor Movement in Memphis During the 1930s," *Labor History* 25 (1984), 533–552; Michael Honey, "The Popular Front in the American South: The View from Memphis," *International Labor and Working-Class History*, 30 (1986), 44–58; Robert Korstad and Nelson Lichtenstein, "Opportunities Found and Lost: Labor, Radicals, and the Early Civil Rights Movement," *Journal of American History* 75 (1988), 786–811; Wells, "The ILWU in New Orleans"; Griffith, *The Crisis of American Labor*.

63. Cf. Christopher L. Tomlins, *The State and the Unions: Labor Relations, Law, and the Organized Labor Movement in America, 1880–1960* (Cambridge, England, 1985); and Howell Harris, "The Snares of Liberalism? Politicians, Bureaucrats, and the Shaping of Federal Labour Relations Policy in the United States, ca. 1915–47," in Steven Tolliday and Jonathan Zeitlin, eds., *Shop Floor Bargaining and the State: Historical and Comparative Perspectives* (Cambridge, England, 1985), 148–191.

64. McMillen, *Dark Journey*, 290.

65. See Nancy Quam-Wickham's essay in the present volume; Kimeldorf, *Reds or Rackets?*, 144–151; Michael Torigian, "National Unity on the Waterfront: Communist Politics and the ILWU During the Second World War," *Labor History* 30 (1989), 409–432.

Who Controls the Hiring Hall?

1. David Brody, "Radical Labor History and Rank-and-File Militancy," *Workers in Industrial America: Essays on the 20th Century Struggle* (New York, 1980), 146–158; Maurice Isserman, *Which Side Were You On? The American Communist Party During the Second World War* (Middletown, Conn., 1982), 137–138.

2. Nelson Lichtenstein, "Ambiguous Legacy: The Union Security Problem During World War II," *Labor History (LH)* 18 (1977), 227; Lichtenstein, *Labor's War at Home: The CIO in World War II* (New York, 1982); James Green, "Fighting on Two Fronts: Working-Class Militancy in the 1940s," *Radical America* 9 (July–August 1975), 7–48; Michael Torigian, "National Unity on the Waterfront: Communist Politics and the ILWU During the Second World War," *LH* 30 (1989), 432.

3. Brody, "Radical Labor History and Rank-and-File Militancy," 157.

4. Paul Heide, "A Warehouseman's Reminiscences," interviewed by Frank N. Jones, Earl Warren Oral History Project, University of California, Berkeley: Regional Oral History Office, 1969, 7; Harvey Schwartz, *The March Inland: Origins of the ILWU Warehouse Division, 1934–1938* (Los Angeles, 1978), 90; International Longshore-

men's & Warehousemen's Union, *Union Busting: New Model,* quoted in Charles P. Larrowe, *Shape-Up and Hiring Hall: A Comparison of Hiring Methods and Labor Relations on the New York and Seattle Waterfronts* (Berkeley, Calif., 1955), 139.

5. Bruce Nelson, *Workers on the Waterfront: Seamen, Longshoremen, and Unionism in the 1930s* (Urbana, Ill., 1988); Howard Kimeldorf, *Reds or Rackets? The Making of Radical and Conservative Unions on the Waterfront* (Berkeley, Calif., 1988).

6. Al Langley, interviewed by Harvey Schwartz, November 19, 1981, ILWU–National Endowment for the Humanities Oral History Project, ILWUA. Unless otherwise noted, all interviews referred to below are part of this project, which interviewed 244 rank-and-file members from eight ILWU locals, recorded between 1981 and 1986. Most of those interviewed were members of the union during World War II; many had been active in the union's formation in the 1930s.

7. Dave Gonzales, interviewed by Schwartz, January 4, 1983; L. L. Loveridge, interviewed by Schwartz, December 9, 1983.

8. Major R. H. Wylie to Henry Schmidt, April 25, 1941, World War II History (hereafter, WW2 History), Box 1, folder Bridges Plan; Statement of C. E. McMillin, [1941], WW2 History, Box 2, folder Waterfront Security; Wylie to Schmidt, April 25, 1941. All manuscript materials cited in this essay are located in the ILWUA.

9. Schmidt, to Bjorne Halling, August 18, 1941, WW2 History, Box 1, folder General History; Stimson to Allen S. Haywood, August 4, 1941, Pacific Coast Maritime Industry Board (hereafter, PCMIB), Box A-3, folder Army Reports; Stimson's anti-labor attitude is well documented in Paul Koistenen, "Mobilizing the World War II Economy: Labor and the Industrial–Military Alliance," *Pacific Historical Review,* 42 (1973), 443–478.

10. Schmidt to Halling, August 18, 1941.

11. Irving Bernstein, *The Turbulent Years* (Boston, 1971), 752–767; Bridges to All ILWU Locals, November 13, 1941, WW2 History, Box 1, folder Bridges Plan.

12. [H. Bridges] Memorandum [to CIO President Philip Murray] Re Plan to Increase Production in Longshore Industry, [1941], WW2 History, Box 1, folder Bridges Plan.

13. Ibid. It is unclear why employers and the government finally adopted the Bridges Plan. Larrowe attributes it to the rumors of sabotage in the destruction of the troopship *Normandie* on the New York waterfront. The poor progress of the war in the Pacific was likely a contributing factor. Larrowe, *Harry Bridges: The Rise and Fall of Radical Labor* (New York, 1972), 254.

14. Richard Criley, interview with author, September 30, 1990.

15. This story is recounted in Larrowe, *Harry Bridges,* 255–256; and Nelson, *Workers on the Waterfront,* 265.

16. Loveridge interview; Bill T. Ward, interviewed by Schwartz, October 27, 1981; Ruben Negrete, interviewed by Daniel Beagle, May 11, 1983; Arthur Kaunisto, interviewed by Schwartz, September 23, 1982; Elmer Gutierrez, interviewed by Schwartz, December 6, 1983; Loveridge interview; Elmer Mevert, interviewed by Schwartz, September 23, 1982; Al Langley, interviewed by Schwartz, November 19, 1981.

17. Pete Grassi, interviewed by Schwartz and Beagle, January 20, 1983, and April 20, 1983; Kathryn Young, interviewed by Schwartz, June 17, 1983; Charles Hackett, interview with author, November 7, 1988.

18. Bill Castagnasso, interviewed by Schwartz, October 8, and October 27, 1982.

19. Sunstedt interview; Langley interview; Grassi interview.

20. *Dispatcher* 2 (March 26, 1943), 5.

21. John Mitchell interviewed by Schwartz, May 23, 1984; Kaunisto interview; Ed Thayne, interviewed by Schwartz, December 8, 1983.

22. Martinez interview; Kimeldorf, *Reds or Rackets?*, 138.

23. Bill Burke, interviewed by Schwartz, February 26, 1986.

24. Hiram ("Buster") Hanspard interviewed by Schwartz, March 25, 1983; Kagel and Halling to Cmdr. G. Keller, February 3, 1942, WW2 History, Box 1, folder Bridges Plan; Rosco Craycraft, "Notes on Meeting with Col. Ross, Seattle, April 21, 1942," WW2 History, Box 2, folder Waterfront Security.

25. Bridges to Kagel, January 23, 1942, WW2 History, Box 1, folder Labor Relations Committee & Pacific Maritime Industry Board Correspondence, 1941/42 (hereafter, folder LRC–PCMIB Corr., 1941/42); Leon Bick, "The Longshore Hiring Hall in San Francisco" (M.A. thesis, University of California, Berkeley, 1948), 139–143; Bridges to Kagel, January 27, 1942, WW2 History, Box 1, folder LRC–PCMIB Corr., 1941/42.

26. George May to Paul Eliel, Chairman, PCMIB, December 22, 1942, PCMIB, Box A-3, folder PCMIB Corr. from locals, 1942–1944.

27. Memorandum to the PCMIB from C. Jackman and H. Schmidt, May 11, 1942, PCMIB, Box A-4, folder PCMIB Manpower Proposals.

28. Bridges to Kagel, January 27, 1942; "Statement of Louis Goldblatt, April 23, 1943, at San Francisco, Before the . . . Senate Committee on Military Affairs," WW2 History, Box 1, folder Downey Committee Hearings; Cole Jackman, "Utilization of Present Dock Seamen," July 6, 1942, WW2 History, Box 2, folder Waterfront Security.

29. For example, more than 400 of 700 ILWU members working at the Naval Supply Depot in Oakland were replaced by nonunion civil servants between September 1943 and February 1944. Louis Goldblatt, "Investigation of the Naval Supply Depot at Oakland," February 3, 1944, WW2 History, Box 1, folder LRC–PCMIB Corr., 1943–1945; "Statement of Louis Goldblatt . . . Before the Senate Committee . . . ,"

30. Homer Dunlap, interviewed by Schwartz, March 18, 1983; Goldblatt, "Investigation of the Naval . . . Depot," February 3, 1944.

31. "Personnel in Charge of ATS Port of Embarkation, San Francisco," [n.a., n.d.], PCMIB, Box A-3, folder Dock Seamen; National Maritime Union *Pilot,* October 23, 1942, quoted in Albert Bendich, "A History of the Marine Cooks' and Stewards' Union" (M.A. thesis, University of California, Berkeley, 1953), 120.

32. Ward interview; "Longshoremen Needed," *Business Week* July 22, 1944, 96; "Closing the Hole," ibid. October 28, 1944, 90.

33. *Bosses' and Stewards' News Letter* no. 9, May 19, 1945; telegram, Schmidt to Craycraft, June 14, 1945, PCMIB, Box A-3, folder PCMIB Corr. all locals.

34. Bridges to Burke, August 20, 1943, PCMIB, Box A-3, folder PCMIB Corr., 1942–1944.

35. Frank Gregory, quoted in the PCMIB, "Minutes of Meeting, March 13, 1945," 16–17, PCMIB, Box A-1, PCMIB Transcript Proceedings binder, January–April 1945. In Los Angeles, employers also used the USES to circumvent established union hiring procedures and discriminate against African-American workers. Here, however, a coalition of black community organizers (led by the Reverend Clayton Russell's Victory Committee) and black labor activists (many of them longshoremen who would go on to form the Afro-American Labor Protective Society in 1946) were somewhat more successful than their white union counterparts in San

Francisco in pressuring the USES into sending black applicants out to jobs. See Walter Williams, interviewed by Schwartz, March 30, 1984.

36. Bridges to Eliel, October 27, 1942, PCMIB, Box A-3, folder PCMIB Corr. all locals.
37. *Dispatcher* 1 (December 18, 1942), 7.
38. Cf. Harvey Schwartz, "A Union Combats Racism: The ILWU's Japanese-American 'Stockton Incident' of 1945," *Southern California Quarterly* 62 (1980), 161–175.
39. Henry Gaitan, interviewed by Daniel Beagle and David Wellman, May 14, 1983; Eugene Lasartemay interviewed by Schwartz[?], 1981[?]. The Pacific Maritime Association (PMA) was the postwar employers association.
40. Williams interview.
41. Walking bosses were ILWU members who supervised dock operations. John Martinez, interviewed by Schwartz, March 29, 1984.
42. Joe Stahl, who was on the same dock the day that Martinez confronted his men, supplies this information about those workers. Stahl, interviewed by Schwartz, December 7, 1983. Odell Franklin, quoted in Victor Silverman, "Left-Led Unions and Racism: A History of the Integration of ILWU Local 10, 1940–1960" (unpublished seminar paper, University of California, Berkeley, 1983).
43. Gaitan interview; Wilson interview; Williams interview; Stahl interview.
44. Tipp, "Daily Inspection Report," December 30, 1942, PCMIB, Box A-3, folder PCMIB Corr, 1942–1946; Henry Schmidt, "Secondary Leadership in the ILWU, 1933–1966," an oral history conducted, 1974–1981, by Miriam F. Stein and Estolv Ethan Ward, Regional Oral History Office, University of California, Berkeley, 1983, 228.
45. Tipp, "Daily Inspection Reports," September 30, 1942, and November 25, 1942, PCMIB, Box A-3, folder PCMIB Corr, 1942–1946.
46. Lasartemay interview; Fannie Walker, interviewed by Schwartz, October 6, 1982; Virginia Wysinger, interviewed by Schwartz, October 13, 1982.
47. Louis Goldblatt noted that warehouse hiring hall dispatchers simply referred "the same man back and back and back" to a job until the employer "would get the point—if he didn't hire this man, he wasn't going to get anybody." Goldblatt, "Working-Class Leader in the ILWU, 1935–1977," an oral history conducted, 1978/79, by Estolv Ethan Ward, Regional Oral History Office, University of California, Berkeley, 1980, 189–190.
48. Bridges to Brother Member of ILWU, Local 8, December 21, 1943, PCMIB, Box A-3, folder PCMIB Corr. Local 8.
49. Sanford Zalburg, *A Spark Is Struck! Jack Hall and the ILWU in Hawaii* (Honolulu, 1979), 16, 122; Goldblatt, "Working-Class Leader," 316, 319–320; Schwartz, "A Union Combats Racism."
50. Paul Ware, interviewed by Beagle, February 14, 1982; John ("Mickey") Mahon and Pete Grassi, interviewed by Schwartz, April 20, 1983; Williams interview.
51. Gutierrez interview; Frank Sunstedt, interviewed by Schwartz, March 26, 1984. A gang head, or gang boss, serves as the leader of his gang, often determines the pace of work, and acts as intermediary between his gang and the walking boss; Kaunisto interview.
52. Langley interview; Local 13 *Bulletin*, July 16, 1945.
53. In some cases, production was down 50 percent between 1934 and 1941. Kimeldorf, *Reds or Rackets?*, 132, 113.
54. Joshua Freeman, "Delivering the Goods: Industrial Unionism During World War II," *LH* 19 (1978), 587.

Black and White Together

1. Sidney Fishman, from Elizabeth, N.J., had studied at New York University, worked in factories, joined a union before the war. After the war, until the early 1950s, he worked as an organizer for FTA and other CIO unions.
2. Reuel worked with FTA for a number of years after he left Charleston. He died in Cincinnati in the 1960s, described by the local press as a one-man agitprop section. For many years he had been handing out leaflets at plant gates urging the workers to unionize and urging them to support the civil rights movement. He was found dead, alone in his room with his typewriter and mimeograph machine.
3. Guy Carawan and Candy Carawan, *We Shall Overcome: Songs of the Southern Freedom Movement* (New York, 1963).
4. Letter in possession of the author.
5. AFL–CIO, Region 8 Papers, Southern Labor Archives, Georgia State University.
6. For a history of the founding of Local 19, see Michael Honey, "Labor and Civil Rights in the South: Black Workers and the Industrial Union Movement in Memphis, Tennessee" (Ph.D. dissertation, Northern Illinois University, 1986).
7. The Southern Organizing Drive is covered in Barbara Sue Griffith, *The Crisis of American Labor: Operation Dixie and the Defeat of the CIO* (Philadelphia, 1988).
8. *Reports of General Executive Officers to Food, Tobacco, Agricultural and Allied Workers Union, CIO* (Philadelphia, n.d.), 39.
9. See Vicki L. Ruiz, *Cannery Women—Cannery Lives: Mexican Women, Unionization, and the California Food Processing Industry, 1930–1950* (Albuquerque, N.M., 1987).
10. The history of Local 22 is discussed in Robert Rodgers Korstad, "Daybreak of Freedom: Tobacco Workers and the CIO, Winston–Salem, North Carolina, 1943–1950" (Ph.D. dissertation, University of North Carolina at Chapel Hill, 1987).

William Sentner, the UE, and Civic Unionism in St. Louis

1. See esp. Harvey A. Levenstein, *Communism, Anticommunism, and the CIO* (Westport, Conn., 1981), and Ronald Filipelli, "UE: An Uncertain Legacy," *Political Power and Social Theory* 4 (1984), 217–252.
2. David Brody, *Workers in Industrial America: Essays on the 20th Century Struggle* (New York, 1980), 176–188; Nelson Lichtenstein, "From Corporatism to Collective Bargaining: Organized Labor and the Eclipse of Social Democracy in the Postwar Era," in Steve Fraser and Gary Gerstle, eds., *The Rise and Fall of the New Deal Order* (Princeton, N.J., 1989), 125–126.
3. "A Yaleman and a Communist," *Fortune* 28 (1943), 213; Antonia Sentner interview with author, San Jose, Calif., June 16, 1989 (all interviews in author's possession except as noted); *Daily Worker*, October 10, 1933, 5; William Sentner FBI File (FBI-HQ), 100-18332-139. All FBI reports are from William Sentner Papers, Washington University Archives (SP). The Sentner Papers are being processed. Where I have referred to items in that portion which had not been processed, I have identified it thus: SP, Box 2u.
4. B. K. Gebert, "How the Unemployed Victory Was Won," *Communist* 11 (1932), 791; *St. Louis Post-Dispatch* (*P-D*) July 8–12, 1932. Ralph Shaw, "St. Louis' Biggest Strike," *Labor Unity* 8 (1933), 8–11; Myrna Fichtenbaum, "The Funsten Nut Strike" (Senior honor's thesis, St. Louis University, 1976); *P-D* May 18, 1933, 1A; Bill

Gebert, "The St. Louis Strike and the Chicago Needle Trades Strike Strike," *Communist* 12 (August 1933), 300–309.

5. FBI-HQ, 100-18332-139; FBI-HQ, 100-18332-33; Sentner interview. During the Third Period, from 1927 to 1935, the CP adhered to the belief that the capitalist system was in collapse and that revolution in many countries was imminent. Reformist measures, many believed, would only delay the coming revolution.

6. Dennis Brunn, "Black Workers and Social Movements of the 1930s in St. Louis," (Ph.D. dissertation Washington University, 1974); FBI-HQ, 100-18332-139; Catherine Risch, "The Effects of Communist Propaganda Among the Negroes of St. Louis" (Master's thesis, St. Louis University, 1935).

7. William Sentner to Brophy, n.d. [mid-1936], SP, Box 2u.

8. C. B. Lord, "The St. Louis Plan," *Industrial Management*, 54 (1917), 44–49; Minutes, January 1, 1917, International Association of Machinists—District 9 Collection, Western Historical Manuscripts Collection, University of Missouri (WHMC), Box 4; "St. Louis as an Electrical Center," *American Industries* 26 (1925), 4–5; "Why St. Louis is Growing," *Greater St. Louis* 1 (1919), 1; Newman comments in "214th Meeting of the Board of Representatives," December 10, 1936, Board Exhibit 5, Case 14-c-34, Transcripts and Exhibits file (T&E), RG 25; "Youth as a Population Element in St. Louis" *Youth Commission Reports* (St. Louis, 1940); Industrial Club of St. Louis, *Industrial Report of St. Louis* (n.p., 1928); *Factory Labor Situation in St. Louis Industrial District* (St. Louis, n.d.), 6.

9. Case 127 case file, Regional Labor Board Records, Region 12, RG 25; Case 83 case file, esp. "Workers of Century Electric" leaflets, Executive Secretary Files, RG 25; Board of Representatives Minutes, 1932–1936, Board Exhibit 5, Case 14-c-34, T&E file, RG 25; Robert Mason [Manewitz] to James Carey, July 24, 1936, UEA, D/8-133.

10. Henry Fiering interview with author, Los Angeles, June 18, 1989 (Fiering claimed Warnick got the directive from the national CP); Manewitz phone interview with author, November 15, 1989; National Metal Trades Association Report, October 27, 1936, SP, Series 1, Box 3, folder 7.

11. Robert Manewitz to James Carey and Julius Emspak, November 4, 1936, UEA, D/8-500.

12. Fiering interview; Sentner to Carey, December 31, 1936, UEA, O/1288.

13. St. Louis *Star-Times* (*S-T*) March 19, 1937, 16; *P-D* March 31, 1937, 10A; *Emerson Equalizer* March 31, 1937, and April 4, 1937, Lloyd Austin Collection, possession of author; Fiering interview.

14. Sentner Organizer's Report (OR), March 27, 1937, SP, Series 1, Box 6, folder 2; unidentified newspaper clipping, Gladys Slate Collection, possession of author; see also Emspak to Sentner, March 17, 1937, SP, Series 1, Box 6, folder 2; *10th Anniversary Journal*, Austin Collection; Lloyd Austin, phone interview, St. Louis, January 5, 1987.

15. Sentner OR, March 27, 1937, SP, Series 1, Box 6, folder 2; *P-D* March 10, 1937, 2A; Speech, "Ladies, Gentlemen, Fellow Workers," n.d., SP, Series 1, Box 5, folder 8.

16. Speech, "Ladies, Gentlemen, Fellow Workers," n.d., SP, Series 1, Box 5, folder 8; *P-D* March 9, 1937, 1A; Official Report of Proceedings, Case 14-c-34, May 10, 1937, T&E, RG 25. The term "workers' rationalization" is used by James Barrett, *Work and Community in the Jungle* (Urbana, Ill., 1987), 155, 270. Robert Zieger, "Toward a History of the CIO: A Bibliographical Report," *Labor History* 26 (1985), 504–510, provides a useful framework in his discussion of internal vs. external control issues in the CIO.

17. Narrative Summary, *Sentner* v. *U.S.* no. 15097, Vol. 2, 884, SP, Series 3, Box 2; Fiering interview.
18. Sentner to Emspak, November 1, 1937, UEA, O/1295; St. Louis District minutes, October 19, 1937, SP, Series 1, Box 5, folder 8, Memorandum, "The History of the Constitution of District 8," UEA, D/8-192; Narrative Summary, *Sentner* v. *U.S.*, Vol. 3, 1023-24, SP, Series 3, Box 2.
19. "Early 1939" speech, SP, Series 1, Box 5, folder 8.
20. 1941 Missouri Industrial Union Council Convention minutes, 24, James Davis Papers, WHMC, folder 24.
21. "A Yaleman and a Communist," 148; District Council Meeting minutes, March 30, 1946, SP, Series 1, Box 6, folder 6; District Council Convention minutes, October 7, 1945, 61, SP, Series 1, Box 6, folder 5.
22. "Open Letter to the Officers and Stewards of UE local Unions affiliated with District 8," UEA, D/8-219; Sentner, speech "Remarks to the State Committee Meeting," May 1948, SP, Series 3, Box 1, folder 9.
23. Sentner interview; Austin interview.
24. Manewitz interview; "A Yaleman and a Communist," 148; *P-D* January 16, 1935, 14A; February 14, 1935, 8a.
25. This summary is based on data collected on 16 UE members who joined the CP; Fiering interview; Logsdon interview with Dennis Brunn, January 22, 1974, WHMC.
26. Fiering interview; Victor Pasche, interview with author, San Francisco, June 16, 1989. Logsdon interview with author, January 8, 1987.
27. History Lecture outline, ca. September 1940, SP, Series 1, Box 5, folder 16; Sentner OR, April 17, 1937, SP, Series 1, Box 6, folder 2; unidentified speech (May Day 1937), SP, Box IUCu.
28. *UE News* April 29, 1939, 3; Typescript, "DeSoto Reconversion Conference," July 31, 1944, SP, Box Waru.
29. On the evolution of industrial democracy concept, see Steve Fraser, "The Labor Question," in Fraser and Gerstle, eds., *Rise and Fall of the New Deal Order*, 56–57. Gerstle outlines the variants of its meanings in *Working Class Americanism: The Politics of Labor in a Textile City, 1914–1960* (Princeton, N.J., 1989), 219; see especially his distinctions between Catholic corporatists and radicals on this issue.
30. Pasche interview; First District 8 Board meeting, October 3, 1937, SP, Series 1, Box 6, folder 5.
31. Local 810 Newsletter, November 1945, SP, Series 1, Box 7, folder 6.
32. Sentner OR, December 25, 1937, SP, Series 1, Box 6, folder 2; District Board Meeting, Nov 3, 1937, SP, Series 1, Box 6, folder 2; unidentified newspaper clippings, SP, Series 1, Box 5, folder 8; Minutes, St. Louis IUC, November 24 and December 22, 1937, SP, Box IUCu; District 8 Board meeting minutes, January 8, 1938, SP, Series 1, Box 6, folder 1; *P-D* May 17, 1938, 2A.
33. Sentner OR, February 19, 1938, March 12, 1938, April 2, 1938, SP, Series 1, Box 6, folder 2. The quotes are from the March 12 report.
34. 14-C-185 file, T&E, RG 25; C-908, Emerson Electric, RG 25; Robert Burns Logsdon to James Matles, August 20, 1938, UEA, O/706; Trial Examiner's Report, C-908 case file, RG 25; President's Report to District 8 Convention, September 3, 1938, SP, Series 1, Box 6, folder 1.
35. Maytag strike material, SP, Series 1, Box 3, folder 16; James Matles and James Higgins, *Them and Us: Struggles of a Rank and File Union* (Englewood Cliffs, N.J., 1974), 89–99.

36. "Resolution Adopted Sept 27, 1939," IUC Minutes, September 27, 1939, SP, Series 1, Box 6, folder 3; *Globe-Democrat (G-D)* September 28, 1939, 6a; speech, attached to Sentner to Matles, September 27, 1939, UEA, O/1307.

37. Sentner to Matles, October 16, 1939, SP, Series 1, Box 6, folder 3; *UE News* October 14, 1939, 11; October 28, 1939, 1.

38. *UE News* November 4, 1939, 8; Matles to Sentner, October 18, 1939, SP, Series 1, Box 6, folder 3; Sentner to Matles, December 13, 1939, SP, Series 1, Box 6, folder 3.

39. It is possible that Sentner resigned because the Party directly or indirectly ordered him to. More than likely, however, Sentner's words to Matles should be taken at face value. But to do so also begs the question, not directly relevant to this time period, of why Sentner did not also resign in 1948 when a good part of the non-CP left in District 8 asked him to do so with the caveat that he could continue to openly discuss socialism. Sentner later came to regret not having made that decision: FBI-HQ, 100-18332-1x2, 100-18332-7. Shortly after he resigned Sentner tried to join B'nai B'rith, indicating his concern for acceptance in the Jewish community despite the rift over the Nazi–Soviet pact: Sentner to Albert Fleishman, January 9, 1940, January 22, 1940, SP, Box 4u. Sentner did not openly fight a resolution condemning the Soviet Union's actions in Poland by District 8 convention: Resolutions, September 24, 1939, UEA, D/8-14. There were no resolutions on foreign policy in the March 1941 convention for instance: Minutes, Semi-annual Meeting, March 15–16, 1941, UEA, D/8-16.

40. Sentner to Emspak, February 16, 1939, UEA, O/1302.

41. Sentner OR, March 25, 1939, SP, Series 1, Box 6, folder 3; Sentner to Emspak, March 1, 1939, UEA, O/1303.

42. W. Stuart Symington to Sentner, February 25, 1939, Sentner to W. Stuart Symington, February 27, 1939, SP, Box 2u, folder Symington; on the garment trades see Steve Fraser, "Dress Rehearsal for the New Deal: Shop-Floor Insurgents, Political Elites, and Industrial Democracy in the Amalgamated Clothing Workers," in Michael H. Frisch and Daniel J. Walkowitz, eds., *Working Class America: Essays on Labor, Community, and American Society* (Urbana, Ill., 1983).

43. *UE News* March 4, 1939, 8; Emspak to Sentner, February 21, 1939, UEA, O/1302; Sentner OR, May 6, 1939, SP, Series 1, Box 6, folder 3; Logsdon to Matles, June 10, 1939, UEA, O/709; Logsdon to Matles, June 23, 1939, UEA, O/709; *UE News* July 22, 1939, 1.

44. Resolution, August 7, 1939, UEA, D/8-493.

45. Sentner to Emspak, October 26, 1939, UEA, O/1308; Sentner to Emspak, November 1, 1939, SP, Series 1, Box 6, folder 3; *UE News* November 18, 1939, 1; Sentner to Matles, October 11, 1939, UEA, O/1307; "Sunday" letter, RBL [Logsdon] to "Bill" [Sentner], SP, Series 1, Box 2, folder 3.

46. Matles to Sentner (transcript of message), October 18, 1939, UEA, O/1307; "Sunday" letter; Sentner to Eustius Brendle, December 23, 1939, SP, Series 1, Box 2, folder 10.

47. "Program on the Emerson Situation," SP, Series 1, Box 2, folder 10; "How a Union Saved 1500 Jobs" pamphlet, "Proposal," and scrapbook, William Reidel Collection, possession of author.

48. Sentner to Matles, March 6, 1940, SP, Series 1, Box 6, folder 3; [W.] Stuart Symington to Carey, March 7, 1940, UEA, D/8-527.

49. [Des Moines?] *Register* March 9, 1940, SP, Series 1, Box 2, folder 10.

50. *P-D* August 23, 1940, 2C; *UE News* September 28, 1940, 8.

51. Century strike documents, especially unidentified newspaper article, July 20, 1940, SP, Series 1, Box 3, folder 9; Logsdon to Matles, October, 19, 31, 1940, UEA, O/716; Semi-annual Officers Report, March 15, 1941, 6, UEA, D/8-148; Sentner to C. I. McNutt, June 17, 1941, SP, Box 4u.

52. Sentner to James J. Matles, November 15, 1945, UEA, D/8-94; Logsdon Report for St. Louis, May 1945, UEA, O/729. District 8 contributed more national organizers than any other district in the UE before 1945, a testament to the emphasis on leadership building.

53. Sentner to Lyle Dowling, November 26, 1941, UEA, O/1320; Logsdon to Matles, December 3, 1941, UEA, O/722, and "Proposed Plan," attached.

54. "What Helps Labor Helps the Nation" speech, SP, Box 4u; Sentner remarks, 1943 Missouri IUC Convention, Davis papers, f 42.

55. Sentner to John Brophy, May 10, 1943, SP, Box Waru; Special District 8 Council Meeting, January 20, 1945, 21, SP, Series 1, Box 6, folder 5.

56. *P-D* May 14, 1944, 3A; Thomas Knowles, interview with author, April 14, 1987, typed notes signed by Knowles.

57. Howell John Harris, *The Right to Manage* (Madison, Wisc., 1981), 97; Lyle Dowling to Sentner, July 20, 1940, SP, Box UE Nationalu; Sentner, "Resolution on Production," SP, Box Waru; *G-D* September 7, 1942, April 22, 1943, May 4, 1943, Feb 8 1943, Jan 3, 1943, *G-D* morgue files, St. Louis Mercantile Library (*G-D* morgue), UE envelope 1; Sentner to War Manpower Commission, January 3, 1943, SP, Box Waru; *S-T* February 23, 1944, 1; "Unemployment Due to Priorities" meeting, October 1941, SP, Box Waru; Report of District President, Annual District Convention, District 8, September 20–21, 1941, UEA, D/8-148; *UE News* September 10, 1941, 1, and November 1, 1941, 8; Sentner to Lyl (Dowling), October 12[?], 1941, UEA, D/8-69; District 8 Executive Board Meeting, March 30, 1943, UEA, D/8-5.

58. Mayor's Committee materials, SP, Box Waru; *G-D* morgue April 23, 1943; *UE News* July 29, 1944, 12; Logsdon to Emspak, March 20, 1944, UEA, D8/125; Sentner to H. E. Klinefelter, September 6, 1944, Naomi Ring to Bill McMurphy, September 26, 1944, Wm. McMurphy to Naomi Ring, October 6, 1944, SP, Series 2, Box 1, folder 1; District 8 Convention, October 7, 1945, transcript, 61, SP, Series 1, Box 6, folder 5; Sentner to William McClellan, August 30, 1944, UEA, D/8-89.

59. *G-D* morgue September 7, 1942; *G-D* July 12, 1942, 3A; *Local Review* May 14, 1943, 2, Jean Paul Collection, possession of author; District Executive Board Report, January 30, 1945, 11, UEA, D/8-5; *St. Louis American* April 2, 1943, 1.

60. FBI-HQ, 100-18332-38; Logsdon interview with author.

61. Pasche interview; Sentner, speech, March 11, 1945, SP, Box 4u; FBI-HQ, 100-18332-33; Sentner to William Z. Foster, June 25, 1945, Sentner to Committee on Discussion on Resolution, June 25, 1945, SP, Series 3, Box 1, folder 5. For a discussion of the Duclos letter and its impact, see Maurice Isserman, *Which Side Were You On?: The American Communist Party During the Second World War* (Middletown, Conn., 1982), chap. 10.

62. Sentner to Matles, October 23, 1945, UEA, D/8-93. Ronald W. Johnson, "Organized Labor's Postwar Red Scare: The UE in St. Louis," *North Dakota Quarterly* 48 (1980), 28–39, covers the basic outlines of the anticommunist drive in District 8, mainly from Click's perspective.

63. FBI-HQ, 100-18332-219.

64. Sentner, Annual Officers' Report, September 25, 1948, UEA, D/8-150.

65. James Davis, interview with Tom Verdot, Columbia, Mo., in possession of Verdot.

The Catholic Church and the Left-Led Unions

1. Two recent exceptions are: Joshua B. Freeman, *In Transit: The Transport Workers Union in New York City, 1933–1966* (New York, 1989); Gary Gerstle, *Working-Class Americanism: The Politics of Labor in a Textile City, 1914–1960* (New York, 1989).
2. Philip Carey, S.J., "Catholic Labor School," n.d., Box Xavier Labor School, folder "History of Roman Catholic Labor Schools," Archives of the New York Province of the Society of Jesus; Rosswurm interview with Mongsignor Charles O. Rice, June 12, 1986, St. Anne's Rectory, Castle Shannon, Pennsylvania (hereafter Rice Interview); *Catholic Action: Priests' Bulletin* February 1942, November 1942; *Our Bishops Speak: National Pastorals and Annual Statements of the Hierarchy of the United States* (Milwaukee, 1952), 138; Dan [Bell] to Bob [Goldsmith], n.d., DBP, Box 4, folder Catholics.
3. *Quadragesimo Anno* (New York, 1939), 22 (¶88).
4. Dietz to John Frey, July 31, 1937, Frey Papers, Box 8, folder 118, LC.
5. *Catholic Action (CA)* September 1939, 20; *Communism in the United States* (Washington, D.C., 1937), 30.
6. *CA* June 1938, 9–11; "Summary of the Priests Meeting at the National Social Action Conference," May 4, 1938, Raymond Clancy Papers (RCP), Box 10, folder 1, ALHUA.
7. Richard M. McKeon, S.J., "The School of Social Sciences St. Joseph College," *Woodstock Letters (WL)* 67 (1938), 103–120; *CA* February 1936, 10–11. I am at work on a book-length study of the relationships between the CIO, the Catholic Church, and surveillance agencies, particularly the FBI. I will not discuss these issues in this essay because many Freedom of Information Act requests are pending. I make an exception in Rice's case because his involvement is so well known.
8. *Labor Leader (LL)*; *Michigan Labor Leader (MLL)*; *Labor Leader* (Chicago) [*LL(C)*]; CORP: Box 8, folder Committee for Industrial Organization, 1937–1940, Box 25, folders 1937, 1938, 1939, Box 22, folder UAW, April 4, 1939; *MLL* November 17, 1939, 1, 2, 4; PPF 5177, FDRL; Patrick J. McGeever, *Rev. Charles Owen Rice: Apostle of Contradiction* (Pittsburgh, 1989), 48, 51, 99; "CIO Padre," *Business Week* July 1, 1944, 99.
9. *Quadragesimo Anno*, 9 (¶31); Michael Harrington, "Catholics in the Labor Movement: A Case History," *Labor History (LH)* 1 (1960), 234; Mel Piehl, *Breaking Bread: The Catholic Worker and the Origin of Catholic Radicalism in America* (Philadelphia, 1982), 160–161; Arthur Juntunen, "Leaven in the Unions," *Catholic Digest* November 1946, 58; Harold Wattel, "The Association of Catholic Trade Unionists" (M.A. thesis, Columbia University, 1947), 19–20; *LL* January 17, 1938, 2; *LL(C)*; the Reverend John M. Hayes to Weber, August 4, 1939, Detroit ACTU Collection (DeACTU), Box 1, folder Chicago–1939, ALHUA; Harry Read to the Reverend Edward Dowling et al., January 24, 1940, DeACTU, Box 8, folder American Newspaper Guild 1940; *LL(C)* February 1941, 1; "Ballot . . . 1947," DeACTU, Box 2, folder Convention 1947. ACTU officially became a national organization with its first convention in 1940, but despite the best efforts of the New York chapter it never became such in reality. I will use the term "ACTU" only when it is fairly clear that all chapters were in agreement with the generalization at hand. Otherwise, I will speak in terms of specific chapters.
10. Paul Ste. Marie to Dear Friend in Christ, [1938], Chancery Collection, folder ACTU, Archdiocesan Archives of Detroit.

11. Surveys, Questionnaires, RCP, Box 1, folder 18; *X-Ray* October 26, 1939; "List of Membership Books Issued," DeACTU, Box 3, folder Parish Captains Minutes 1939–1941; *ISO Service Bulletin (ISOSB)* October 1941, 6; "Minutes of Regional Meeting of the Committee on Industrial Relations of the ISO," April 15, 1944, attached to Father Daniel Lord, S.J., to Father William Smith, S.J., May 23, 1944, folder Industrial Relations Committee, Missouri Jesuit Provincial Archives (MJPA).

12. Sharon Hartman Strom, "Challenging 'Woman's Place': Feminism, the Left, and Industrial Unionism in the 1930s," *Feminist Studies* 9 (1983), 371; Leslie Woodcock Tentler, *Seasons of Grace: A History of the Catholic Archdiocese of Detroit* (Detroit, 1990), 64–66, 169, 172–175, 179, 402–405.

13. Cf. Douglas Seaton, *Catholics and Radicals: The Association of Catholic Trade Unionists and the American Labor Movement from Depression to Cold War* (Lewisburg, Pa., 1981).

14. Philip Dobson, S.J., "The Xavier Labor School, 1938–1939," *WL* 68 (1939), 270; Freeman, *In Transit*, 137–146; Rice to Father Thomas Darby, June 13, 1946, CORP, folder 139.

15. Weber, "Memorandum to ACTU–NY re Intra-Union Organization," [late 1938 or early 1939], DeACTU, Box 2, folder New York 1939–1943.

16. *MLL* January 26, 1940, 4; Carey to Bert MacLeech, July 28, 1950, Box Xavier Labor School, folder Correspondence 1942–1943.

17. Read to Father Hayes, [July] 15, 1942, Harry Read Papers (HRP), Box 3, folder Clergy, CUAA; Read to Monsignor [Hillenbrand?], Sunday, Catholic Council on Working Life Papers (CCWLP), Box 1, folder 1941–1943, CHS.

18. *Wage-Earner (WE)* June 25, 1943, 4; Richard Deverall to Philleo Nash, April 8, 1943, Deverall Papers, OWI, II, 151–152, CUAA; *WE* June 9, 1943, 3; Deverall to Clarence Glick, June 28, 1943, Philleo Nash Papers, Box 29, folder Race Tension—Daniels file—tension, HSTL.

19. *MLL* September 27, 1940, 2; "Confidential ACTU Newsletter," November 1, 1943, Carl Haessler Papers, Box 8, folder 17, ALHUA.

20. Social Action Department, "A Report of the Conference on Labor Schools held at Cleveland, Ohio, September 13–14, 1943," Masse to Edward [Marciniak], January 1, 1945, CCWLP, Box 1, folders 1941–1943, 1945.

21. Patrick W. Gearty, "Diocesan Labor Institute, Diocese of Hartford" (M.A. thesis, Catholic University of America, 1947), 15, 16–18; *Waterbury Democrat* October 1, 1942, 4; Donnelly to Editor of *WE*, October 23, 1942, DeACTU, Box 21, folder Mine, Mill 1942–1947.

22. Donnelly, "Working with Workers," *American Eccesiastical Review (AER)*, 113 (July 1945), 5; Donnelly, "Diocesan Labor Institute," Report to Bishop Henry J. O'Brien for July 1, 1944–June 30, 1945, CCWLP, Box 1, folder 1945.

23. "Diocesan Labor Institute," adopted June 12, 1944, attached to Donnelly, "Diocesan Labor Institute"; ibid.

24. *ISOSB* October 1944, 1–9, and November–December 1944, 1–2; *Crown Heights Comment* September 15, 1944; Smith to Marciniak, October 10, 1944, CCWLP, Box 1, folder 1944; *America* November 4, 18, 25 and December 16, 1944.

25. This generalization is based upon a large number of documents in the Archdiocesan Archives of Chicago (AAC).

26. Samuel Cardinal Stritch to Monsignor Thomas P. Bona, November 17, 1943, Chancery, Box 2952, AAC; *Our Bishops Speak*, 126–130.

27. This generalization is based upon *Work; WE; Our Sunday Visitor; Catholic Review; ISOSB; LL; CA;* DeACTU; CCWLP; AAC; *Our Bishops Speak.*

28. Archbishop Spellman radio address, March 22, 1942, FBIHQ 94-1-20733-67; Father

Edgar Schmiedeler, "The Wedding Ring," March 15, 1943, Chancery, Box 2956, folder NCWC, AAC; *ISOSB,* October 10, 1944, 5; Read to Monsignor [Hillenbrand?], May 9, 1943, CCWLP, Box 1, folder 1941–1943; *WE* May 14, 1943, 8.

29. *Crown Heights Comment* November 11, 1945; Twomey to Murray, November 12, 1945, and December 8, 1945, Louis Twomey Papers (LTP), Loyola University of New Orleans; Smith to Daniel Cantwell, December 15, 1945, Daniel Cantwell Papers (DCP), Box 1, folder 5, CHS.

30. "Minutes of Regional Meeting of the Committee on Industrial Relations of the ISO"; [Philip] Carey, S.J., to Editor, *WE* [1944], DeACTU, Box 11, folder Philip Carey; Freeman, *In Transit,* 253–254; *Fortune* November 1946, 188; Wattel, "Association of Catholic Trade Unionists," 108–128; Joshua Freeman and Steve Rosswurm, "The Education of an Anti-Communist: Father John F. Cronin and the Baltimore Labor Movement" (unpublished manuscript); Father George Higgins to Clancy, January 8, 1945, RCP, Box 1, folder 14; Clancy to Cantwell, December 10, 1945, Cantwell to Smith, December 5, 1945, DCP, Box 1, folder 5; Cronin to Higgins, July 10, 1945, and July 17, 1945, Social Action Department Collection, Box 9, folder 3, CUAA.

31. Donnelly, "The Junior Clergy Look at Organized Labor," *AER* 115 (1946), 1.

32. "The Story of Disruption," April 3, 1947, International Fur and Leather Workers Union Papers, Box 12, folder 19–20, LMDC; Vernon Jensen, *Nonferrous Metals Industrial Unionism, 1932–1954* (Ithaca, N.Y., 1954), 193; John Brophy, "Instructions to the Chicago Industrial Union Council," April 26, 1945, DeACTU, Box 12, folder Chicago IUC—Brophy Instruction, 1945; Phil Dobson to Twomey, October 26, 1946, LTP.

33. Murray to Julius Emspak, March 18, 1948, CIOSTO, Box 62, folder UE 1948. The generalization on the UAW and USWA raiding is drawn from material in CIOSTO; UEA; Walter Reuther Papers, ALHUA; UAW Secretary-Treasurer Papers, ALHUA; Harry Block Personal Papers (microfilm), University of Pittsburgh Library; *New York Times;* Arthur W. Hepner, "Union War in Bessemer," *The Reporter* July 5, 1949, 12–14. Cf. Harvey J. Clermont, *Organizing the Insurance Workers: A History of Labor Unions of Insurance Employees* (Washington, D.C., 1966), 118.

34. Ronald Filippelli, "A Second Oral History Interview with Monsignor Charles Owen Rice," April 5, 1968, 15–16, HCLA.

35. *1950 IUE Convention Proceedings,* 21; Rice Interview.

36. CORP; McGeever, *Rice,* 120; Charles Owen Rice Papers (microfilm version) (CORP[m]), HCLA; "Statement of William H. Peeler, Sr.," August 28, 1952, D6-308, UEA; McGeever, *Rice.*

37. Thomas E. Crehan, "Father Charles Owen Rice" (M.A. thesis, Duquesne University, 1964), 75; Rice Interview (cf. Rice to Rosswurm, April 13, 1988); *The Voice of the UE* August 11, 1949, 3; "Peeler Statement"; Sigmund Diamond, "Labor History vs. Labor Historiography: The FBI, James B. Carey, and the Association of Catholic Trade Unionists," in *Religion, Ideology, and Nationalism in Europe and America* (Jerusalem, 1986), 324 (cf. 326 n19); James T. Fitzpatrick to Carey, July 14, [1949], IUEP, A2.05; *Pittsburgh Post Gazette* January 13, 1950, 13; Rice to Bishop Dearden, May 13, 1950, CORP, Box 23, folder UE—Voice of the UE, 1949–1950; Suzanne M. Rini to Rosswurm, June 29, 1986; Harrington, "Catholics in the Labor Movement," 257; "A Second Interview with Rice," 14; Rice Interview.

38. CORP, folders 520, 522, 523.

39. Rice to R. A. Kerstein, August 26, 1948, CORP, Box 25, folder 1948; Rice Interview; Rice to Reverend Andrew Dzmura, July 3, 1948, CORP, Box 22, folder UE 1947–1948; Rice Interview (cf. Rice to Rosswurm, April 13, 1988; *LH* 31 [1990], 402–403).

40. CORP(m), reel A; CORP, Box 11, folder Farm Equipment and Metal Workers Union, Box 22, folder United Auto Workers; *Cub* December 29, 1949, 2; Ronald Schatz, *The Electrical Workers: A History of Labor at General Electric and Westinghouse, 1923–1960* (Urbana, Ill., 1983), 204–217; *Pittsburgh Catholic* (column) June 9, 1966, clipping, no. 601 Records, Box 4, folder "Leaftlet ACTU," AIS; Rice, "The Tragic Purge of 1948," *Blueprint for the Christian Reshaping of Society* February 1977, 3; Rice Interview.

41. Read to Higgins, December 27, 1948, HRP, Box 3, folder NCWC.

42. Brown Papers, MJPA; Brown to Rice, June 28, 1946, CORP(m), reel C; Rosemary Feurer interview with Robert Logsdon, January 8, 1987 (courtesy of Feurer); interview with Logsdon, January 22, 1974, Western Historical Manuscripts Collection, University of Missouri at St. Louis (courtesy of Feurer); Feurer interview with James Click, July 28, 1987; unidentified report of conversations with Brown, William Sentner Papers, Washington University (courtesy of Feurer); Darby, *Thirteen Years in a Labor School: The History of the New Rochelle Labor School* (n.p., 1953), 26, 29–43; "Xavier Labor School, 1945," Minutes of the Convention," April 10, 1946, Box Xavier Labor School, folder Correspondence, 1945–1946, folder Xavier Labor School Annual Conventions, 1942–1960; "Combatting Communism Side by Side with the Worker: A Report on the Work of Association of Catholic Trade Unionists," July 15, 1945—June 30, 1946, Chancery, Box 2969, AAC; *ISOSB* October 1944, 19.

43. *Newark Evening News* (*NEN*) November 21, 1949, 17; Albert Fitzgerald to the Most Reverend Thomas N. O'Leary, October 22, 1946, EDP, Box 14, folder 5; *NEN*, November 21, 1949, 17; *Berkshire Eagle*, May 10, 1950, clipping, unidentified newspaper clipping in envelope addressed to Rice, Rice to Bishop Christopher Weldon, May 12, 1950, CORP, Box 8, folder Communism in Labor, Box 22, folder United Electrical Workers 1947–1949, Box 25, folder 1950; Rice to John Callahan, May 15, 1950, Weldon to Rice, May 15, 1950, CORP(m), reel A.

44. *NEN*, November 28, 1949, 1; *Daily Compass*, December 2, 1949, clipping, CORP(m), reel B; "Editor's Notes," CORP, Box 8, folder Communism in Labor Movement, 1947–1950; Steven P. Gietschier, "Limited War and the Home Front: Ohio During the Korean War" (Ph.D. dissertation, Ohio State University, 1977), 151; Father Bill O'Connor to Cantwell, January 14, 1955, handwritten notes on back of [?] to Don, January 17, 1955, DCP, Box 3, folder 1, Box 15, folder 2; "Labor Management Forum," June 10, 1949, CORP, Box 22, folder UE; Ken Peterson to Carey, n.d., Les Finnegan Memorandum to Al Hartnett, n.d., IUEP, A2.02, B1.19; Jackson to Carey, November 24, 1953, GJP, Box 13, folder Carey; [Cantwell] to Father Andryaskiewicz, June 19, 1949, CCWLP, Box 2, folder June–October, 1949; FBIHQ 100-71906-209.

45. Twomey to Jim, [October 15, 1946], CIOSTO, Box 111, folder Hearings . . . Mine Mill; Joseph Verdu to Twomey, October 3, 1946, Twomey to Dobson, October 15, 1946, Dobson to Twomey, October 26, 1946, Richard T. Deters, S.J., to Dear Father, [September 1946?], Angleo Verdu to Twomey, October 12, 1948, LTP; *ISOSB* December 1946, 3–4; Edward Radden to Bernard W. Stern, March 20, 1947, CIOSTO, Box 111, folder Hearings . . . Mine, Mill; [Bishop] Gercke to Priests of Diocese, April 12, 1954, Stritch Personal Papers, Box 2840, AAC; Vicki Ruiz, *Cannery Women—Cannery Lives: Mexican Women, Unionization, and the California Food Processing Industry, 1930–1950* (Albuquerque, N.M., 1987), 112; Clermont, *Organizing the Insurance Workers*, 101–102; "Combatting Communism Side by Side with the Worker"; Edward J. Dolan to Rice, May 19, 1947, CORP, folder 520; *Endicott Daily Bulletin*, April 12, 1947; "Monthly Report of San Francisco Chapter of ACTU—

March, 1950," "Monthly Report of the San Francisco Chapter of ACTU—February, 1950," DeACTU, Box 1, folder ACTU—California, 1950–1951; Thomas O'Brien, S.J., to [Philip] Carey, S.J., October 2, 1949, attached to Carey, S.J., to O'Brien, October 31, 1949, Box Xavier Labor School, folder XLS Correspondence, 1942 and 1943.

46. Bernard Lazerwitz, "Some Factors Associated with Variations in Church Attendance," *Social Forces* 39 (1960), 303; Andrew Greeley, "Some Information on the Present Situation of American Catholics," *Social Order* April, 1963, 18, 19; Thomas A. Kselman and Steven Avella, "Marian Piety and the Cold War in the United States," *Catholic Historical Review* 72 (1986), 403–424. This generalization is also based upon extensive research in the AAC.

47. These generalizations are based upon much NCWC-related material and documents on the conservative grouping in AAC.

48. Virtually any issue of the *WE* may be examined for Weber's writings on "economic democracy." For examples of praise for Weber's writings, see Read to Hayes, December 16, 1941, HRP, Box 3, folder Clergy; *Crown Heights Comment* March 2, 1948.

49. *WE* December 4, 1942, 6; October 29, 1943, 8.

50. Karl Alter, "Industry Councils," *Sign* May 1950, 50–53; Thomas T. McAvoy, *Father O'Hara of Notre Dame* (Notre Dame, Ind., 1967), 332. The generalizations again are based upon a large number of documents in the AAC.

51. "The Catholic Viewpoint on Industry Councils," *AER* 122 (1950), 114.

52. This generalization is based upon much periodical literature; for the kinds of developments Catholics found encouraging, see Ed Marciniak, "Some U.S. Approximations to the Industry Council Idea," *American Catholic Sociological Review* 16 (1954), 24–29.

53. Schatz, "Connecticut's Working Class in the 1950s: A Catholic Perspective," *LH* 25 (Winter 1984), 83–101; Gutiérrez, *A Theology of Liberation: History Politics, and Salvation* (Maryknoll, N.Y., 1988), rev. ed., 120.

54. *ISOSB* November–December 1944, 1.

McCarthyism and the Labor Movement

1. For a more detailed exploration of the connection between anticommunism and national security, see Ellen W. Schrecker, "McCarthyism Revisited: The Case of Gerhart Eisler," paper presented at the Annual Meeting of the Organization of American Historians, April 1991, Louisville, Ky.; CIOSTO, Boxes 109–114.

2. Steve Rosswurm, Introduction to the present volume; Fred A. Hartley, Jr, *Our New National Labor Policy* (New York, 1948), 179; Harvey Levenstein, *Communism, Anti-Communism, and the CIO* (Westport, Conn., 1981), 235, 242; James Forrestal, *The Forrestal Diaries*, Walter Millis, ed. (New York, 1951), 280; James Carey to Harry S. Truman, October 18, 1950, IUEP, A1.08.

3. Vernon H. Jensen, *Nonferrous Metals Industry Unionism, 1932–1954* (Ithaca, N.Y., 1954), xiii; Robert Denham to John M. Houston, July 5, 1950, Box 696, National Labor Relations Board, Record Group 25-60-A-387 (RG 25). On the defense industry strikes, see Nelson Lichtenstein, *Labor's War at Home* (New York, 1982), 49–63.

4. Athan Theoharis and John Stuart Cox, *The Boss* (Philadelphia, 1988); Kenneth O'Reilly, *Hoover and the Un-Americans* (Philadelphia, 1983).

5. On the committees, see Walter Goodman, *The Committee* (New York, 1968); Telford Taylor, *Grand Inquest* (New York, 1955); and Frank Donner, *The Un-Americans* (New York, 1961).

6. Otto Kirchheimer, *Political Justice* (Princeton, N.J., 1961); "Fact Sheet on the Christoffel Case," n.d., David Scribner to Harold Christoffel, September 22, 1952, reel 3, Press Release, February 23, 1950, "The Case of Harold Christoffel, II," reel 20, Civil Rights Congress papers, [microfilm] Arthur Schomberg Collection, New York Public Library, New York; Roger Keeran, *The Communist Party and the Auto Workers Unions* (Bloomington, Ind., 1980), 266–78.

7. F. S. O'Brien, "The 'Communist-Dominated' Unions in the United States Since 1950," *Labor History* 9 (1968), 204; George Morris Fay to David Scribner, October 31, 1950, Scribner to Thomas Quinn, December 20, 1950, May 6, 1952, Albert J. Fitzgerald to Fellow Union Member, March 28, 1951, all in Thomas J. Quinn Papers (TJQP), AIS; Louis Goldblatt, Oral History, Columbia University (CU), 623, 662, 713–725; Abram Flaxer, Oral History, 91–92, Robert Wagner Labor Archives (RWLA), TI; Joseph Kehoe to Edward Barlow, September 5, 1957, American Communications Association Papers (ACA), Box 23, folder 12, SHSW.

8. Ronald Schatz, *The Electrical Workers: A History of Labor at General Electric and Westinghouse, 1923–60* (Urbana, Ill., 1983), 177; Robert Korstad and Nelson Lichtenstein, "Opportunities Found and Lost: Labor, Radicals, and the Early Civil Rights Movement," *The Journal of American History* 75 (1988), 801–803; Barbara S. Griffith, *The Crisis of American Labor: Operation Dixie and the Defeat of the CIO* (Philadelphia, 1988), 150–152; "UE on Evansville," pamphlet in Hymen Schlesinger Papers, Series I, folder "UE, Local 601, Current Matters," AIS; Bud and Ruth Schultz, *It Did Happen Here* (Berkeley, Calif., 1989), 123.

9. Thomas J. Fitzpatrick et al. to John S. Woods, August 7, 1949, Box 1, folder A-2, UE 601, AIS; "Voice of the UE," August 11, 1949, TJQP; Ronald L. Filippelli, "UE: An Uncertain Legacy," in Maurice Zeitlin and Howard Kimeldorf, eds., *Political Power and Social Theory*, vol. 4 (Greenwich, Conn., 1984), 239; William D. Andrew, "Factionalism and Anti-Communism: Ford Local 600," *Labor History* 20 (1979): 228–254.

10. Bruno Stein, "Loyalty and Security Cases in Arbitration," *Industrial and Labor Relations Review* 17 (1963), 106.

11. Stein, "Loyalty and Security Cases," 96–114; Joseph D. McGoldrick, Arbitration Decision, February 4, 1955, TJQP; Goldblatt, Oral History, 714–16; UE Press Release, February 5, 1955, Box 201, folder 18, International Union of Mine, Mill & Smelter Workers Archives (IUMMSW), Western Historical Collections, University of Colorado, Boulder; ACA Press Release, May 12, 1958, ACA, Box 10, folder 3; James Carey to Charles Thomas, May 26, 1954, IUEP, A1.08.

12. William Preston, Jr., *Aliens and Dissenters* (Cambridge, Mass., 1963), deals with early cases; for later ones, see Stanley I. Kutler, *The American Inquisition* (New York, 1982), 118–51, and Ellen W. Schrecker, "No Golden Door: McCarthyism and the Foreign Born," paper presented at the Annual Meeting of the Organization of American Historians, March 1988, Reno, Nev.

13. Schrecker, "No Golden Door"; Stanley Nowak to "Friends," n.d., *The Lamb*, July 1946, Nathalie Gross, memo, May 7, 1946, Abner Green to Ugo Carusi, May 20, 1946, IUMMSW, Box 109, folder 28; Green to "Friend," n.d., IUMMSW, Box 112, folder "American Committee for Protection of Foreign Born"; Howard B. Gliedman, affidavit, September 27, 1956, UE mimeo, "News of the Matles Case," October 1956, November 20, 1956, ACA, Box 10, folder 9; Schatz, *The Electrical Workers*, 184; Levenstein, *Communism, Anti-Communism, and the CIO*, 266; Filippelli, "UE,"

244; O'Brien, "The 'Communist-Dominated' Unions," 204; George Bott to Board, December 1, 1952, RG 25, Box 692; Warren Olney III to Bott, November 3, 1953, RG 25, Box 693.

14. Mark McColloch, *White Collar Workers in Transition* (Westport, Conn., 1983), 72; George Lipsitz, *Class and Culture in Cold War America* (S. Hadley, Mass., 1981), 169; Albert J. Fitzgerald to Truman, and encl., August 24, 1948, Schlesinger Papers, Series I, folder "UE Dist. 6, Union Miscellany"; Carl Bernstein, *Loyalties* (New York, 1989), 173–258; James J. Matles and James Higgins, *Them and Us* (Englewood Cliffs, N.J., 1974), 174–180.

15. Ralph S. Brown, Jr., and John D. Fassett, "Security Tests for Maritime Workers: Due Process Under the Port Security Program," *Yale Law Journal* 62 (1953), 1163–1208; Goldblatt, Oral History, 561, 618–623, 674; clipping, *New York Times*, April 3, 1960, IUMMSW, Box 201, folder 21.

16. "Communist Domination of Certain Unions," Part II, *Report of the Subcommittee on Labor of the Committee on Labor and Public Welfare*, U.S. Senate, 82nd Congress, 2nd session, 1952, 4–48 (hereafter Humphrey Report); "NLRB Summary of Section 9(h) Problems," undated memo, RG 25, Box 694 (hereafter cited as "NLRB Summary"); Sigal to Carey, November 1, 1950, Carey to Humphrey, November 28, 1951, IUEP, A1.08.

17. Stein, "Loyalty and Security Cases," 106–113; Henry Mayer, "How the Loyalty–Security Program Affects Private Employment," *Lawyers Guild Review* 15 (Winter 1955/56), 126–127; Porter Mechling, Memo to Defend the UE Committee, May 29, 1950, Box 1, folder A3, "What Is the Answer?" IUE mimeo, UE 601.

18. Michal R. Belknap, *Cold War Political Justice* (Westport, Conn., 1977), 152–278; Olney to Bott, November 3, 1953, RG 25, Box 693; Salvatore Cosentino to Murdock, January 13, 1955, RG 25, Box 694; Goldblatt, Oral History, 624–626, 633–644, 711–712, 737; Maurice Travis, memo, December 1, 1949, January 26, 1950, IUMMSW, Box 109, folder 11; Julius Emspak, Oral History, 14, CU.

19. Sigmund Diamond, "Labor History vs. Labor Historiography," in *Religion, Ideology and Nationalism in Europe and America* (Jerusalem, 1986), 299–328; Steven Rosswurm, "The FBI and the CIO from 1940 to 1955" (paper presented to the Organization of American Historians, Philadelphia, 1987); O'Reilly, *Hoover and the Un-Americans*, passim; Athan Theoharis, ed., *Beyond the Hiss Case* (Philadelphia, 1982); Russell R. Miller to Kenneth C. McGuiness, September 16, 1955, RG 25, Box 692.

20. Harry A. Millis and Emily Clark Brown, *From the Wagner Act to Taft–Hartley* (Chicago, 1950), 286–295, 311–314, 342–361, 545–556; R. Alton Lee, *Truman and Taft–Hartley* (Lexington, Ky., 1966), 32–38; Susan M. Hartmann, *Truman and the 80th Congress* (Columbia, Mo., 1971), 22–24, 80–101; Hartley, *Our New Labor Policy*, 16–20, 51–61; James T. Patterson, *Mr. Republican* (Boston, 1972), 356–364; Gerard D. Reilly, "The Legislative History of the Taft–Hartley Act," *George Washington Law Review* 29 (1960), 298–299.

21. Labor Management Relations Act of 1947, 61 Stat. 136, 146, 29 U.S.C. (Supp. III).

22. Patterson, *Mr. Republican*, 362–364; Philip Taft, "Internal Affairs of Unions and the Taft–Hartley Act," *Industrial and Labor Relations Review* 11 (1958), 357; Millis and Brown, *Wagner Act to Taft–Hartley*, 540–541, 546, 555; John A. Morgan, Jr., "The Supreme Court and the Non-Communist Affidavit," *Labor Law Journal* 10 (1959), 36–37; "NLRB Summary"; Lee, *Truman and Taft–Hartley*, 89–96, 161–164; Victor Rabinowitz, Oral History, 68–70, CU.

23. Lipsitz, *Class and Culture*, 135; Martin Halpern, "Taft–Hartley and the Defeat of the Progressive Alternative in the United Auto Workers," *Labor History* 27 (1986), 211–

13; Francis A. Cherry, Recommended Decision, December 26, 1961, in *Robert F. Kennedy* v. *International Union of Mine, Mill and Smelter Workers*, SACB, 55–56, IUMMSW, Box 537, folder "Recommended Decision"; Levenstein, *Communism, Anti-Communism, and the CIO*, 218, 231, 265; McColloch, *White Collar Workers*, 69.

24. Millis and Brown, *Wagner Act to Taft–Hartley*, 553; Rabinowitz, Oral History, 65–66, 68–71; Morgan, "The Supreme Court and the Non-Communist Affidavit," 30–36; *American Communications Association* v. *Douds*, 339 U.S. 94 (1950).

25. Father Charles O. Rice to editors of *Counterattack*, June 5, 1948, to Charles O'Brien, May 5, 1950, CORP, Box 18; Rice to Walter Reuther, April 3, 1948, to "Dear Father," December 8, 1949, CORP, Box 22; Douglas Seaton, *Catholics and Radicals: The Association of Catholic Trade Unionists and the American Labor Movement, from Depression to Cold War*, (Lewisburg, Pa., 1981), 164–167, 194–195; Andrew, "Factionalism and Anti-Communism," 238; David Brody, *The Butcher Workmen* (Cambridge, Mass., 1964), 232; Jensen, *Nonferrous Metals Industry Unionism*, 69–73, 93–193; Levenstein, *Communism, Anti-Communism, and the CIO*, 265.

26. Keeran, *The Communist Party and the Auto Workers Unions*, 279–283; Jensen, *Nonferrous Metals Industry Unionism*, 214–225; Horace Huntley, "Iron Ore Miners and Mine Mill in Alabama: 1933–1952" (Ph.D. dissertation, University of Pittsburgh, 1977), 126–138; Cherry, Recommended Decision, 55–56; Staff Report, April 23, 1948, Department Store Workers Union, Local 1S, RWDSU papers, Box 2, Folder 2, RWLA.

27. Levenstein, *Communists, Anti-Communists, and the CIO*, 269–278; James T. Fitzpatrick to Les Finnegan, August 24, 1949, IUE, Box A2.05, folder "UE Locals Disaffiliating"; Millis and Brown, *Wagner Act to Taft–Hartley*, 458–459, 524, 533, 645; Lipsitz, *Class and Culture*, 161; McColloch, *White Collar Workers*, 71; "NLRB Summary."

28. Lee, *Truman and Taft–Hartley*, 187–202; Millis and Brown, *Wagner Act to Taft–Hartley*, 629–630.

29. Jensen, *Nonferrous Metals Industry Unionism*, 222–223; Korstad and Lichtenstein, "Opportunities Found and Lost," 804; Lipsitz, *Class and Culture*, 155–156, 165–168; Millis and Brown, *Wagner Act to Taft–Hartley*, 556–559, 584, 643; Vivian McGuckin Ranieri, "UE Local 735 Confronts a Hanging Judge," Ann Fagan Ginger and David Christiano, *Cold War Against Labor* (Berkeley, Calif., 1987), 349–373; Frank G. Hoover to Robert Taft, April 5, 1949, James W. Greene and Harold Habner to friends, May 5, 1949, Robert Taft Papers, Box 728, folder "Non-Communist Affidavits," LC.

30. "NLRB Summary"; Goldblatt, Oral History, 474, 648; Jensen, *Nonferrous Metals Industry Unionism*, 248–250, 269, 274–292; Millis and Brown, *Wagner Act to Taft–Hartley*, 492–493, 584; Executive Board Statement, July 20, 1949, IUMMSW, Box 65, folder 42, Nathan Witt to Elizabeth Sasuly, July 22, 1949, IUMMSW, Box 65, folder 41.

31. Allen P. Haas to Ross M. Madden, February 24, 1956, T. C. Kammholz to Board, December 5, 1956, RG 25, Box 697; Denham to Board, November 25, 1949, RG 25, Box 692; "NLRB Summary"; John A. Hull, Jr., to Murdock, February 19, 1954, RG 25, Box 693; Victor Rabinowitz, interview with the author, April 10, 1990; Reid Robinson to Civil Rights Congress, American Committee for the Foreign Born, National Council for Soviet–American Friendship, July 27, 1949, IUMMSW, Box 65, folder 42.

32. David I. Shair, "How Effective Is the Non-Communist Affidavit?" *Labor Law Journal*

1 (1950), 941–942; O'Brien, "The 'Communist-Dominated' Unions," 192; "NLRB Summary"; Murdock to Frank M. Kleiler, May 28, 1955, RG 25, Box 692.

33. Denham to Board, November 25, 1949, RG 25, Box 692; "NLRB Summary"; McGuiness to Regional Directors, November 15, 1955, RG 25, Box 695; Kleiler to Miller, June 25, 1954, Kammholz to Board, December 5, 1956, RG 25, Box 697.

34. Denham to Board, November 25, 1949, RG 25, Box 692; Denham, press release, June 14, 1949, "NLRB Summary"; Denham to James M. McInerney, March 24, 1950, RG 25, Box 696; Richard Neustadt to Stephen J. Spingarn, June 29, 1950, Stephen J. Spingarn Papers, Box 31, folder Internal Security File, National Defense and Individual Rights, Vol. I, HSTL.

35. Frank W. McCulloch and Tim Bornstein, *The National Labor Relations Board* (New York, 1974), 61; Harold L. Richman to Charles Douds, July 2, 1952, RG 25, Box 693; Howard F. LeBaron to Murdock, December 12, 1952, RG 25, Box 694; NLRB Order, February 4, 1954, RG 25, Box 695.

36. "Notes of NLRB hearing," May 12, 1954, George A. Downing, Order, June 7, 1954, IUMMSW Box 63, folder 36; NLRB, Determination and Order, February 1, 1955, RG 25, Box 695; Al Pezzati to Local Unions, February 24, 1954, IUMMSW, Box 63, folder 19; Miller, September 15, 1955, NLRB, Supplemental Decision and Order, February 28, 1957, RG 25, Box 692; *Leedom et al.* v. *International Union of Mine, Mill and Smelter Workers*, 352 U.S. 145.

37. Undated list of Section 9(h) affidavits sent to the Department of Justice, Ellery Stone to Charles B. Murray, October 3, 1952, RG 25, Box 693; Denham to McInerney, March 24, 1950, RG 25, Box 696; McGrath statement, in Morgan, "The Supreme Court and the Non-Communist Affidavit," 43; Murray to the attorney general, October 22, 1952, James P. McGranery Papers, Box 80, LC; Travis, memos, December 1, 1949, January 26, 1950, IUMMSW, Box 109, folder 1; "122: Labor Management Relations Act, 1947," in NARS, "Appraisal of the Records of Use, FBI," in Athan Theoharis, ed., "Federal Bureau of Investigation: Filing Records and Procedures," microfilm, 1985; Neustadt, memo to Spingarn, June 29, 1950, Spingarn papers, Box 31, folder "Internal Security File, National Defense and Individual Rights," Vol. I (2 of 2).

38. Attorney General's Report, January 17, 1953, McGranery Papers, Box 84; Sigal, memo to Carey, March 8, 1951, IUEP, A1.08. Besides Valentino, the indicted officials were Walter C. Lohman and Ernst Hupman, UE local officials in Ohio, and Olga Zenchuk, a former Packinghouse Workers local official in Detroit. Ralph Helstein and Lewis J. Clark to Locals, January 4, 1952, Highlander Research and Educational Center Papers, Box 74, Folder 2, SHSW; Bott to Board, date unintelligible [probably November 1952] RG 25, Box 695; "Documents and memoranda pertaining to UE Local 801 and trial and conviction of Ernst Melvin Hupman," n.d., "Documents and memoranda pertaining to UE Local 768 and trial and conviction of Walter C. Lohman," n.d., RG 25, Box 694.

39. Brownell to Taft, February 27, 1953, Taft Papers, Box 821, folder "Taft–Hartley Communists, 1953"; testimony of Arthur G. McDowell, December 21, 1953, in "Hearings on Subversive Influence in Certain Labor Organizations," Senate Internal Security Subcommittee, 83rd Congress, 1st session, 37–38; Stone to Murray, October 3, 1952, McGuiness to Wm. F. Tompkins, May 23, 1953, RG 25, Box 693; Guy Farmer to Tompkins, January 31, 1955, RG 25, Box 693; Tompkins to Director, FBI, September 20, 1954, FBIHQ 122-837-8.

40. Olney to Bott, November 3, 1953, RG 25, Box 693; press release, November 16, 1956,

ACA, Box 10, folder 8; Vivian McGuckin Ranieri, "United States vs. Marie Reed," in Ginger and Christiano, *Cold War Against Labor,* 671–678; "The Cleveland Taft–Hartley Conspiracy Case," pamphlet, n.d., IUMMSW, Box 120, folder "Haug, Fred and Marie."

41. Chas. F. Herring to Harvey Matusow, February 5, 1954, Matusow, affidavit, January 20, 1955, copy in UE Organizers Bulletin, February 1, 1955, TJQP; Matusow, *False Witness* (New York, 1955).

42. *Jencks v. U.S.,* 353 U.S. 657 was the key case. See also Miller to McGuiness, August 25, 1955; *Travis v. U.S.,* 44 LLRM 2707, August 31, 1959, in RG 25, Box 695; Olney to Bott, November 3, 1953, February 17, 1954, RG 25, Box 693; *Fisher v. U.S.,* 37 LRRM, 2600-6, in RG 25, Box 694; Murdock to Kleiler, March 2, 1955, RG 25, Box 695; Oliver Gasch to Tompkins, April 17, 1957, Wm. P. Rogers Papers, Box 56, folder U.S. Attorney Correspondence (A-K), Dwight D. Eisenhower Library (DDEL); A.C. Skinner to Joseph Selly, June 23, 1966, ACA, Box 10, folder 8.

43. Herzog to Taft, November 26, 1952, Taft papers, Box 821, folder, "Taft–Hartley Communists 1953"; Bott to Board, November 24, 1952, Bott to Herzog, March 18, 1953, RG 25, Box 692; Press Release, October 23, 1953, Motion of NLRB to dismiss complaint in *International Fur and Leather Workers Union v. Guy Farmer et al.,* November 18, 1953, RG 25, Box 694; *Lannom and Leedom et al.* v. *Mine, Mill and Smelter Workers* U.S. 145 (1956); *Meat Cutters and Butcher Workmen* v. *NLRB* 352 U.S. 153 (1956); McGuiness to Regional Directors, January 23, 1957, RG 25, Box 692.

44. Hartley, *Our New Labor Law,* 174, 180; Lee, *Truman and Taft–Hartley,* 172–176; "NLRB Summary"; Olney to Rogers, February 17, 1953, Taft Papers, Box 821, folder "Taft–Hartley Communists 1953."

45. Sigal to Carey, November 1, 1950, Carey to Humphrey, November 28, 1951, in IUEP, A1.08; "Legislative History of S. 3706," IUMMSW Box 916, folder "SACB Leg. History"; Humphrey Committee Report; "NLRB Summary."

46. Roger Jones to Bernard M. Shanley, September 3, 1953, Shanley to Jones, September 24, 1953, Dwight David Eisenhower, Official Files, (hereafter DDE OF) Box 659, folder 133 E—Internal Security Subversive Activities (1), DDEL; Press release, August 24, 1954, in DDE OF, Box 660, folder 133-E-1 1954 (2), DDEL; Miller to McGuiness, August 8, 1955, RG 25, Box 695.

47. Brody, *Butcher Workmen,* 259–261; Olney to the attorney general, February 12, 1953, Olney to Rogers, February 17, 1953, both in Taft Papers, Box 821, folder "Taft–Hartley Communists 1953"; Cherry, Recommended Decision, December 26, 1961.

48. Rogers, "Report . . . with Respect to the Subversive Activities Control Act, June 1, 1959, DDE OF, Box 662, folder 113-E-10, Blacklisted Organizations (6); Skinner et al. to Selly, June 23, 1966, ACA, Box 10, folder 8; Ellen W. Schrecker, "Introduction," *Records of the Subversive Activities Control Board, 1950–1970* (Frederick, Md., 1989).

49. R. Alton Lee, *Eisenhower and Landrum–Griffin* (Lexington, Ky., 1990); "158: Labor Management Reporting and Disclosure Act of 1959," in NARS, "Appraisal"; A. J. McGrath, memo to Mr. Rosen, February 26, 1960, FBIHQ 158-00-43; J. Walter Yeagley to the director, June 23, 1965, FBIHQ 158-00-81; *U.S.* v. *Brown,* 381 U.S. 437 (1965); Brief of Respondent in *U.S.* v. *Archie Brown,* U.S. Supreme Court, October term 1964, in IUMMSW, Box 916, folder Kapp–Kay, Instructions Brown.

50. For a fully developed presentation of the triumph-of-the-law thesis, see Kutler, *American Inquisition.*

51. Levenstein, *Communism, Anti-Communism, and the CIO,* 314.

52. Travis to Clark et al., May 4, 1954, IUMMSW, Box 109, folder 12; Clark to Dear Friend [January 1960?], Selly to Albert J. Fitzgerald, September 14, 1965, both in ACA, Box 10, folder 8; summary, income and disbursements, Mine-Mill Defense Fund, IUMMSW, Box 538, folder Eastland Committee; Rabinowitz, Oral History, 83.
53. Carey, statement, June 13, 1952, IUEP, A1.06; press release, January 16, 1950, IUEP, A2.04.
54. Keitel, "Merger," 37; Levenstein, *Communism, Anti-Communism, and the CIO*, 314; Goldblatt, Oral History, 718–719.
55. Brody, *Butcher Workmen*, 260–261, Keitel, "Merger," 36–43; Levenstein, *Communism, Anti-Communism, and the CIO*, 322–325; McColloch, *White Collar Workers*, 77; O'Brien, "The 'Communist-Dominated' Unions," 191–197; Goldblatt, Oral History, 457, 609, 718–719; Rabinowitz, Oral History, 103, 160.

Fighting Left-Wing Unionism

1. *Leather and Shoes* December 16, 1950, 6.
2. Local tanners had been organized since the early 1930s, but in 1945 they formalized their union by incorporating as the Tanners Association of Fulton County and hiring a professional labor-relations expert, John Forster.
3. For a more extended analysis of Local 202 and its antagonists, see both Philip S. Foner, *The Fur and Leather Workers Union* (Newark, N.J., 1950), 668–673, and my " 'Communism Is No Bug-a-Boo': Communism and Left-Wing Unionism in Fulton County, New York, 1933–1950," *Labor History* (forthcoming).
4. Howell John Harris, *The Right to Manage: Industrial Relations Policies of American Business in the 1940s* (Madison, Wisc., 1982).
5. Actually, only 19 tanneries were members of the association in 1946, and 18 during the strike of 1949/50.
6. John J. Maurillo was a CIO subregional director based in Syracuse, New York. See Foner, *The Fur and Leather Workers Union*, 671.
7. George O. Pershing was director of District 3 of the IFLWU, covering New York and Pennsylvania. Myer Klig was a Russian-born Canadian organizer for the IFLWU, quite active in organizing in the Northeast around this time.
8. Harold Pozefsky was Local 202's lawyer. He was a labor lawyer with a reputation for supporting left-wing causes.
9. The Tanners Council was a national informational and lobbying association of tanners based in New York City. In the late 1940s and early 1950s, it, along with the New England Tanners Association, helped finance campaigns against the IFLWU.
10. Bernie Woolis, at the time, was a Party member and an International organizer assigned to aid Local 202 during the strike of 1949/50. He was a close personal friend of Clarence Carr.
11. Meyer is referring to the NLRB election held on December 9, 1949. The final results were as follows: "Neither," 493 votes (536, if 43 challenged votes are included); "CIO Textile Workers Union," 180 votes; the "AFL United Leather Workers Union," 144 votes.
12. Carr ran for Congress under the CPUSA ticket in 1934 and 1936.
13. Sutliff is a bit off on the date. The union affiliated with the IFLWU in the summer of 1940.

14. By this time Local 202 had disaffiliated with the IFLWU. The NLRB, however, ruled that the local union had failed to achieve a truly independent status, and thus under Taft–Hartley, as a satellite of the Communist-led IFLWU, could not participate in the certification election.
15. Peter Aversa was a CIO organizer at the time. Previous to his work in upstate New York, he was active in the Farm Equipment Union in the Chicago area until his expulsion from the FE.
16. Haywood was CIO vice president and director of organization.

The Shop-Floor Dimension of Union Rivalry

1. For a sample of the former view, see W. J. Usery, "Epilogue," in Richard B. Morris, ed., *The U.S. Department of Labor Bicentennial History of the American Worker* (Washington, D.C., 1976), 296–298. For an extreme formulation of the latter view, see David Gartman, *Auto Slavery: The Labor Process in the American Automobile Industry, 1897–1950* (New Brunswick, N.J., 1986), 275.
2. Ronald W. Schatz, *The Electrical Workers: A History of Labor at General Electric and Westinghouse, 1923–60* (Urbana, Ill., 1983), 76, 225.
3. Schatz, *Electrical Workers*, 232–233, is by far the most sophisticated. He argues that the UE grasped at unacceptable terms offered by Westinghouse but calls it no worse than the IUE. Harvey Levenstein, *Communism, Anti-Communism and the CIO* (Westport, Conn., 1981), 313; Bert Cochran, *Labor and Communism: The Conflict That Shaped American Unions* (Princeton, N.J., 1977), 293, and Jules Backman, *The Economics of the Electrical Manufacturing Industry* (New York, 1962), 213, have less detailed treatments.
4. Levenstein, *Communism*, 312.
5. James Matles and James Higgins, *Them and Us* (New York, 1974), 304.
6. 1951 UE Policy, p. 27, UEA, CPol 8.
7. James Carey Keynote Address, September 28, 1953, UEA, Red 130.
8. IUE Resolutions, 1956, p. 2, UEA, Red 130.
9. 1953 IUE Convention Summary, p. 1, UEA, Red 130.
10. Schatz, *Electrical Workers*, 139, has no citations here, but I think this is an excellent summary.
11. Ibid., 140. Schatz claims that the UE "dropped all reservations about the principle of incentive pay. Instead they endorsed it enthusiastically and called on union members to work as fast as they could." There is no citation here, and I believe that this is a one-sided, extreme formulation of the UE's position at the time.
12. Ibid., 142.
13. Ibid., 146–147.
14. 1950 UE Policy, p. 13, UEA, CPol 7.
15. UE–Westinghouse Contract, April 1, 1948, UEA, CB-W9.
16. Ibid.
17. Ibid.
18. Ibid.
19. *UE News* May 15, 1950, 11.
20. Charles Zober report, April 15, 1950, UEA, O-1662.
21. *United Front* February 2, 1950, 1, UEA, CBW-684.
22. "An Open Letter," April 20, 1950, UEA, D/7-975.

23. *UE News* March 20, 1950, 4.

24. "Press Release," May 3, 1950, UEA, PR-35.

25. *UE News* June 26, 1950, 3.

26. *UE News* August 7, 1950, 3.

27. *IUE CIO News* April 7, 1950, 10; July 31, 1950, 1.

28. "Why Is Your Pay Raise Being Held Up?" 1950, UEA, CBW-429. This was a Westinghouse mailing to UE members. The mailing added that "when management desires to use cameras for other purposes, the reason will be discussed with the union representative in advance."

29. "W Says These Are Trivial," 1950, UEA, PL-28.

30. *UE News* August 7, 1950, 5.

31. Westinghouse–IUE Contract, July 19, 1950, UEA, CBW-92.

32. *UE News* November 13, 1950, 1.

33. UE–Westinghouse Contract, November 1, 1950, UEA, CBW-13.

34. Ibid.

35. "Support," 1953, UEA, DD6-L21; and "Westinghouse Incentive Rates for Various Local Unions," 1951, IUEP, 1.03.

36. *Union Generator* May 7, 1952, 1; "Statement of the IUE–CIO Programs," April 1, 1954, IUEP, G1.08#2.

37. *UE News* June 11, 1951, 9. This would have been bad enough for a group of incentive workers, but all the production workers at the Cheektowaga plant were on daywork! In other words, without using the term, Westinghouse had instituted a form of measured daywork at this plant.

38. Ibid.

39. *IUE CIO News* April 23, 1951, 1; Mike Fitzpatrick Report to the IUE Westinghouse Conference Board, 1951, IUEP, G1.09.

40. *Voice of the IUE* May 24, 1951, 4. To cite an example of the cuts, the old taping rate in department B-32 was $1.15; Westinghouse proposed to cut it to 97.6 cents; after the lockout, it was restored to $1.03.

41. John Baldwin to James Carey, January 8, 1953, IUEP, G1.09#1; Joseph Hawkins to All IUE Locals, June 18, 1953, IUEP, F1.22#1.

42. Contract, IBEW Local 1136–Westinghouse, January 16, 1952, Supplement, IUEP, B1.05; *The Assembler* 1954, 6, IUEP, B1.05; Summary Collective Bargaining Strength at End of 1953, 1953, IUEP, F1.22#1.

43. *Local 107 News* August 1953, p.3; East Pittsburgh Twenty-Seventh Keysheet, July 1, 1953, UEA, DD6L11; Earl Kipp to David Lasser, January 13, 1951, IUEP, G1.05.

44. *UE News* September 15, 1952, 5; "The Nuttall Strike," 1952, UEA, PA-281; Edward Matthews to Westinghouse Locals, September 10, 1952, UEA, CBW-155.

45. *UE News* March 17, 1952, 3; James Matles to general executive board members, April 10, 1952, UEA, PM-253.

46. *UE News* July 27, 1953, 1.

47. *UE News* July 26, 1954, 1; Matles to International representatives, September 13, 1954, UEA, PM-308. The proposed speedup clause, dropped by Westinghouse on the last day of negotiations, read: "the Union recognizes that improved methods and increased rates of production are desirable, as long as the health and safety of the employees are not endangered. The Union will cooperate in making effective immediately any method or change established by the Company but may file a grievance in any case where it believes the health and safety of the employees is endangered."

48. *UE Policy: 1951–52*, 15, UEA, PC-15; *UE Policy: 1954–55*, UEA, PC-17 16. The union

called for the strengthening of safeguards where incentive systems existed but urged the locals to work for the elimination of incentive, called for a ban on the introduction of new piecework payment, and denounced incentive pay as inherently evil and destructive. This is one of many illustrations of the inaccuracy of the claim that "while UE spokespersons criticized management attempts to cut piece rates after World War Two, they never revived the traditional moral arguments about incentive pay." Schatz, *The Electrical Workers,* p. 156.

49. "Contract Ratified," September 13, 1954, UEA, DD6-PL10.
50. Thomas Quinn to East Pittsburgh Workers, September 27, 1954, UEA, DD6-PL10.
51. *IUE CIO News* October 10, 1955, 3; Peter Abbondi to UE Westinghouse Locals, August 17, 1955, UEA, DD6-M2; Company Proposal, 1955, IUEP, C1.12#1.
52. *IUE–CIO News* September 26, 1955, 3.
53. Ibid.; IUE Westinghouse Conference Board Minutes, September 14, 1955, IUEP, G1.09.
54. *UE News* October 31, 1955, 1.
55. *IUE News* January 16, 1956, 3; January 30, 1956, 11. With about 6,000 strikebreakers at the IUE plants, several hundred at the UE plants, the largely nonstriking IBEW and IAM plants, and a few unorganized shops subtracted, about 80 percent of the production workers struck and stayed out until the end.
56. 1959 UE Policy, p. 8, UEA, CPol 16.
57. UE Westinghouse Conference Board to UE Westinghouse Locals, November 28, 1955, UEA, DD6-M3.
58. "Comparison Between Present UE and IUE Contracts," March 1956, UEA, DD6-M3.
59. Ibid.; "The Westinghouse Strike and the Westinghouse Peace," 1956, IUEP, G1.07#2.
60. *UE News* March 6, 1956, 1; August 20, 1956, 4; "Local 107 Wins," August 17, 1956, UEA, CBW-522. The prestrike incentive takeout average had been 178 percent. While about one-third of those switched to daywork jobs that were lower paid, the incumbent workers had their rates "red-circled" so that they did not lose money. The average worker gained about $7\frac{1}{2}$ cents per hour. Still, about 20 percent of the workers voted to continue the long strike.
61. Joseph Dermody to Westinghouse Locals, July 30, 1958, UEA, DD11-M8.
62. *Pittsburgh Press* March 1, 1957, 1; *UE News* March 4, 1957, 5.
63. *UE News* March 18, 1957, 5.
64. "Proposed Understanding for the Movement of the Power Circuit Breaker Department to Trafford," February 21, 1957, UEA, CBW-186; *Pittsburgh Press* March 10, 1957, 1.
65. Quinn to Matles, August 24, 1959, UEA, DD6-D62.
66. *Pittsburgh Post Gazette* April 29, 1960; "Speedup," April 29, 1960, UEA, DD6-PL18.
67. *Pittsburgh Post Gazette* July 18, 1957, 12; "Increasing Unemployment," January 31, 1959, UEA, PA-356.
68. IUE Westinghouse Conference Board Minutes, November 15, 1956, and August 8, 1957, both IUEP, G1.09.
69. "Membership Meeting," February 2, 1959, UEA, DD11-PL47.
70. UE General Executive Board Minutes, January 7, 1958, UEA, D/6-326.
71. Dermody to Westinghouse Locals, August 29, 1960, UEA, DD6-M6.
72. UE–Westinghouse Contract, April 1, 1948.
73. Ibid.
74. Ibid.; Schatz, *Electrical Workers,* 116–117.

75. Schatz, *Electrical Workers*, 127; Ruth Milkman, *Gender at Work: The Dynamics of Job Segregation by Sex During World War Two* (Urbana, Ill., 1987), 146.
76. *UE News* July 10, 1950, 11; "To Westinghouse Locals of IUE–CIO," June, 1950, IUEP, G1.05.
77. Ibid.
78. Ibid.
79. "Announcement," September 25, 1950, UEA, DD6-L9.
80. Westinghouse Conference Board Minutes, October 7, 1950, UEA, CBW-36.
81. Westinghouse–IUE Contract, July 19, 1950.
82. Ibid.
83. Westinghouse–IUE Local 202 Contract, 1950, IUEA, C1.02.
84. Ibid.
85. Mansfield Works Local Supplement, October 1, 1950, IUEP, F1.22#1.
86. "The Crisis in Buffalo," November 28, 1951, IUEA, G1.09.
87. *Buffalo Courier Express* December 12, 1951, 2.
88. *Buffalo Evening News* December 14, 1951, 1.
89. Ibid.
90. Unidentified newsclipping, December 18, 1951, UEA, D/3-705.
91. "Let's Clean House," 1954, UEA, DD6-L21.
92. Ibid. In both IUE Locals 601 and 617 the new leaderships were composed primarily of younger, secondary leaders from the 1945–1950 period. Most came from the old IUE side, but some from the former UE. They came to power mainly on the basis of their expression of dissatisfaction with the fruits of the breakup of the old UE.
93. *Union Member* April 2, 1954, UEA, CBW-808. The *IUE–CIO News* April 14, 1954, distorted the information about the origin of the old seniority agreement, calling it a UE deal. Right-wingers in UE Local 617, who became the leaders of IUE Local 617, had tried to push the agreement through, but it was disallowed by the UE national office. When the IUE won at Sharon, discrimination against married women was immediately implemented by the IUE Local officers.
94. *IUE CIO News* February 16, 1953, 3.
95. Ellis Hockenberry to All IUE–CIO Westinghouse Locals, September 24, 1954, IUEP, G1.09.
96. Quinn to John Nelson, October 15, 1954, UEA, DD6-D47.
97. Quinn to Peter Abbondi, October 13, 1954, UEA, DD6-D47.
98. *Union Generator* December 14, 1954, UEA, DD6-P39.
99. Ibid.
100. Dermody to Westinghouse Locals, September 21, 1960, UEA, DD6-M6.
101. *Pittsburgh Post-Gazette* January 12, 1959, 1.
102. "Employment Security for the Westinghouse Employees," September 9, 1958, IUEP, G1.07#2.
103. *Pittsburgh Press* May 10, 1956, 1.
104. Ibid. October 10, 1957, 21.
105. *Union Generator* November 29, 1957, UEA, DD6-P41; "The Campaign," 1959, UEA, DD6-L22.
106. *Spark* July 30, 1958, UEA, DD6-P36; *News in Brief* September 16, 1959, UEA, DD6-P33.
107. Quinn to "Dick," January 9, 1959, UEA, DD6-D51.
108. IUE Local 601 Supplement—Westinghouse, May 6, 1958, UEA, DD6-L515.
109. Ibid.

110. See, for example, *Seven Eleven News* March 1959, UEA, DD7-PP4. At the Mansfield plant, men with seniority dates of 1950 were being recalled while women with 1947 dates were still off the job. Or "Highlights IUE Convention," 1958, IUEP, C1.02 for Sharon, where men with 11 years of seniority were currently being laid off, while joblessness reached back to $15\frac{1}{2}$ years for women.
111. J. Babcock to All Raleigh Plant Employees, November 9, 1956, IUEP, 2.06.
112. "IBEW and Company," 1958, IUEA, 2.06.
113. Benjamin Sigal to Carey, October 6, 1959, IUEP, 2.06.
114. Dermody to Westinghouse Locals, April 17, 1957, DD11-M6.
115. *1956–57 UE Policy*, 13, UEA, PC-19; Dermody to Westinghouse Locals, September 21, 1960, UEA, DD6-M6. Other unions in the chain did not pick up this theme, and little headway was made.

CONTRIBUTORS

Steve Rosswurm teaches history at Lake Forest College and is the author of *Arms, Country, and Class: The Philadelphia Militia and the American Revolution*.

Rosemary Feurer is a doctoral candidate at Washington University in St. Louis, where she is completing a dissertation on UE District 8. She has published several articles on labor history and is producer and host for the cable TV show "Laborvision."

Karl Korstad worked with the Food, Tobacco, Agricultural and Allied Workers Unions, CIO, in the mid-south and the southeast as a business agent, organizer, and regional director, from 1945 through 1951.

Mark McColloch is Associate Professor of History at the University of Pittsburgh at Greensburg. He is the author of *White Collar Labor in Transition* and coauthor of *Forging a Union of Steel*. He is currently at work on a study of Westinghouse workers in the 1950s and a study of basic steelworkers in the 1945–1970 period.

Bruce Nelson teaches history at Dartmouth College. He is the author of *Workers on the Waterfront: Seamen, Longshoremen, and Unionism in the 1930s* (University of Illinois Press, 1988).

Nancy Quam-Wickham has worked oil barges, fish boats, and deep-sea vessels. She was educated at Antioch College and San Francisco State University. She is working on her dissertation, "Petroleocrats and Proletarians: The Southern California Oil Industry, 1917–1940," at the University of California, Berkeley.

Ellen W. Schrecker is Associate Professor of History at Yeshiva University. She is the author and editor of several books, most notably *No Ivory Tower: McCarthyism and the Universities.* She is presently working on a general study of anticommunist political repression during the early years of the cold war.

Gerald Zahavi is a member of the Department of History at the University at Albany, State University of New York. He is the author of *Workers, Managers, and Welfare Capitalism: The Shoeworkers and Tanner of Endicott Johnson, 1890–1950* (1988). He is currently working on a monograph focusing on the local and regional history of labor and communism in twentieth-century America.

INDEX

communist affidavit, 149, 151, 153; and SACB, 151, 155; and shop-floor militance, 121; social composition of, 2, 4; as threat to "national security," 141

Japanese-American workers, 60, 64
Japanese workers, 3
Jesuits, 122, 124, 128, 129, 133, 134
Jim Crow, xi, 29, 40, 41, 45, 71, 93. *See also* segregation
Johnstown, New York, 159
Jones, Ben, 21, 27, 29, 30

Kauisto, Art, 52, 65
Kimmel, George, 99, 100, 101
Kimmel, Lou, 99, 101
Klig, Meyer, 169
Knowles, Thomas, 113, 117
Koger, Mary Lou, 88

labor priests, 122–123, 124, 127, 131. *See also* Catholic Church
labor schools, 122, 123–124, 136–137. *See also* Catholic Church
LaFarge, Father John, S.J., 137
Landrum-Griffith, 155
Lane, Harold, 77
Langley, Al, 49, 53, 54, 65, 66
Lannon, Al, 21
LaPorte, Camela, 190
Lasantemay, Eugene, 61, 63
Lathan, Robert, 89
Latino workers, 48
Leiserson, William, 35
Less, Fred, 88
Lewis, John L., 21, 22, 102
Logan, Charles, 30, 34, 37
Logsdon, Robert, 99, 104, 106, 112–113, 115
Los Angeles, 218n35
Loveridge, "Chick," 52, 53
Lovestone, Jay, 13

McGrew, Earl, 100
McKay, Marshall, 167, 171
Mahon, Mickey, 65
Maider, Lydon, 161, 162, 170, 172; oral history of, 163–168
Manewitz, Robert, 99, 101, 103
Maritime Federation of the Pacific, 22, 43

Marshall, Father Eugene, 133
Marshall Plan, 13
Martinez, John, 54, 61
Masse, Father Benjamin, S.J., 127
Matles, James, 12, 107–108, 145
Maurillo, John, 168
measured daywork, 189, 192, 193, 199, 237n37. *See also* daywork
Memphis, Tennessee, 44, 75–83
mental labor, xv
Merrill, Louis, 6
Mevert, Elmer, 53
Mexican-American workers, 4, 5, 48, 59–66
Meyer, George, 162; oral history of, 168–173
Mitchell, John, 54
Mobile, Alabama, 27–28, 35, 36, 40, 41, 42, 44
Murray, Philip, ix, x, 4, 95, 126, 129, 130, 163, 176
Murray Plan, 51

National Association for the Advancement of Colored People, 38
National Industrial Recovery Act (NIRA), 26, 99
National Labor Relations Board (NLRB), xiii–xiv, 28, 32, 33, 43–44, 88, 92, 106
National Maritime Union of America (NMU), 22, 33, 43, 145
National Negro Labor Council, 83
National Union of Marine, Cooks & Stewards (NUMCS), 2, 3, 145, 153
Needle Trades Workers Industrial Union, 160
negotiated class struggle, 16
Negrete, Ruben, 52
Nelson, Burt, 32, 33
Nelson, John W., v, xvi, 132
Netter, Harvey, 29
New Orleans, 19–45
New Rochelle Labor School, 132–133
non-communist affidavits, of Taft-Hartley, 147, 148, 149–150, 160–161, 165
North American Aviation Strike, 49–50
no-strike pledge, 10, 47, 52–55, 66, 112–113

DUE DATE

			Printed in USA